Surrogacy Was the Way

Zara Griswold

SURROGACY WAS THE WAY

For information about Nightengale Press please
visit our website at www.nightengalepress.com.
Email: publisher@nightengalepress.biz
or send a letter to:
Nightengale Press
5250 Grand Avenue, Suite 14-110
Gurnee, IL 60031
Library of Congress Cataloging-in-Publication Data

Griswold, Zara,
    Surrogacy Was The Way/ Zara Griswold
    ISBN:1-933449-18-7
    Parenting/Women's Health

Copyright Registered: 2005
First Published by Nightengale Press in the USA

January 2006

10 9 8 7 6 5 4 3 2 1

Printed at
Lightning Source Inc.
1246 Heil Quaker Boulevard
La Vergne, Tennessee 37086

Surrogacy Was the Way

"Zara Griswold's book encapsulates the human experience and life stories of couples who have built their families with third party reproduction. The book highlights the obstacles and journeys of real people on their way to parenthood using technologies that were not widely available until recently. Congratulations to Ms. Griswold for highlighting this important option for many seeking to overcome infertility."

—*Michael M. Alper, M.D.*
Medical Director, Boston IVF
Assistant Clinical Professor of OB/GYN
Harvard Medical School

"This book provides an intimate look at the lives of couples and their experiences with surrogacy. Well written and comprehensive, it discusses the emotional and medical issues families go through. I will recommend this wonderful book to all my patients considering surrogacy."

—*Camran Nezhat, M.D., FACOG, FACS*
Stanford University Medical Center
Center for Special Minimally Invasive Surgery

"Not only does Ms. Griswold give us a clearly written and precious window into the intimate lives of all those engaged in the "way" of surrogacy, she illuminates, at the deepest level, Man's (woman's) humanity to woman (and men and children). This book does more than restore hope for those who have lived in despair about the prospect of never being a parent, although this is its aim and it does this very well. These stories shine a sunbeam on the tendrils of hope that there can, someday, be a rebirth in the public, day-to-day arena, of the confidence that the basis of humanity, is in fact, good."

—*Carol Ann Munschauer, Ph.D.*
President of the Psychoanalytic Society of Upstate New York
Author, "How to Bounce Back when You Think You Can't: The
P.R.I.D.E. Factor" (co-authored with Dave Hood)
Frequent writer and speaker for RESOLVE and infertility sufferer herself

"There is a wealth of important information in these twenty stories to help potential intended parents planning to use surrogacy to achieve their dream of having a family."

—*Arthur L. Wisot, M.D.*
Reproductive Partners Medical Group
Author, "Conceptions and Misconceptions"

"I highly recommend Zara Griswold's poignant book. It imparts wisdom obtained through loss but it also shines with the light of hope and faith. In its pages, the voices of women who became mothers through surrogacy tell stories of how they healed heartache through dreams, determination, and resolve. Women and couples considering surrogacy will find these stories affirming and empowering. Their friends, family members as well as professionals in the field will find an honest and touching depiction of building one's family with the help of surrogacy."

—*Silvia Schneider Fox, Psy.D.*
Licensed Clinical Psychologist

"Because each person can be the beginning of a universe of possibilities, each birth is a miracle. Zara Griswold's book has allowed us to peer into a world of miracles where women who can carry a pregnancy have given the ultimate gift by helping couples who cannot carry their own pregnancies achieve the goal of parenthood."

—*Harvey J. Kliman, M.D., Ph.D.*
Yale University School of Medicine
Reproductive and Placental Research Unit
Department of Obstetrics, Gynecology and Reproductive Sciences

"The stories told in *Surrogacy Was the Way* are an excellent demonstration of the value that clinical surrogacy has in helping intended parents create their families. This book will be an asset not only to the infertile community, but to anyone interested in the ways in which third party reproduction has created options for so many people."

—*Mark W. Surrey, M.D.*
Southern California Reproductive Center

"Surrogacy offers significant hope allowing deserving couples to establish their family. These 'larger than life' experiences come to life in *Surrogacy Was the Way: Twenty Intended Mothers Tell Their Stories.* Women helping women to be mothers—these heartfelt stories demonstrate this fundamental bond that exists between women. *Surrogacy Was the Way* leaves one with tears of joy. The world is a better place for these miracles of love in our midst."

—*William P. Hummel, M.D.*
San Diego Fertility Center

"This heartwarming collection of personal stories is an excellent starting point for anyone considering surrogacy to grow their family. *Surrogacy Is The Way* is an encouraging message to those who may have given up the hope of having a child bless their lives—don't miss it."

—*Thomas Pinkerton*
Third Party Reproduction Attorney

"Poignant and powerful are Zara Griswold's stories of twenty determined women and their partners who find their way to parenthood through surrogacy. Although surrogacy has been written about since biblical times, this book tells the modern, highly personal journey through reproductive loss, high technological interventions, and the gift of life that is shared between very special women—the "intended" mother, the "gestating" mother and, at times, the woman donating her eggs. It is a courageous, heartfelt collection of stories that will provide inspiration and assistance to other infertile couples considering surrogacy."

—*Sharon N. Covington, M.S.W., L.C.S.W.-C.*
Director, Psychological Support Services
Shady Grove Fertility Reproductive Science Center
Co-author/Editor, "Infertility Counseling: A Comprehensive
Handbook For Clinicians"

For Noah and Isabella, our beautiful miracles
May you always chase after your dreams,
whatever they may be.

Acknowledgments

I would like to first thank my husband, Mike, who has been practically wifeless while I have been writing this book for the last two years. Every time I wanted to give up, every time I almost veered off into another project, you reminded me to keep plugging along. As much as I wanted to be a mommy, I wanted you to be a daddy, because I knew what a phenomenal one you would be. And I was so right.

To my wonderful parents. It is because of you that I had the confidence to go forward with my dream of writing this book. You are always proud of me, even when I've done something most would consider mediocre. Your continual support in whatever I do has made me believe that the sky is the limit in life. I am so grateful for that. Everybody should be as fortunate as I am to have parents like you.

Grandma Blanche, thank you for your words of wisdom throughout the years—they have come in handy. Thanks also for teaching me how to roll with the punches. You are the best.

Thank you to Ashley* and Juliana, two incredible women who were totally dedicated to making me a mom. Ashley, you were the greatest surrogate any intended mother could ask for. I am forever thankful to you for being a true partner in my quest to have children. Juliana, few people on this earth are as selfless as you. You went way beyond what most people would do for a friend. Every day when I look at Bella and Noah, I thank my lucky stars that both of you found your way into my world.

To Staci, my intended mother-advisor in writing this book. From the moment I shared the concept with you to the final stages of the writing process, you have given me invaluable feedback and constant encouragement. Of the many great things that have

---

*All of the stories told in this book are true and all of the people mentioned throughout are real people. However, in order to protect the privacy of all parties, aside from the author's name as well as the members of the author's family, all of the other names have been changed.

happened to me due to having children through surrogacy, you are definitely one of them.

Thank you Julie for planting the seed. You and I have certainly been in each other's lives for many reasons. Melanie, thanks so much for being there for me when I needed you most—and for your offerings of help time and time again.

There are many people out there who I have met on the Internet—other intended parents and surrogates—who were such a huge source of help as I went through my own surrogacy journey. I would especially like to thank the people I have met on the Parents Pursing Surrogacy (PPS) Online support group and all of the amazing women who have contributed their stories to this book. All of you have been an inspiration to me.

And to so many others who were there for me as I went through my cancer experience, my infertility struggles and my journey through surrogacy. Some of you were there in ways you don't even realize. Some of you were there by just being in my life. To all of you who have walked along beside me through good times and bad, I thank you. I may not be naming all of you, but you know who you are.

Author's Note

Acronyms and abbreviations are used throughout for commonly mentioned infertility and medical terms, associations, websites and Online support groups. Please consult the back of the book for a complete list and explanations of the above.

Preface

The idea for this book came to me almost a year before my children were born. Like many women who are infertile, I had spent many years worrying and wondering if I would ever become a mom. I knew adoption was an alternative all along, but once I learned that surrogacy was another realistic possibility I became convinced that it was the way I wanted to create my family.

I had a hysterectomy when I was twenty-three years old due to ovarian cancer; therefore, from that point on I knew I would never experience pregnancy or childbirth. I was certain I would love any child who came into my life, so of course the next logical choice was to adopt. My husband and I went to two adoption agency orientations——the first one was a few months before we were married and the second one was a year after our wedding. Both times we were told we would have to wait to start the process until we reached the "number of years married" requirement. Needless to say, it was upsetting to me that other people were controlling my destiny. Okay, that's putting it nicely——I was pissed! But I just didn't think I had any other choice.

In the spring of 2002, a friend suggested surrogacy and I began researching the subject. Immediately, I felt like, "This is the answer I have been looking for."

Until this conversation with my friend, doing surrogacy had never crossed my mind. I had always been very open about my infertility and my strong desire to be a mother——yet over the course of eight years, not one person had suggested the idea of surrogacy to me. I suffered with an unnecessary burden on my shoulders simply because I thought I had so few options.

My desire to have children via surrogacy was based on many factors. I wanted to go to ultrasound appointments and to experience a pregnancy from beginning to end. I wanted to live vicariously through someone else, since it couldn't be me who was the pregnant one. And when I found out that through surrogacy my husband could have a biological child, even if I could not, it was the icing on the cake for me.

I was astonished when I found *Surrogate Mothers Online* (SMO) and saw that hundreds of women out there actually wanted to have a baby—for someone else! The first time I read through the message boards on SMO, I felt like I was in the Twilight Zone or something. It was an underworld of sorts.

When I stumbled upon PPS, an Online support group specifically for *Parents Pursuing Surrogacy*, I finally felt like I was not alone. And as I learned about the experiences of others, the more I realized their stories—our stories—needed to be heard. The epiphany suddenly came to me that so many others would benefit by reading about what these women went through. Of course, my superstition would not allow me to actually start the project until our babies were born, so throughout the entire pregnancy the idea simply brewed in the back of my mind. But within weeks after Bella and Noah's birth I plunged right in, and I have been obsessed with writing and completing this book ever since.

Surrogacy Was the Way includes a series of true stories that give a realistic view into the world of an intended mother, the term for the "mother to be" in a surrogacy arrangement. The women whose journeys are chronicled throughout this book have resorted to surrogacy for a variety of reasons, from Mayer-Rokitansky-Kuster-Hauser syndrome (MRKH) to cancer to everything in between. Some of the journeys have gone rather smoothly, while others have been filled with one obstacle after another. Several of the women already have children and want to add to their families, while most are attempting to become mothers for the first time. The level of involvement between the surrogates and intended parents differ as well; from remaining extremely close, to keeping things business-like, to relationships gone completely awry. What they do have in common, regardless of the variations in their personal experiences, is that all of the women featured eventually become mothers through surrogacy.

There are many roads to family building in today's day and age and surrogacy is not necessarily the right choice for everyone. For a growing percentage of the infertile population, however, and for the twenty women who tell their stories in the pages to follow, surrogacy was the way.

"There is no chance, no destiny, no fate, that can hinder or control the firm resolve of a determined soul."

-Ella Wheeler Wilcox

One

My Story

As I was growing up, there was really only one thing I knew for sure about myself: I wanted to be a mom someday. I would imagine what it would be like to be pregnant, to have my husband feel my belly, to send him out in the middle of the night for ice cream and pickles. I'd envision going into labor and taking the mad dash to the hospital. I'd picture myself giving birth and shedding tears as the baby was placed on my chest. Having children in life was something I just assumed would happen. I just never imagined it would happen the way it did.

It all started in January 1994, eight months after I graduated from college. Out of nowhere I was chronically fatigued, oftentimes nauseous, and I didn't have much of an appetite. I was also getting persistent migraines.

When I was on the way to work one morning in early March, I had piercing pains in my abdomen and took myself to the emergency room. It turned out I had a hernia. I scheduled myself for the first opening they had for surgery, which was two days later.

My abdomen started swelling within days after the surgery. I figured it was some kind of after-effect—I even laughed to myself and thought, "Maybe they dropped a surgical instrument in me or something."

After about a week of my abdomen growing noticeably larger by the day, I realized something was terribly wrong. I didn't think it was so comical anymore.

I scheduled an appointment with my family doctor and he did a pelvic exam. He was visibly concerned when I described my symptoms to him. "Am I going to be okay?" I asked him. You're scaring me." He looked at me with a very serious facial expression and suggested I get an ultrasound as soon as possible.

I had the ultrasound the next day. When the doctor gave me the results he said there were definitely masses on my ovaries, but only a biopsy would determine whether they were cancerous or not. He referred me to a gynecologist, Dr. C, who would take over from that point.

My mom came with me to meet with Dr. C a few days later. After a quick pelvic exam she asked us to have a seat in her office. With my ultrasound results in front of her and a diagram of the female reproductive organs, she explained what the possible scenarios were. She described the various stages of cancer and used her pen to point to the organs in the picture.

According to Dr. C., stage one would mean it was contained to either one or both ovaries. That would be the best-case scenario because the cure for stage one ovarian cancer is around ninety-five percent. Stage two would mean it went beyond my ovaries, perhaps to my fallopian tubes. If it was stage three, it would have spread to all of my female organs, and stage four would mean it had reached my vital organs.

As I tried to digest this information, I was in a total state of shock. I felt like I was in a movie or something—like in those scenes when the doctor tells the patient, "You have cancer," and then the music plays to emphasize the horror of the moment.

I had the surgery on March 25, 1994, and it wasn't until I woke up from the anesthesia that I knew what the results were. Still drugged up, I opened my eyes to see Dr. C standing above me.

"I'm sorry, honey," she said, "but we had to take everything."

She added something about the surgery going well—they were able to remove the tumors and most of the cancer cells that had spread. The fluid that had built up in my stomach was actually caused by the tumors and that in turn is what caused the hernia.

Before I dozed off again, I thought to myself, "I can't have children now."

Then it hit me, "Why am I even thinking about having children—am I even going to live?"

Later that day, Dr. C and the oncologist, Dr. Y, gave me my diagnosis. I had third stage ovarian cancer, which meant it spread to all of my female organs: my ovaries, fallopian tubes, uterus, cervix, the whole shebang.

I spent the next eight days in the hospital. Every time my family would walk into the room, even though they tried to put on chipper faces, I knew they were so upset and worried. It made me more depressed than I already was.

I'd pretend I was sleeping when visitors came, even though I was usually wide-awake. I didn't want to see anyone. I was totally blindsided by the fact that I had cancer, especially since I had been reasonably healthy my entire life and nothing like this had ever happened to me. But I just couldn't grasp the fact that I just had a complete hysterectomy at twenty-three years old.

On my last day in the hospital, the doctors told me that the pathology results would be available about a week later. All I could do was go home and await my fate. I spent the entire week lying on the couch in a depression. I was terrified.

When my mom and I went to see Dr. C for the pathology results, she had great news for us: the biopsy showed that even though the cancer was third stage, it was a certain kind of cancer cell called "low malignant potential". This meant that although it spread while the tumors were present, when the tumors were removed the remaining cells would likely die off.

In other words, the hysterectomy was probably sufficient treatment and I wouldn't have to go through chemotherapy or radiation treatment. The survival rate was eighty-five percent with low malignant potential cancer at the third stage. Not one hundred percent—but hey, I'd take it.

Over the next few years most of my friends got married and started having babies, and although I didn't want to be jealous—I couldn't help it. I hated myself for feeling the way I did. It was also painfully obvious that it was awkward for my friends, especially when they would call to share news of a recent pregnancy. I would hear in their voices that they were walking on eggshells in a sense because they knew how desperately I wished I could be in their shoes. I felt guilty that they couldn't share happy news with me freely, without having to worry about how it was affecting me emotionally.

As a young woman without any female organs, I felt like a freak. I felt empty, physically and mentally. I figured I would never find somebody who was willing to marry me.

When I would start feeling sorry for myself that I couldn't have children, I would remind myself how fortunate I was that this was the worst of it. I never took for granted, after such a horrific cancer scare, that I was at least alive. My feelings during this time were complex because I knew things could have been much worse and I felt grateful that I was spared. Still, I was incredibly saddened because of what I had been through and because of the repercussions of my hysterectomy, and I simply cannot discount that.

Two years after my hysterectomy, in March of 1996, I met Mike at a restaurant that I was working at part-time. I told him I couldn't have children on our second date. I could see myself with him long-term and I didn't want to get attached if he was going to have a problem with my infertility. In October 1997, he got a new job, which required that he move to Michigan. He asked me to come with him. I said, "Yes!" I was ecstatic.

I constantly asked him why he'd want to be with someone like me, someone who couldn't have children. He'd reassure me that he loved me regardless and that it didn't matter to him. He would always add that if it came down to it, he'd rather be *with* me and childless than without me. All along, he said he was fine with adopting or whatever we ended up doing.

We got engaged in March 1999 and shortly thereafter I began researching adoption. I knew it would potentially take several years to adopt and figured it would be a good idea to start the process before we got married.

Meanwhile, I decided to go back to school to get my secondary education degree and I started taking classes at Eastern Michigan University that May.

A few months before our wedding, we went to an adoption agency orientation in Farmington Hills, Michigan. It was my idea, actually; I knew the adoption process could take a long time so I figured we should get a head start. We sat through both the domestic and international adoption meetings and then we stayed to talk to one of the social workers when the meetings ended.

She told us we'd have to be married for one year before we could start the adoption process through this agency. I cried the whole way home.

I knew surrogacy existed, but I never considered it as the way we'd create our family. I didn't know anybody who had been a surrogate or who had worked with a surrogate; my gynecologist had never suggested the idea—*nobody* ever suggested the idea. I remembered the "Baby M" case, but that was about it.

Shortly before our wedding, which was in August 2000, Mike got a new job in Illinois. I needed somewhere to live while I finished my classes in Michigan, so we decided to ask our friends, Juliana and Ron, if I could stay with them during the weekdays while I finished my last semester of school. Without hesitation, they said, "No problem."

As I completed my classes, I stayed at Juliana and Ron's house Monday through Thursday every week. Although we had known each other for the previous two years, Juliana and I became much closer than we had been previously. While I was taking my teaching courses, she was getting her business degree, so we'd often stay up late doing our homework together and talking about everything under the sun. One of the things we talked about frequently was my desire to be a mother and the hole I felt within because I couldn't bear children.

I moved back to Chicago when the semester ended and began my student teaching assignment. In March, when Mike and I had been married for seven months, we went to another adoption agency orientation. We figured this agency—The Cradle—would have the same requirement as the agency in Michigan, to be married for a minimum of one year.

It turned out The Cradle required that we were married for two years. I left that orientation meeting devastated. Once again, somebody else was telling me when I could start my family.

After a few days of feeling sorry for myself, I tried to look at the situation optimistically. I had just crammed in one hundred hours of college into two years so that I could get my teaching degree in the shortest time possible. I figured since we had no choice but to wait to start the adoption process, this would allow me to focus entirely on finding a job and getting through my first year as a teacher.

A few months later, I was hired at a nearby high school to teach English for the upcoming 2001 school year. Even though I was frustrated that we had to wait another year to adopt, once I knew how demanding and stressful the first year as a teacher is, I realized that maybe our "forced wait time" was a blessing in disguise.

One day, I was talking to my friend Jodie on the phone and she mentioned that the mom of a little boy in her son's pre-school class was a surrogate mother.

Then she asked me if we had ever thought about doing surrogacy and I said, "Absolutely not!"

I became intrigued though and asked her a few more questions, like, "Does that lady seem okay about not keeping the baby?"

"Oh yeah," Jodie said, "She's totally fine with it." After we hung up the phone, I really didn't think much more about it.

A couple of months later, Jodie called me again to tell me that Maureen had a baby girl. I was like, "So what happened? Was everything okay?" I waited for her to tell me about a pending legal battle or some disaster that resulted.

She said, "Oh yeah. Everything went fine. The couple was with her when she gave birth and they took the baby right home from the hospital." And before we hung up the phone, she added, "If you ever want to call Maureen, I'm sure she'd be more than happy to talk to you."

I said, "Well maybe someday, I'll let you know."

Within a day after this conversation, I hopped on the computer and did a search for "surrogate mothers". I clicked on one of the websites listed, *Surrogate Mothers Online* (SMO) and there before me was a world I never knew existed.

In the classified ads section, there were many women interested in being surrogates. They were asking fees—and some of them quite large, but all of a sudden this whole idea seemed like a possibility. I became obsessed and started combing the classified ads and reading the message boards several times a day.

In the meantime, I decided we should begin to look for a surrogate and put the adoption idea on the backburner.

About a week later, Mike and I were standing in the kitchen and I said, "You know, we have other options besides adoption."

"Like what?"

"We could do surrogacy. You know, someone else would carry the baby. The only thing is we would have to find an egg donor."

"Are you nuts?" he responded, right off the bat. "There's no way something like that would work…especially for us."

"Why not?" I asked. Do you think we are doomed or something? I think it could work, and you know what—I want to do it."

"It's too expensive," he said. "There's no way we can afford it."

He was right. From the research I had done up until this point, I knew that surrogacy and egg donation could be very costly. But I also knew there were ways to cut corners for people, like myself, who were willing to do a lot of the legwork.

I learned quickly that one of the most expensive aspects of surrogacy, in addition to the surrogate's compensation, is the IVF costs and medication expenses.

If we were going forward with surrogacy, we had a budget and we had to stick with it. We really had to sit down and figure out, "Is this a realistic possibility, financially."

One thing I knew for sure was that if we had to pay for all of the IVF expenses out of pocket, it would not have been an option for us. We had to find out if we had infertility coverage through our insurance.

I told Mike, "I'll look into the insurance and see if we're covered for infertility treatment, and if we are, I really think we can do this."

"Let's just adopt," he suggested. "I don't want to risk doing surrogacy and have something go wrong. Plus, I really think it's going to end up costing a lot more than you think it will."

I had always carried this guilt with me that Mike couldn't have a genetic child because of my defect. He never made me feel that way—I just did. When I learned that with the help of an egg donor Mike would be able to have a biological link, I thought, "That would be so awesome."

But the genetic issue wasn't really a selling point for him. He told me, during this initial conversation, that if the baby was only going to be half his biologically, he'd rather adopt. He felt bad that he would have a biological connection and I would not. I assured him that it wouldn't bother me. I figured just because I could not pass on my genes, it wasn't fair that he wouldn't have the opportunity to do so.

A couple of weeks later, we went to Michigan to visit Ron and Juliana. We were at their house chatting and Juliana asked, "So do you guys still plan to move forward with adoption soon?"

I said, "Well actually, we were thinking about doing surrogacy instead. The only thing is that we'd need an egg donor."

"I'll do it," she responded immediately.

I asked her, "Are you sure?"

"Positive," she said, and then she jokingly added, "Well that's assuming you'd even *want* me to be your egg donor!"

The concept of "choosing" genetics to pass down to a potential baby was rather odd. But if we wanted to do gestational surrogacy, this was something we had to consider——strange or not.

Juliana is from Argentina and she shares a lot of my physical characteristics; brown hair, brown eyes, similar completion. Whether or not this seems shallow to some, the fact that her features would potentially be passed on to a future child appealed to me. It wasn't only that Juliana's is a beautiful person on the outside; she is also incredibly intelligent, she has a great sense of humor and strong moral character. Taking everything into consideration, I believed she would be the perfect egg donor for us, and I felt a combination of joy, relief and shock that she actually offered to do it.

She was totally confident that she wouldn't have a maternal emotional attachment to any future child. She has a son, who was eight years old at the time, and she explained that he fulfilled her desire to be a mother. She said that because we were good friends, she would feel a connection to any child that we had——whether it was the "natural" way, through adoption, whether she was the egg donor or not. And although being our egg donor might cause her to feel an extra bond of sorts, it wasn't anything that she felt would be overwhelming or uncomfortable for her. I trusted that she knew what her emotional capabilities were. If this is what she was telling me——I believed her.

When we got home, I resumed my activity on SMO and I met a potential surrogate named Alison. She was thirty-five years old, she had four children and she lived about ten minutes from our house. She seemed like a great match from what I could tell.

I called Juliana to find out what her time frame would be. She told me that since she was going to Argentina for the summer to visit her family, she wouldn't be able to do the egg retrieval until the fall.

Meanwhile, Alison and I were emailing each other almost daily for about two weeks before we decided we should meet in person.

On a Sunday morning, Mike and I went to meet Alison and her husband at a nearby IHOP. During breakfast, Alison mentioned that she didn't plan to tell any of her kids that she was a surrogate until she was far enough in the pregnancy that she was showing. I thought this was sort of odd, but I figured she had her reasons and didn't want to pry.

While we were driving home after breakfast, Mike said he didn't feel like we clicked with Alison and her husband. I assumed it was his skeptical side talking, and even though I agreed with him deep down, I insisted that it would be fine.

I had asked around, and was referred to an adoption and third party reproduction attorney in downtown Chicago. Mike and I had a consultation with her shortly after we met Alison. One of the things she advised was that we find out whether or not we had infertility coverage through our insurance, and if we did, to get a letter confirming this in writing.

There were two infertility clinics on our HMO plan; one of them was a part of a university hospital in Chicago and the other one was Fertility Centers of Illinois (FCI), a large clinic with several locations throughout Chicago and the suburbs. We decided to go with FCI.

When I called to schedule our initial consultation, the nurse at FCI suggested she send Alison a packet of information so that she could get started on the paperwork.

I said, "Sure that would be great, except I don't know her home address." The nurse offered to call Alison for her address and I thought it was a good idea. That way, I figured, Alison could ask her any questions that she may have.

About two days later, I was surprised to open up my email and see an e-card from Alison. I thought, "Hm, what could this be?"

The message on the e-card said she had decided not to work with us after all because, in so many words, we had not honored her wishes.

I was like, "Huh? What's she even talking about?"

I tried calling her but got her answering machine. Then I emailed her and asked what we had done wrong.

She emailed back and said she was upset because the nurse from FCI called her and left a message on her answering machine. She reminded me that she didn't want her kids to know she was going to be a surrogate, and even though none of them actually heard the answering machine message, they could have.

I tried explaining that it was an honest mistake. She had made up her mind though, so all I could do was apologize and wish her the best. I wasn't going to beg her to give us another chance.

In tears, I told Mike about Alison's email. He hugged me and said, "Hey, then we weren't meant to work with her. Don't worry, we'll find someone else." Then he suggested we go for a long drive into the country, which is something both of us love to do. As we drove down the country roads on this warm, rainy spring day, I pondered all that had happened in my life up until that point. By the end of the day, I was fine. I knew in my heart that we would eventually find the right match.

I began looking for another surrogate on SMO the next day, but instead of only replying to other people's ads, this time I posted my own ad too.

After a few weeks, I had it narrowed down to a few potentials. One of them was named Kathy. Kathy and I chatted for a week or so and she seemed great, but she wanted to wait a year to start her journey while we were ready to get started within a few months. We parted ways as friends.

A few days later, Kathy emailed me and said that she had met another woman through SMO who was looking for intended parents—her name was Ashley. Would it be okay if she emailed me?

I replied, "Send her my way!"

Ashley emailed me a day or so later and we clicked immediately. She was twenty-three, married, and had a two year old son. She lived in Michigan, about three and a half hours from us, which was close enough that we could be included in the pregnancy as we wished.

Of course one of the questions I asked her as we were getting to know each other, is what prompted her to want to be a surrogate. She told me that about a month before we met, she dreamt that she was pregnant, but that she wasn't carrying her own baby. She woke up the next morning and went Online to research what she'd need to do to become a surrogate mother.

One Saturday morning, a couple of weeks after Ashley and I started chatting Online, I decided to give her a call.

The phone conversation went very well and we agreed we wanted to go forward. We decided she should come to Chicago the following Friday, so that we could meet each other and so she could begin the necessary preliminary testing at FCI.

I took the day off of work that Friday and went to pick her up at the train station in downtown Chicago. I didn't see her when I first walked through the doors at Union Station, so I yelled out, "Ashley?" All of a sudden, her voiced echoed out, "Zara?"

We hugged and laughed about how funny and strange this whole thing was. Our "hellos" had to be quick though. We had to get Glenview for her appointment with our RE, Dr. L. She was scheduled to have an HSG, a procedure in which fluid is injected into the reproductive organs and they are x-rayed to make sure everything is normal.

By the time our appointment was over, it was already 4:30 and her train was going back to Michigan at 6:04.

Rush hour traffic in the Chicago area, especially on a Friday, is atrocious. Miraculously, I got Ashley to Union Station by 6:01, and she had three minutes to run through the train station and catch her train back home.

After she flew out of the car and into the train station and we quickly said, "goodbye," I sighed with relief that we made it on time. Even though I was so glad we hit it off—just as I thought we would—I was exhausted. It had been a long day and I had a pulsating migraine.

The following week, Mike and I drove to Michigan to meet Nick, Ashley's husband, and their son, Andrew. We had pizza at their house and talked until midnight before we went back to our hotel room.

On the way home the next morning, I asked Mike what he thought of them. He said they seemed nice and that he could see himself being comfortable with Ashley as our surrogate. We also both liked Nick, which was a good thing, because it was important that we were comfortable with our surrogate's husband too.

It was the summer of 2002. Ashley and I talked on the phone and emailed almost every day. We were both very active on SMO and we each belonged to a Yahoo support group for surrogates and intended parents who lived in the Midwest. We started Online journals to document our surrogacy journeys. Both of us lived and breathed pregnancy and surrogacy.

As the summer came to an end and the school year was approaching, a lot of my energy went into preparing for my classes. At the same time, we continued plans for our upcoming egg retrieval and transfer.

Juliana was due back from Argentina at the end of August and we were hoping she'd be able to do the egg retrieval in September.

Since she was still in school at the University of Michigan, she would need to look at her syllabi and talk to her professors before she knew when she could miss a week of school. We would start planning the specifics once we knew her time-frame.

We had to coordinate Juliana's blood work and screening, which she would do at a clinic in Ypsilanti, Michigan, just outside of Ann Arbor. I didn't want to bother her in Argentina though, so instead I called Ron who had stayed home in Michigan. I figured he could relay my message to her.

When I got a hold of Ron, he said, "Well actually, I was going to call you. Juliana's father died yesterday so she won't be coming back for a couple more weeks." Then Ron explained what had happened; it turned out Juliana's father had had a heart attack and died almost immediately. He was only fifty-eight years old.

I didn't want to ask about the egg donation, but I had to know if she was going to call it off in case we had to come up with a "Plan B". I obviously would have understood if she changed her mind—but I have to admit, I would have been disappointed.

Ron assured us that she still wanted to go forward with us, but since she would be prolonging her trip to Argentina, we'd have to delay the egg retrieval until October.

Regardless of what Ron was telling me, I had my own theory. I figured that while Juliana was in Argentina for two months, she had thought about it more thoroughly and decided there was no way she could go through with her offer. Also, since her father had just passed away, I was certain she would be too distraught to go forward. I felt selfish for even worrying about the egg donation situation, but at the same time I had to know either way. After all, it wasn't just me who was involved in this process—I had to consider Ashley's role as well.

I decided it would be a good idea to check out egg donor agencies just in case. I looked Online and found several in the Chicago area, but when I contacted them I learned their fees were upwards of $9,000.00. I said to myself, "Well forget that idea."

I told one of my best friends, Megan, who I've known since my freshman year in college, about my dilemma. She said that she would be more than happy to be our egg donor if Juliana had changed her mind.

I also posted on the egg donation forum of SMO with my concerns and ended up meeting a woman named Claire, who said she'd be our egg donor if things didn't work out with Juliana or Megan. Then Meredith, anther lady I had met Online, offered to be our egg donor if needed.

It turned out all of my fears were for naught. Juliana called me in mid-September, the day after she returned home from Argentina, to tell me she was ready to get started. I told her I would totally understand if she had changed her mind, especially after losing her father so recently and so unexpectedly. She explained that they weren't super close anyway, and although she was of course very sad that he died, it in no way changed her desire to help us. She assured me that in a sense, because she knew she was doing something so profound, preparing for the egg donation and planning the trip to Chicago would probably help to take her mind off of things.

And then she said something that I will never forget. She said, "Zara, how many people have the opportunity to do something this significant in a lifetime? After all is said and done, no matter what else I do, I will be able to look back at my life and know that I helped you and Mike to have a family, something that you want more than anything in the world. This is my chance to do something that I will feel good about forever. I want to do this for you."

Juliana and Ron drove to Chicago on October 10, 2002. She had already begun the protocol for the egg retrieval a couple of weeks previous and she was being monitored at the Michigan clinic as planned. But we were getting closer to the retrieval date and FCI required that she come to the clinic every morning for the final week to closely monitor her follicle growth.

As the retrieval date was approaching, I felt like the weight of the world was on my shoulders. I'd wake up in the middle of the night thinking, "What if she doesn't produce many eggs? What if the embryos aren't good quality? What if her ovaries hyperstimulate and she ends up getting really sick?"

Ron and Juliana stayed at a hotel in downtown Chicago so they could be close to FCI, and Mike and I joined them every morning when she went in for monitoring.

We'd all look at Juliana's ovaries on the screen as the nurse explained her follicle growth progress. She was responding well to the egg stimulation medications and everything was right on track.

The egg retrieval was on October 16 and there were twenty-five eggs retrieved. The results boosted my confidence that things would work out after all, but I knew we still had a lot of hurdles to cross.

As we said our goodbyes in the parking lot at FCI, there was no way for me to verbalize my deep appreciation to Juliana for what she had just done for us. All I could muster up, as I squeezed her tightly, was "Thank you."

We watched them drive out of the parking lot and down the street, and I thought to myself, as I took a deep breath, "We've made it to another step."

We didn't know if we'd be having a three-day or a five-day transfer, so we decided Ashley should come to our house on Friday—two days after the egg retrieval—just in case in ended up being a three-day transfer.

On Saturday morning, Dr. L called to tell us the embryos were growing nicely and we'd be having a five-day transfer.

I knew this meant we'd only be transferring two embryos and I wondered if that would decrease our chances of a pregnancy resulting.

Dr. L said that the odds of achieving pregnancy were the same whether we transferred three embryos on day three or two embryos on day five. But he encouraged choosing the five-day route, because by transferring three embryos we'd be increasing our chances of all three taking. He said, in so many words, that if I were his daughter he'd give me the same advice. That was the clincher for me.

Finally the day came that we had been planning for so long. I was excited, but also very nervous. Mike had to work and Nick had to stay back with Andrew, so it was just Ashley and I at the transfer. Staring at the monitor and holding hands, we watched the two blastocysts travel into her uterus. I don't think either one of us was prepared for the wonder and magnitude of the moment.

The embryologist told us that out of seventeen embryos that had resulted from the egg retrieval, thirteen had made it to day five; this meant that after transferring two we would still have eleven embryos remaining. I hoped most of them would be good enough quality to freeze. Although I shuttered at the thought, I was acutely aware that the transfer may not work. If Ashley didn't get pregnant, we would definitely have wanted to do a frozen embryo transfer—so knowing we'd even have that option was extremely important. After all, it wasn't like I could just go through an egg retrieval myself, and I surely wouldn't have asked Juliana to do it again.

We came back to our house and Ashley was on bed rest for the next two days. She and her family went back to Michigan on Wednesday afternoon, two days after the transfer.

After Ashley, Nick and Andrew went home, I called FCI to find out how many of our embryos they were able to freeze. They said there were five. I had hoped that out of eleven embryos more would make it to freezing stage, but I was still relieved that we at least had enough left for one or two frozen embryo transfer attempts—if it came to that.

On Friday of that week I was driving home from work and my cell phone rang. It was Ashley. I could tell immediately that she was very excited. Suddenly she blurted out, "I know this is crazy, but I took a home pregnancy test and there is a really light line!"

I just lost it. I started laughing and crying at the same time, and all I could say was, "Are you sure?" She described how she took the pregnancy test outside to look at it in the sunlight and then she had Nick look at it too. Nick said he could barely see the line, but admitted nonetheless that there was something there.

It was only four days past our transfer date. I knew it was way too early to start celebrating and I didn't want to get my hopes up only to be disappointed. But after all of the effort it had taken to get to this point, I did allow myself to enjoy the moment. I finally let myself experience some feelings of optimism and relish in the happiness I felt I deserved so much.

As the days went on, Ashley took more tests and the lines got darker and darker. We were pregnant!

Seven days after the transfer, Ashley went to a clinic near her house and had her blood drawn. She couldn't stand waiting and wanted to know what the beta number was. As soon as she had the results she called me with the number—it was ninety-seven, on the higher end for that time frame. She was convinced it was twins.

I didn't want to jinx us by even allowing the luxury of thinking it was twins, so I assumed it was one baby and was very appreciative of that fact. I was just so happy that we actually *had* a pregnancy.

About two weeks after the transfer, Mike and I went to visit some friends in Texas. When we returned, I opened up our email to see a message from Ashley.

It said, "Roses are red, violets are blue, July is the month, your twins will be due," and she attached an ultrasound picture showing two gestational sacs.

She went on to explain that she thought she had a bladder infection, so she went to the hospital to make sure everything was okay with the pregnancy. It turned out that she didn't have a bladder infection; she had tried a new soap and it was causing her some irritation.

The night before we were to go to Michigan for our first ultrasound, about a week after we got the email announcing it was twins, Ashley called around 11:00 p.m. from her cell phone. She was on her way home from the hospital.

Ashley and Nick were out to dinner and she started spotting. The bleeding was heavy enough that she went to the emergency room, but the doctor who normally did the ultrasounds wasn't there. They sat in the waiting area for a couple of hours before they were told they'd have to wait until midnight for the next doctor on duty to arrive.

Ashley was worried because she didn't want us to drive all the way to Michigan only to find out that we had lost the pregnancy.

But Andrew was with them and it was late at night, so they had no choice but to go home.

Needless to say, Mike and I did not sleep that night. We left before 6:00 a.m. the next morning to drive to the doctor appointment in Michigan. I had been crying all night, and both of us were mentally and physically exhausted. Naturally, we were assuming the worst.

When the ultrasound technician put the wand on Ashley's belly, we saw two heartbeats beating away. To say we were relieved would be an understatement.

Although there were several more spotting episodes throughout the first trimester, we didn't worry like we had the first time. We talked to other women on our surrogacy support groups and learned that spotting in IVF pregnancies, especially during the first trimester, is actually fairly common.

Everything was going along smoothly and from the beginning we could not have asked for better results; however, I refused to let myself be "too" happy. I believed that once I started celebrating it would somehow be taken away from me.

I knew that most of the time, even with twin pregnancies, things turned out fine. But since my life at that time revolved around surrogacy and childbirth, I also knew, unfortunately, how much could go wrong. It was hard not to obsess about the "What ifs."

Mike was never as worried about losing the pregnancy as I was. His theory was, "If it's going to happen, it's going to happen," and he felt we shouldn't make ourselves crazy unnecessarily. But he also believed, as did I, that some risks were more avoidable than others.

When I first started talking to Ashley, she mentioned that she planned on taking some college classes that winter. I didn't think much of it at the time. I was like, "Oh that's nice."

The classes were scheduled for two nights a week, but since they weren't available at the campus ten minutes from her house, she'd have to go to the other campus—a fifty-minute drive each way.

I wasn't thrilled with the prospect of her driving in winter weather so far and so late at night, but I didn't know how to ask her to not take the classes or delay taking them until the following semester when it would be spring-time.

I bit my tongue and just hoped that everything would be okay. I imagined that the nights she had classes, I'd be on pins and needles wondering if she was going to make it home safely. I figured those nights would be nerve wracking but I'd just have to deal with it.

Around thirteen weeks into the pregnancy, Mike and I went to Michigan to attend the next ultrasound appointment. Both babies looked great. We made it to the end of the first trimester—another major hurdle crossed.

After the appointment, we all went to Applebees for lunch, and Ashley nonchalantly mentioned that her classes were starting in a couple of weeks.

Mike was like, "Huh?"

"Oh, didn't Zara tell you?" she asked.

I thought to myself, "Oh shit." I knew this was not going to go over well with Mike.

Although there was tension between Mike and I throughout lunch, we managed to make it through. Then we said, "Goodbye" and got back on the road to head home to Illinois.

It was beginning to snow hard and it was immediately apparent that the roads were very icy. Mike is a confident driver, but even he was uneasy driving in these conditions.

Southwest Michigan gets a lake effect from nearby Lake Michigan which causes a thick fog and terrible visibility. This was the case as we began our ride home, and if we weren't already struggling with the "driving to school issue" our fears were further magnified.

About five minutes after we got on the road Mike said, "I cannot believe you didn't tell me she was taking these classes…" and this led to an argument that lasted the entire drive home—

which ended up being over five hours because the weather was so bad.

I realized that I should have told him in the first place. I knew he would think it was a horrible idea and that he'd expect Ashley to change her plans. I also knew this would upset her which is obviously something I did not want to happen.

I agreed with him completely that it was not a good idea for her to be driving late at night, fifty minutes each way, on rural roads that aren't lit well. But I didn't know want to offend her or make her feel as if we were trying to be controlling—so I felt like I was in a lose-lose situation. Mike offered to discuss it with her, but I told him I wanted to talk to her instead.

The next day, I asked her if there was any way she could take her classes during the daytime. She said for the classes she wanted, there wasn't anything available during the day.

I asked her if she was sure there weren't any classes she could take at the campus near her house, so at least the drive wouldn't be so far—even if it did have to be at night.

"No," she said, the classes she needed were only offered at the campus that was farther away.

She said she'd see if there were any other possibilities—but it was very clear she was unhappy about the situation.

We were stuck between a rock and a hard place. I was so stressed out; I didn't know what to do. I felt like I was on the verge of a nervous breakdown.

As if I wasn't already freaking out, I opened my email a couple of days after our visit to Michigan to find out that a woman I had met through my RESOLVE infertility support group had just lost her triplets at twenty-one weeks into the pregnancy. I literally fell onto the floor. I was a total basket case. Much of this was due to the sadness I felt for my friend, but it was also the culmination of all of the stress I'd been feeling for the last several months. I made an appointment with my doctor and got a prescription for an anti-anxiety medication for the first time in my life. It was just too overwhelming.

A few days after our initial conversation, Mike talked to Ashley and explained our point of view. He told her we truly were not trying to be controlling—we applauded and understood completely that she'd want to take college classes.

Then he added, "Ashley, we cannot have children. You have our babies inside of you. If you were to have a miscarriage, that is something you cannot control. We realize that could happen any time and it wouldn't be anybody's fault. But driving in the middle of the winter in crappy weather, late at night, on dark country roads—is a controllable and avoidable risk. Can you just put yourself in our shoes?"

She was sympathetic, but still didn't agree with us that it was as dangerous as we thought it was. She told us time and time again that she was a safe driver. We went back and forth about it for over a week.

Fortunately, this was really the only major conflict that we encountered throughout our journey. But we were not prepared to deal with something like this; it was something that we did not think of beforehand. I've talked to many intended mothers who have come across similar circumstances. It feels awkward to ask someone "not to do" something that she'd normally do otherwise, but as an intended mother, it's incredibly difficult to sit back and not say anything when it's something you wouldn't do yourself if you were the pregnant one.

To say we came to a compromise wouldn't be fair—it wasn't really a compromise, it was "our" way. But Ashley had our babies inside of her and even though it was totally uncomfortable for us to ask her to alter her life, we felt it was our only option.

She agreed to make the concession and was able to find some classes she could take from home instead. Although not thrilled with this solution, she was willing to make the sacrifice because she knew how important it was to us. Mike and I paid the fees to drop the classes and that was the end of that.

When Ashley was about twenty-eight weeks along, Mike and I decided we really needed some stress-relief and we planned a five-day trip to Jamaica. We figured it was safe to go away for a few days since she didn't have any indications that she would be going into labor any day soon.

She had an appointment with her periontologist on our second day in Jamaica and called us afterwards to give us the update: the doctor checked her cervix and said it was dilated to between one and two and thinning. She was put on bed rest for the remainder of the pregnancy.

We felt bad for her that she had to be on bed rest, but as far as her going into labor, we weren't too worried about it. Plus, we figured, if she were to go into labor, even though it was early, at least we knew the chances of the babies surviving were very good.

Something that we admitted to nobody else but each other, was that we were both secretly happy she was stuck at home. Mike used to joke with her that we wished she was in a bubble—although, he was only partially kidding.

The school year ended on May 29. I had already told my boss, the English Department Chair, that I wouldn't be coming back the next year—I was going to be a stay at home mom.

We went to Michigan to visit Ashley the day after the school year ended. It was a Friday. We had planned on staying in a hotel near her house for the weekend and assessing the situation before we went home on Sunday. She was thirty-four weeks and four days along.

She was pretty sure she didn't feel any labor coming on, but since the doctor told her she could go off of bed rest, we knew it could happen at any moment.

We discussed it for a couple of hours, back and forth. Should we go? should we stay? what should we do?

We agreed that Mike and I should head back home and if Ashley felt the slightest sign of labor she'd call us immediately. That night, we went out to dinner in downtown Chicago to celebrate my mom's birthday, which was the following day—Monday, June 2.

On our way home, when we were about two minutes from our house, Mike's cell phone rang.

It was Ashley telling us that she was in labor and on her way to the hospital.

I just started laughing and I kept on saying, "No way!"

I couldn't believe that after all we had gone through preparing for this moment and after all I had been through, personally, as I waited for this dream to come true, Ashley was really in labor and I was finally going to be a mommy.

We arrived at the hospital around 5:30 a.m., and went up to Ashley's room to be with her while she labored.

At 9:30, her water broke, and by 12:20 the labor pains were really starting to kick in. After several more intense contractions she asked me to go get Dr. H, and when the doctor showed up Ashley was dilated to between eight and nine. She was determined all along that she'd deliver the babies without any drugs, but when Dr. H asked her if she wanted an epidural after all, Ashley said "Yes!" It was too late though—she was delivering naturally whether she wanted to or not.

Suddenly, Ashley screamed out, "He's coming!" and I ran into the hall and yelled, "They're coming!" Next thing we knew, there were a bunch of staff members charging into the room, including Dr. H and Carmen, the midwife.

Me, Ashley and Mike had discussed the birth plan several times, and Ashley told both of us that we were welcome to watch the babies come out. Mike wasn't sure if he'd actually be able to go through with it, but from the beginning, I knew it was something I wouldn't miss for the world.

I was standing a few feet back but could see our son's head crowning, so I quickly motioned Mike over to where I was standing. He turned to Nick and asked, "Is it okay?". Nick who was videotaping for us, said, "Sure".

Just a couple minutes later, at 1:52 p.m., Noah Michael made his appearance. At 5 lbs. 6 oz., he came out crying and absolutely perfect.

I didn't know what to do first because it was so chaotic. Mike and I ran over to look at Noah and we were in such awe. We watched the nurses clean and weigh him, and we held him briefly before he was put in the warmer. Then we ran back to watch Isabella being born.

Isabella Alina arrived at 1:59 p.m., seven minutes after her brother. When I saw her head crown I yelled out, "Look at her full head of hair" and at 6 lbs. 3 oz., out she came. She was the most beautiful little thing! Within a few seconds, she too let out a cry, and then she was whisked off to be cleaned and weighed. We took turns holding her, then one of the nurses handed Noah over to us so we could hold both of our babies.

Before they were taken out of the room to have their apgars done, Mike and I each gave Ashley a hug and thanked her. I had such admiration for what she had just done for us; I will never forget that moment. It is burned in my brain forever.

After expressing our gratitude to Ashley we left the room to be with our babies. Then we called our families to tell them the good news. My parents said they were on their way to the hospital and they'd be arriving in three hours. Before I hung up the phone I said to my mom, "By the way, happy birthday Grandma!"

Both babies went to the NICU because they had slight breathing issues and needed some oxygen help. Noah was off the oxygen after a few hours, but Bella needed to have it overnight. By the next day they were bottle-feeding and they were in the regular care nursery by the third day.

I stayed with Ashley in her room for the first two nights and Mike slept at a hospitality house near the hospital. On the first night, after Mike left for the hospitality house and I said "Goodnight," I started walking towards the parking lot. I was headed towards our car to get a book to read.

As I flung open the hospital doors, I stopped in my tracks and thought, "Hey, wait a second. My babies are here. Why in the world would I read a book now?" It barely had sunk in to the point that I almost didn't realize that they were really here. I could see them anytime I wanted now.

Then all of a sudden it hit me like a ton of bricks. They're here. My babies are finally here. I spent the last nine years wondering if I'd ever be a mom and I worried for the entire pregnancy that something would go wrong and my dream would be taken away from me. I went into the bathroom and had a good cry; then I looked at myself in the mirror and said, "You did it. You are finally a mommy."

We left the hospital and headed home to Illinois in the early afternoon of June 7, a Saturday. Summer in the Midwest had just begun; the sun was shining and the sky was bright blue. Mike drove and I sat in the backseat between Noah and Bella, who were so tiny as they slept in their infant car seats. We were quiet during that ride home—overwhelmed with contentment and gratitude. Our babies were here and our hearts were finally full.

Postscript

From the moment our children came into our world, I have felt a sense of peace and fulfillment that I never dreamed possible. The day they were born, it was as if the weight that had been on my shoulders for over nine years had been lifted. The anxiety medication I had taken for the last five months of the pregnancy was no longer needed—I literally took my last pill the day before Bella and Noah were born.

Mike loves being a daddy, and just as I imagined, he is a wonderful one. Sometimes, I get lost in watching them together; laughing, playing, cuddling. When I hear the depths of his laughter and see the expression of pure joy on his face as he interacts with our children, it warms my heart in a way that I cannot even put into words.

Would I ever have wished cancer upon myself? Certainly not. But the fact that I had cancer and a hysterectomy, led my life down a road that I never would have envisioned. I have met people who I would have known otherwise, and I have learned so much about human nature and the genuine goodness of so many.

Noah and Bella are typical two and a half year olds now. Both of them look like a combination of Juliana and Mike, and with brown curly hair and brown eyes, Bella looks very much like me as well. Their vocabulary is extensive and we are now having full-blown conversations with them. Their latest kick is telling us many times a day, "I love you so, so, so, so much!"

They like all sports, especially golf and hockey. They love to go outside and "ride their bikes" and they're into matchbox cars and anything else with wheels. They like to play "kitchen" and feed their dolls and stuffed animals fake pasta that they made on their toy stove. They help their mommy make cakes and eat the batter with spoons. They love when we read to them. They love music, dancing and singing. They love to snuggle with their mommy and daddy.

Instead of waking up to a silent house every day, I wake up to their voices echoing through the hall, "Mommy? Where are you?"

Our house is an absolute pigsty. There are toys and crumbs everywhere. The shade on a lamp in our family room is now covered with red and yellow crayon. The couches are covered with little spots of crusted milk. Our carpets are pretty much ruined. We are the luckiest people in the world.

Ashley has since had a second son and is she is currently a surrogate again for another couple. I still talk to her frequently on email and occasionally on the telephone, and we have managed to get together a couple of times a year since Bella and Noah were born. Besides being a former intended mother and a former surrogate, we are good friends. I believe we will stay in touch indefinitely.

Juliana and I are also still very close. We try to get together once or twice a year and we talk frequently on email and on the telephone when we both have time. She and Ron are divorced now and she's engaged to a man named Perry. She recently asked me to stand up in her wedding next year. Bella and Noah are going to be in the wedding too.

I have already started telling our children what bits and pieces they can comprehend as two year olds—they know they were "In Ashley's belly because Mommy's belly was broken," and although they don't completely grasp it at this time, we plan to always be honest with them about the way they were brought into this world.

Whatever path took me to Bella and Noah, even though it was filled with much pain at times, I believe it was a road I was meant to walk down. When I look at my children I cannot help but think they were meant to be mine. But I also know that none of this would have happened if I didn't initiate all of the steps that had to be taken; if I didn't refuse to accept childlessness as an option.

I don't know why bad things happen to good people. I don't know why I had cancer at such a young age and I don't know why all of the women whose stories are told in this book faced other obstacles in life. What I do know, however, is that as humans we have choices. And I believe wholeheartedly that almost anything is possible if we want it enough.

The trend for women to wait until "later" in life to have children has perhaps contributed to the number of those seeking fertility treatment today. Egg quality declines over time; therefore, when a woman in her late thirties or older is having difficulties conceiving, poor egg quality may be the root of the problem. Of the six intended mothers in this book who were over forty years old when their babies were born, five of them did gestational surrogacy with donor eggs. Karen, the woman featured in the following chapter, tried to get pregnant with assisted reproduction for several years before she found out why it would never happen. An Endometrial Function Test® (EFT®) performed in the laboratory of Dr. Harvey J. Kliman, M.D. Ph.D., Yale University School of Medicine's Department of Obstetrics, Gynecology and Reproductive Sciences, confirmed that she lacks MAG, one of the substances that is normally produced by the endometrium to promote implantation. Dr. Kliman and Dr. David L. Keefe, M.D., Professor and Chair of the Department of Obstetrics and Gynecology at the University of South Florida College of Medicine, ran a study to determine the effects abnormal or absent MAG levels had on implantation. In their 2002 article, "Implantation: The Challenge of Assessment and Treatment", where they discuss the results of this study, it is stated, "only 18% of the patients with abnormal MAG levels became pregnant and none of the patients with absent MAG expression became pregnant." Karen's EFT® results proved that even if she did have some good quality eggs, despite her age, the embryos could not implant in her body. She and her husband went through years of failed IUI's and IVF's, several miscarriages, and almost seventy embryos before the cause of her infertility was determined. But even with this realization, Karen had no intention of giving up on her dream.

Two

Karen
Los Angeles, California

Before I got married I was ambivalent about having a child. I had resigned myself to the fact that I may never meet a man and figured I would never have a baby on my own. So I just didn't indulge myself in that fantasy.

I met Matt when I was thirty-seven and we got married one month before I turned forty. We decided to start trying to get pregnant on our wedding night; he's old fashioned and believed we should wait until we were married. We figured once we started trying, it would take one, two, three months and that would be it.

My gynecologist's wife got pregnant while using birth control at age forty-two and he always assured me, "Don't worry, it will happen."

Six months later it still hadn't happened. My gynecologist told us nothing was wrong and suggested we do IUI for better results. He said, "We'd normally do the insemination on the day you ovulate, which falls on a Saturday this month, but since we aren't open on the weekends we'll just have to do it Friday and Sunday instead."

"That's not very good," I thought, "We need to find someone who is open on the weekends." We decided it was time to see a RE.

The RE suggested we go straight to IVF but I wanted to continue trying fertility drugs and IUI attempts instead. Month after month went by and I still wasn't pregnant, so we finally took the doctor's advice and did an IVF cycle.

To everyone's surprise, I produced eggs like a twenty year old. I made twenty-three eggs at my first egg retrieval, which was amazing statistically given that I was forty-one years old.

The doctors and staff at our clinic were confident it would work; they all told us, "This is going to take for sure."

Our first IVF attempt didn't take, but on the second try I got pregnant with triplets. Only one of them had a heartbeat and it was a weak heartbeat. A week later we went back and the heartbeat was gone. It never occurred to me this could happen. I always thought once you are pregnant, that's it.

The doctors were very optimistic. They kept saying, "The hardest part is getting pregnant."

We did a third IVF and soon found out I was pregnant with twins, but I miscarried one baby before the first ultrasound. The second baby looked great though and there was still a strong heartbeat at six and a half weeks. At the seven-week ultrasound, however, the heartbeat was gone.

This time I guess I was a little more prepared. The whole infertility process is devastating; it seems like your life is always on hold waiting for the next cycle and your whole existence revolves around trying to get pregnant. It's very draining.

Finally, my doctor suggested, "Maybe there is something wrong."

They did a hysteroscopy and said, "Oh, it looks like you have a septum, an extra tissue in your uterus. Maybe that's the problem." They removed the extra tissue and we tried another attempt.

This transfer led to a chemical pregnancy. The doctors suggested we try again, so we transferred another set of frozen embryos. I didn't get pregnant.

Finally, our RE bluntly said, "You have gone through sixty-three embryos and you have no baby to show for it. Even though you are older, we believe that one-third of your eggs should be good and you should have a pregnancy by now."

"I think you should look into surrogacy because we cannot figure out what is wrong with you. There should have been some good eggs in there."

As a television producer, it may sound like I make a lot of money. I work on cable shows though, and while we are comfortable, we are not exactly rolling in the money. We were just married and this took an enormous financial toll on us. I really don't know how we figured we were going to pay for a surrogate.

I began researching surrogacy agencies on the Internet to find out what they charged and what services they provided to warrant their fees. I learned about how they worked and that overall expenses through an agency could be upwards of $70,000.

I thought to myself, "I can do this myself. I mean, really, what do they do? They get all the players and they put them together...that's what I do for a living."

I began searching websites for information about surrogacy. One of the best ones was SMO, where women post ads if they want to be surrogates and people post ads if they are looking for a surrogate. I posted an ad and got five or six responses. One woman, Tanya, lived about a half hour drive from us. I thought, "Okay, well she's the one." I figured since she lived nearby, we were "meant" to work together.

Tanya and I met at a coffee shop. She was twenty-one years old and had one daughter. She wasn't married, but lived with her daughter's father. She was very overweight. My doctor didn't think her weight would be a problem, however, because she was so young. I could just tell that she was very honest and sincere about wanting to be a surrogate. It felt right.

We took our remaining six frozen embryos and transferred them into Tanya. She did not get pregnant.

Our RE said, "Your eggs are old. Maybe we should do a fresh cycle instead of another frozen embryo transfer." It had been five months since I miscarried the twins and I was forty-one years old.

In the interim, our doctor suggested Matt do a Sperm Chromatin Structures Assay (SCSA) test, which analyzes sperm DNA. It looks for some things that a normal microscope can't see. We were told that oftentimes, when there is a miscarriage, or when it just seems the woman can't get pregnant, there is actually a sperm problem. It turned out that Matt's sperm wasn't too great, but he had also been on antibiotics, which can affect sperm quality. He went off the antibiotics and we did a fresh cycle with Tanya again.

We decided to be really aggressive this time and transferred embryos into both Tanya and myself. We assumed at least one of us would get pregnant. But about twelve days later we had our betas and they were both negative.

It seemed the problem was likely my eggs and Matt's sperm. The doctors suggested we get an egg donor and a sperm donor and transfer the embryos into me instead of our surrogate.

We were ready to move on to a different RE by then. Not that he or his staff did anything wrong, but I just think we kind of overstayed our welcome. We still continued to recommend people to them because we believe they are highly competent, but Matt and I were just ready to move on.

We switched to another clinic and they sent Matt to a male infertility specialist. Although it was an option, he wasn't interested in using donor sperm. The new RE took a look at Matt and discovered that he had a varicose vein running through his scrotum. Basically what this means, is that one of the valves that runs from his heart through his scrotum isn't pumping properly. The blood pulls down in his scrotum heating the sperm to a higher temperature than it should be, and this harms the sperm.

With our previous attempts, one hundred percent of the eggs fertilized—even without ICSI. Matt didn't have any pain so there were no indicators that this problem existed.

He has been very supportive. He has a son from a previous marriage so he doesn't have the same need I do to have another child, but he went under the knife to have his condition repaired because he knew how important it was to me that we have a baby together.

Ironically, it turned out that his sperm was fine after all of this, but the RE told us we would have to wait three months after Matt's surgery before we could go forward with another fresh transfer attempt.

We sat down with the RE to discuss our next step, and he told us that early miscarriage is sometimes a sign that a woman has an abnormal endometrium. Then he added, "I'd like to send you to take some samples and do an Endometrial Function Test® (EFT®), a new test that Yale is doing. I've sent twenty people and nobody has had a problem so far, but I'd just like you to check and see."

He said the EFT® was like an endometrial biopsy, where they scoop out some of the uterine lining on the fifteenth and the twenty-fifth day of a woman's cycle. It was a good thing I had the EFT® done, because the results explained why I was not getting pregnant. It turns out that I am missing a glue-like protein called MAG in my endometrium, a protein that is essential to support implantation. There is no cure and currently there is no known reason why some women have this condition. This was obviously disappointing news to say the least, but I was relieved to finally have an answer after all of this time.

Once it was clear that I would never become pregnant, the RE suggested we try again with a gestational surrogate. Because of my age, we also knew that my egg quality could be poor, so just as the previous RE had suggested a while back, Matt and I decided to look into egg donation as well.

Shortly after we received the EFT® results, I called Tanya to see if she would be willing to do another attempt with us in a few months, but she had already found a new set of intended parents. I would have to begin searching for a new surrogate.

I placed another ad on SMO but I was much more specific than I was the first time. I actually got about forty responses. I had a chart to keep track: their screen names, their ages, whether or not they had a significant other, and little stories about things we talked about. It can feel like such an artificial thing sometimes.

I emailed several women for about five weeks and then I finally said to Matt, "I'm talking to a bunch of potential surrogates and after New Years I want to put out some offers." I had narrowed it down to seven potentials.

One woman, Julie, had already been a surrogate through an agency. I emailed her and said, "You're probably not going to be interested in working with us, because we cannot afford to pay agency fees." We had already spent over $120,000 trying to achieve pregnancy by this point.

She emailed back and said, "That's not what this is all about for me. I'd like to continue talking."

I was just getting to know people. So I made her an offer that I assumed she wouldn't accept. She accepted it. I made an even lower offer to the other two women thinking they wouldn't accept either. They did. Matt and I decided to meet all three of them.

We met Julie, who was married with one child, and we just loved her. She was upfront, warm and open. We could laugh together and I could just be myself.

Then, we met the second potential surrogate and her boyfriend. Her boyfriend smoked which bothered us, and I don't know, we just didn't feel like it was a fit. As terrible as it sounds, you are sizing them up. And they are doing the same to you—as they should be. You can't just look at her and say, "I like her but not her boyfriend." He is part of the package.

As we were getting ready to go meet the third one, Matt said, "I'm tired of this, don't you like the first woman?"

I said, "Yeah, I really like Julie, let's just go with her." It felt so right with her from the beginning.

After New Year's 2003, I made Julie an offer and she accepted. She was ready to begin immediately but we hadn't found an egg donor yet. I had been trying to find someone independently for a couple of months, but everybody I met lived out of state and we wanted to find someone local. Eventually we decided to go through an egg donor agency.

At this point, I was forty-three years old and tired of failure. I just wanted a baby and I didn't care if I would be genetically related or not.

Meanwhile, we did the contracts and everything went smoothly. It was important to Matt and I that our potential surrogate was willing to reduce if necessary. Everyone must be on the same page; surrogates and intended parents need to talk about everything before going to the lawyer, not after the lawyer is involved. Nobody wants surprises.

Our doctor co-stimulated the donor and myself, so we were still able to use my eggs. We actually mixed them with the donor eggs.

In April 2003, we transferred three embryos created by my eggs and Matt's sperm, and three embryos created by the egg donor's eggs and Matt's sperm, into Julie. Since my eggs were old, we knew the chances of them actually taking were slim——but we figured we'd put them in too just in case. I'd refer to them as "throwaways" and it would upset Julie.

She'd say, "You are going through so much effort to get them. I wish you were more positive."

I'd reply, "You know, you haven't been through what I've been through."

I was confident the transfer would work. Julie started doing home pregnancy tests and she was getting negatives at first, but then she suddenly got a positive. I thought, "This is it! I'm going to be a mom!"

Then she went in for the beta test and the number was eleven. I knew it was a chemical pregnancy. The beta went down to nine a few days later. We were all crushed and we couldn't figure out why it didn't work.

Our RE said, "I'd like to run a blood panel on her."

The results of the blood test showed that she had blood clotting and immune issues. I couldn't believe I found myself a surrogate with infertility problems. The RE said Julie was fortunate that she got pregnant so easily with her own children.

He told us, "You have two options. One, you can get a new surrogate and that would probably be my first recommendation. Or two, what we do with women who are trying on their own is we give them heparin, which is a blood thinner and pregnazone, which is a steroid, to keep them from miscarrying. What would you like to do?" I told him I'd get back to him.

I said to Matt, "I can't take this anymore. This is too much. I'm burnt out, I'm devastated, I have no feeling left anymore. We have three embryos created by donor eggs and three created with my own eggs, let's just try another attempt with Julie if she's willing."

Julie was glad that we wanted to try again with her, and we were relieved that she was willing to take the heparin and do everything she needed to do. We went right into another cycle. She was on a variety of drugs; fortunately she had no problem with shots. We did the transfer on May 17. I hardly talked to her for the two-week wait because I was so certain it was going to fail.

I was Online one day and she sent me an instant message. She asked if we could talk and I said, "Of course."

"I feel like I can't talk to you about this pregnancy and about how I'm feeling, and if I'm feeling cramps or twinges."

Unjustifiably, I felt frustrated with her that she had these problems. I asked her not to take any home pregnancy tests because I was afraid they'd be negative and I just didn't want to know. All of this bothered her because I didn't have the same level of excitement as I did during the first attempt.

When I told some of my friends that Julie's feelings were hurt by my lack of enthusiasm, they responded, "What about you, what about your feelings—doesn't she know what you've been through?"

I'd say, "No, that's not the dynamic. She's doing something enormous for me and her job is not to think about how I feel. Not that she isn't compassionate, but she's telling me I need to be there for her. I need to cast aside my emotions and give her what she needs."

I called her over the next few days and acted as if I was excited and optimistic, which I was not.

I'd get off the phone and sob, "We're never going to have a baby. We're not pregnant, I know we're not pregnant."

The morning of her beta test she called me and I asked her how she felt. She said, "Not pregnant."

I asked her if she took a home pregnancy test and she said "No."

She went to the doctor and the nurse called me later and she sounded kind of happy. I thought, "This is really cruel."

She said, "Julie's beta was positive! Do you want to know the number? It's 213!" I asked her if she thought there was more than one baby but she said, "No, I think it's just one."

Julie was bummed because she had a fantasy of how she was going to tell me and she didn't get the chance to do that. The next beta, about a week later, was 1186 and she finally had a way to surprise me by giving me this good news.

A week or so later we went in for the first ultrasound and they put in the wand. They weren't sure if we were going to see a heartbeat because we were only five weeks and six days along. Not only could we hear the heartbeat, we could even see the yolk sac. We were thrilled!

Then the doctor pushed the wand around a little more and remarked, "This is interesting."

"What do you mean?" I asked.

It turned out that he saw another yolk sac and inside that sac were two more heartbeats.

I was like, "Oh no…" because we had talked about selective reduction and Julie said she would do it if we requested.

We all agreed to reduce if there were more than two because of the health risks involved to the babies. At the time, though, we didn't realize the reality of it. There are just too many complications with triplets and our goal was to bring home a healthy baby. Research shows that the mortality rate for triplets is high, as is the chance of miscarriage. Oftentimes the birth weights are very low—some babies are under a pound—and this increases the chances of birth defects. Plus, we had identical twins in there so that presented a whole new array of problems.

We went back two weeks later when we were seven weeks and six days pregnant to have an ultrasound. All three of the babies had strong healthy heartbeats. It was incredible.

We are grateful that we have a pregnancy, but we are also sad because we are probably going to reduce. This Monday, we are going in for CVS and this will diagnose any abnormalities affecting the fetus. Part of the reason we want to do this is that the embryos created with my forty-year-old eggs are in there too. We want to make sure there aren't any chromosomal abnormalities. The decision will be easier for us if something is wrong with one or two of them. It's very hard—we never imagined this would happen.

The irony is that only two took, but one of them split. Nothing has been easy. We haven't had an ultrasound since we were seven weeks and six days pregnant, and Julie will be over eleven weeks when we have the CVS test. I know she isn't happy about the situation—none of us are. She's even offered to carry all three of the babies, but all of the doctors we've consulted are very bleak about the scenario. It doesn't feel good to make this decision. All of these decisions require taking someone else into consideration too. She's another person and now she's my friend.

Everyone who I've spoken to who was in a position where they had to reduce said that once you do it it's a relief. Until we do this, I feel I can't get too attached to the pregnancy. I mean, I don't know if I should be getting attached to one baby or two or what.

Pregnant women will say to me, "Oh, you are so lucky you don't have to go through the pregnancy."

They have no idea what it's like being an intended mother; they don't understand how difficult it is to have zero control of the pregnancy and they don't realize how emotionally draining the whole thing is.

I think the core issue is, to me, that yes there is gratefulness that there are other options out there besides adoption. I have one friend who had three adoptions fall through before she finally got her baby. The biggest reason that I like the idea of surrogacy is that once the surrogate is pregnant, that baby is yours. That is the difference between surrogacy and adoption. In a surrogacy scenario, the baby is created with intent. The baby isn't being "given up", rather, it's "intended" for someone.

I think my situation is pretty common nowadays. People wait until they are older to try and get pregnant, and then when it's not working out they have to figure out another way to have a baby.

My mother keeps on saying, "I still don't understand why she'd want to do this for a stranger."

There is so much suspicion about why surrogates would want to do this. I think my journey may be happening to prove how much I really want to be a parent. I haven't told too many people yet——I'm curious to see what the reactions are going to be when people find out that we are becoming parents this way.

Postscript

Julie ended up having placenta abruption at twenty-eight weeks gestation, so to everybody's shock, at 3:00 a.m., on November 14, 2003, she gave birth by emergency c-section to Karen and Matt's identical twin boys. They were born twelve weeks premature, at 3 lbs. 1 oz and 2 lbs. 7 oz. and had to spend about three months in the hospital hooked up to ventilators and struggling to survive. One of the boys had a collapsed lung and needed surgery. They were both quarantined for three additional months after they arrived home and only allowed out for doctor appointments. They also needed shots for their lungs for their first two winters.

Today Justin and Landen are healthy, growing boys. They have some developmental delays but Karen and Matt are very optimistic that these smiling, happy, beautiful children will continue to catch up and reach their potential. They have also become soap opera stars on "The Bold and The Beautiful" appearing as one character, R.J., once or twice a month.

Karen says she has learned a lot throughout her infertility and surrogacy journeys. She has been able to take all of her experiences—from starting a support group with other women going through infertility, her own IVF and surrogacy failures, having CVS and going through selective reduction, and finally the premature birth of her twins—and she has started her own surrogacy agency, Agency for Surrogacy Solutions, Inc. In less than a year of incorporation she already has over twenty-five clients, and the agency is expanding to help in other areas of infertility. Karen hopes that she can continue to use her past experiences, as well as her new ones, to help more and more people.

Vivian and Jessica never even attempted to get pregnant; they knew from a young age that it would never happen for them. Along with two more intended mothers featured later in the book, both Vivian and Jessica were born with a condition called Mayer-Rokitansky-Kuster-Hauser Syndrome (MRKH). Vivian learned at eight years old that she had this condition, while Jessica, like most women with MRKH, found out when she was in her teens. In a Magic Foundation article titled, "What is Mayer-Rokitansky-Kuster-Hauser Syndrome?", Tom Mazur Psy. D. of The Children's Hospital of Buffalo, New York and Ellen Jones, M.Ed., Magic Foundation Division Consultant, define MRKH as "an uncommon variation in the prenatal development of the female genital tract, with features that include an absent or very short vagina and a uterus that can be absent or immaturely formed." They add, "the incidence of MRKH syndrome is approximately 1 in 4,000 - 5,000 female births. Although it has been determined that the absence of a vagina and uterus is a result of the Mullerian ducts failing to form properly early in embryonic development, its underlying cause is unknown." The majority of women with MRKH still have functioning ovaries; therefore, thanks to gestational surrogacy, both Vivian and Jessica were able to use their own eggs and have biological children. The following two stories demonstrate that knowing about ones' infertility early in life does have one benefit—the opportunity to plan ahead.

Three

Vivian
Volant, Pennsylvania

When I was eight years old, I was diagnosed with Mayer-Rokitansky-Kuster-Hauser syndrome (MRKH). As a result, I have certain physical issues common in MRKH patients; specifically, I have no cervix and my uterus is undeveloped. So I've known from childhood that I would never bear children.

Most women don't discover they have MRKH until they are in their teens or twenties. I found out because I had a kidney problem. The doctor eventually did some x-rays, then he told me I only had one ovary. Several years later I found out that I actually have two—they are just higher up and smaller than a "normal" woman's ovaries.

One morning before school, when I was ten years old, I saw on television that the first "test tube baby" was born. I didn't completely understand the technology at the time but it gave me hope that I too could have a baby in the future.

Although I was inspired by the prospect of having a test-tube baby someday, I was also discouraged because I knew that it was probably quite expensive. We were a regular, middle-class family, and I didn't think I'd ever be able to afford something like that.

Still, I figured I should start saving money just in case. To be honest, I have been conservative, financially, all of my life in order to save for IVF and surrogacy.

As I was growing up, my friends would talk about what it would be like when they had babies one day. Occasionally I would join in and pretend that I was just like all of the other girls, even though I knew I'd never give birth, but most of the time I tried to avoid these types of conversations.

I was very bitter and angry about it but I never confided in anybody about my feelings. I didn't even talk to my parents about how I felt because I figured they wouldn't be able to help me anyway. As far as I know, they never considered putting me in counseling or anything like that.

I didn't really even start confiding in people about it until about five years ago. I didn't share my feelings with a soul—not even my best friend. My husband's family didn't even know there was a problem. They just assumed we didn't want kids, I guess.

Once I started talking about it, I felt so much better. It was like a weight was lifted off my shoulders. It was sort of embarrassing to tell people that I wasn't a "normal" woman, but it was better than keeping it all to myself. It was better than trying to hide a big secret.

I met my husband, Eric, when I was nineteen years old, but I waited five years to tell him I couldn't have children. I actually didn't tell him until the year before we got married. I was afraid to tell him—I didn't want to lose him.

It was really difficult for me because Eric refused to talk about how we were going to have kids. He wouldn't discuss adoption or surrogacy. That really upset me; I needed him to be my partner in this. I think I would have been more open with his family if he was willing to talk to me about it too.

Meanwhile, everyone around me was having babies and I felt awful. Keeping all of my feelings to myself made it worse.

When I was twenty-nine, four years after we got married, we decided it was time to tell the whole family. I emailed my mother-in-law and sister-in-law and told them what was really going on. They were in disbelief but tried to be supportive for the most part. Not only did we drop the bomb that I was infertile, we added that we were researching surrogacy at the same time.

To be honest, because we were so worried about the cost, my true motive for telling everyone was that I hoped a family member would offer to be our surrogate.

Initially, my sister-in-law offered to carry for us but she ended up changing her mind. Then Eric's cousin was going to do it, but her husband wasn't supportive of the idea so she changed her mind too.

I have a sister and always thought she should have offered to be our surrogate. She has three children but had lots of problems in her pregnancies, and she didn't want to take the risk that something would go wrong if she were pregnant with our child. I used to think she was being selfish, but now I realize that she did have our best interests at heart. She was actually the first person that I ever told about my dreams to have a baby via surrogacy. Although, I have to say that she wasn't very optimistic that it could actually happen for us.

I decided to try and find a surrogate mother Online, through the classified ads on SMO. I met a potential candidate named Wendy who lived only about an hour and a half from us.

Wendy and I were both anxious to move forward so we got started with all of the necessary screening. We became friends over the course of the next year. Although we didn't talk on the phone very often, we did email each other on a frequent basis. She'd also pop into my work when she was in the area. We have these huge outlet stores where we live, so Wendy would go shopping and then stop by my work unannounced.

The fire department where I volunteer puts on occasional craft shows and Wendy came to those too. One time, when she came to a craft show, my sister was there and she said, "I don't want to see my sister hurt. I hope you are serious about doing this."

Wendy said, "I'm totally serious about it."

The reason she wanted to be a surrogate was because she had an abortion when she was younger and she felt very guilty about it. She was recently married and had no kids, which ended up being the reason she changed her mind about being our surrogate.

She shared this with me in an email, saying something along the lines of, "I'm sorry, I have some bad news to tell you. I can't be your carrier right now because Jim and I want to have our own children first."

I tried to act like I wasn't upset because I did honestly think she was a great person for even attempting to be a surrogate for us. I was incredibly saddened though.

I have to admit, the whole experience with Wendy was kind of weird. She was only twenty-one years old, so when I think back on it, I realize that maybe she was just too young. Maybe she was just looking for a friend or something. We stayed in contact for a while and she was always interested in how our search for a new surrogate was going, so I do think she meant well for the most part.

After the experience with Wendy, I went into a slump and decided to unsubscribe from the PPS list-serv, another Online support group to which I belonged. I was convinced that surrogacy was never going to happen for us, that we would never find anyone. I thought we should just give up. It ruined me for probably about eight months or so. I was pissed off and I was hurt.

I eventually re-joined the PPS list-serv. I also decided to start looking for another surrogate, and went back on SMO to do another search through the surrogate classified ads.

I stumbled upon the ad of a lady who was only charging $5,000.00, and thought, "Hm, maybe we can afford her?"

She was from Arizona and she called herself, "Chandra." She seemed normal when we talked on the phone but it turned out she was a total fruit loop.

She said she was going to college in Arizona and was a surrogate twice, having twins for the first couple and another baby for the second couple. She even had a website.

I thought, "Even though she lives far away, since her fee is on the low side it will be worth it to work with her." Actually, when I first started this journey, surrogates were asking for between $5000.00 and $10,000. Now they charge much more.

One day, Chandra emailed me and said, "I can't be your surrogate anymore because my children, my husband, my mother-in-law, and father-in-law, were all killed in a car accident over Fourth of July weekend."

I was like, "Oh my God!", and of course, totally horrified.

I told the girls at work and they said, "No way is that true." I had to admit that something was fishy about her story so I began to search the Internet and the newspapers. I couldn't find any information proving her story was true.

When I told people on SMO and PPS what had happened with Chandra, many other women emailed me and said they had heard of her before. Apparently, she had a reputation as a scammer.

The girls at work kept telling me that I should find someone who also lived in Pennsylvania, someone who was stable. They didn't realize that money was a huge factor in who we worked with as our surrogate. At the time, we felt that if our surrogate lived farther away and was charging a lower fee, it was preferable to finding a surrogate close by who was charging more money.

Finally, we just gave up the search for a little while. Eric and I decided to concentrate, instead, on saving as much money as we could to build our house. We figured, once we had enough for the down payment, we'd take out a loan to pay for surrogacy.

Over a year later, when I was thirty-three, we were in the process of building our new house. I decided to start looking for a surrogate again, and that's when I met Kelli Online. It was spring, 2002—I think April or May.

Kelli lived in Pennsylvania, just three hours from us. She was married, twenty-five years old, and she had two children—a boy and a girl. Although she was charging what would be considered "average" compensation, which was more than we wanted to pay, we felt she was the perfect match for us.

Because of my past experiences, I was very skeptical when I was first talking to Kelli Online. I called myself, "Amanda" and gave her an alternate email address that I created just for conversing with potential surrogates.

She was very honest and that's what I liked about her. When I asked her why she wanted to be a surrogate, she said, "I'm doing it because I want to do it, to help somebody. But I'm doing it for the money too—to help my own family."

Kelli and her husband came to our house, and Eric, who is a real skeptic about everything, even liked them. She told us that she originally realized she wanted to be a surrogate when one of her aunts couldn't have children and asked Kelli if she'd carry a baby for her. The aunt changed her mind, but the idea was already planted in her head.

We were going to do the transfer at a clinic in Pittsburgh, but they refused to work with us because I met Kelli Online. It wasn't that they had a problem with surrogacy—it was the way we met each other.

We switched to Cooper Center in New Jersey. It was a six-hour drive, but they didn't have any issues with our situation and they had a good success rate with infertility treatment.

Our first cycle was in November 2002. My eggs matured too fast though and I over-stimulated. Since Kelli's body wasn't ready for the transfer yet, the cycle had to be cancelled. We were disappointed and we were upset that we wasted so much money on the medications. We started our next cycle in December to prepare for a transfer in early January 2003.

Actually, the doctors at Cooper Center are the ones who informed me that I had two ovaries, not just one as I was told as a child. Since they are small and high up in my body, when I had the egg retrieval on January 2, it was done trans-abdominally. My thirty-fourth birthday was January 4 and we had the transfer the next day. It was a great birthday present.

About ten days later, the beta confirmed we were pregnant. Our six-week ultrasound appointment showed two gestational sacs and two heartbeats—we were absolutely elated!

The weird thing was that I always knew there would be twins. I just had a gut feeling. But I was still really surprised that it worked on our first transfer.

Kelli is so wonderful. I know that she's doing the best job she can. She really tries to eat healthy—heck, she won't even it chocolate! There was some protein in her urine so her blood pressure is on the high side right now, but otherwise everything is going along just fine with the pregnancy.

I can't believe how close we are to having the babies. We are thirty-four weeks and four days pregnant and I'm so excited I can hardly stand it.

Some days I am completely fine and just go about my daily business, but other days I am kind of freaking out. I worry if I can handle twins. I worry if I can even handle one baby!

You know, I am kind of embarrassed to admit this, but when we initially found out we were having twin girls, I was disappointed that we weren't having boys. I feel like such an awful person admitting this, like I'm ungrateful or something.

Throughout the first trimester of the pregnancy, after we spread the word that we were having twins, everyone kept on guessing that it was two boys. I actually thought it was going to be a boy and a girl at first.

When we found out at the eighteen-week ultrasound that we were having two girls, I was kind of in shock. It just wasn't what I had envisioned in my mind. I guess that's another reason I reacted the way I did.

Nobody could ever picture me with girls because there are all boys in our family. My sister only has boys, and I love them so much that I just felt like I wanted a boy.

I mean, I don't feel that way at all anymore. I'm totally thrilled that we have two girls on the way. But at first, I felt like my husband would want a boy to carry on his name. He is a Junior so I thought that would be really neat. I kept on telling my husband, "I want a little you. I want a little Eric."

I also think that part of what bothered me was that I was worried that something would be wrong with a girl, like what is wrong with me.

Now, I can't wait to meet our little girls! I really do feel horrible about how I was when we first found out. I just pray to God that they're healthy, especially with the guilt I feel for wanting a boy at first.

When I called Coopers to donate the medications we had left over from our cycle, I told the nurse that I was unsure what to do with our frozen embryos. She asked me, "What did you end up with?" and I told her, "Two girls." I told her that at first, we were hoping for a boy and a girl or two boys, and she said, "I understand, I see this all the time. People picture something for themselves and it ends up differently." She advised me to hang onto the medicine in case we want to try for a sibling down the road.

I'm experiencing a lot of anxiety right now because, since Kelli is three hours away, I'm afraid we'll miss the birth.

I've become obsessed with planning for the girls' arrival. I am constantly cleaning, I've put together the bouncy seats, our birth certificates are ready and our bags are packed. The babies will be delivered in Altoona, Pennsylvania, not too far from where she lives.

If we make it to the hospital in time, we'll be there in the delivery room with her. This could happen any day now!

I just want people experiencing infertility to know there is hope. I went through a lot, emotionally, worrying about whether or not I'd ever have children, but things are working out after all.

I'd like people who are looking for a surrogate mother to know, if you have doubts—that should be a "no". I had doubts with Wendy and Chandra, but I was basing my decision on the financial factor and the fact that they were charging lower than average fees. It doesn't pay to be cheap when it comes to choosing a surrogate. It's more important to choose someone based on chemistry and instinct. It's important to feel that she will be responsible before and throughout the pregnancy.

I feel like my life before was never quite right. I have always felt so abnormal because I have MRKH, but many other women have other problems that prevent them from getting pregnant. What it boils down to, regardless of the issue—is that if you can't have kids, you can't have kids. It doesn't matter, "why". Actually, I just feel lucky that I have my ovaries so I was able to use my own eggs. Lots of women can't even do that.

I do regret keeping the problem to myself for most of my life. I probably would have helped me to talk about it with others.

But now, everything is falling into place—at thirty-four years old. We built the house we wanted and we are having twins. I really do feel triple blessed that my dream of being a mommy is finally going to come true.

Postscript

On August 30, 2003 at 3:00 a.m., Vivian and Eric got the call that Kelli's water broke and off to the hospital they went. At approximately 9:00 a.m, Brooke was born at 6 lbs. 10 oz. and her sister, Bethany, followed nine minutes later at 5 lbs. 12 oz. Both girls were delivered vaginally and everything went as smooth as could be. Kelli was totally calm throughout the entire delivery; in fact, she later told Vivian it was easier than delivering her own two children.

Vivian and Eric were crying with joy, and all Vivian could think to herself was, "Oh my God, how perfect!" The second she saw their daughters she realized everything was the way it was meant to be.

The family came home and naturally fell into a routine. Vivian admits that she was exhausted, especially because Brooke and Bethany didn't sleep much, but she was so happy to be a mom that her lack of sleep didn't bother her whatsoever. She recalls how wonderful it felt to be called "Mommy" after all she had been though.

She is so happy with her girls and cannot even imagine having boys. When she remembers her initial concern about having girls instead of boys, she feels completely ridiculous. She attributes her thoughts at that time to hormones and says several of her girlfriends, including Kelli, told her that even though she wasn't the pregnant one, her hormones were definitely out of whack. She laughs about it now.

Vivian thoroughly enjoys watching Brooke and Bethany with Eric and says he is a wonderful father who is very involved in their daughters' lives. The girls' favorite thing to do is play outside. They love animals and looking for deer in the woods with their daddy. Vivian and Eric take them to animal parks and petting parks as often as possible. They also enjoy books and children's shows like The Wiggles, Blues Clues, and Homeward Bound.

Vivian and Eric love being parents; taking Brooke and Bethany to family reunions, taking them to swimming lessons, or doing whatever it is they do. She loves walking through the door and hearing them say, "Mommy, Mommy!" She loves Mother's Day and Father's Day. Everything in life is better now.

Vivian and Kelli are still very close. They see each other about twice a year, which isn't as much as they would like, but they do stay in touch via phone and email. Vivian says they are almost like sisters and definitely meant to be in each other's lives.

She advises others who are considering surrogacy to read up on everything and obtain as much knowledge as possible. "The journey," she says, "is definitely worth it. And through perseverance and prayer, you'll get there."

Most of the intended mothers in this book found their surrogate mothers either Online or through surrogacy agencies. Jessica and Krystal, however, had family members offer to help them achieve their dreams of motherhood. Certainly not in all cases, but much of the time when a relative is the surrogate she does not require the intended parents to pay compensation. This is a major benefit of course. While there are certainly many other expenses involved, subtracting the surrogate's fee out of the equation makes surrogacy a more realistic possibility for many potential intended parents. There are other advantages as well. If everyone can withstand the stress involved, chances are that relationships that were already strong will become even stronger. This was the case with Jessica and Krystal, who went to surrogacy for different reasons but both ended up with the same happy results.

Four

Jessica
West Bloomfield, Michigan

I still hadn't started my period at sixteen years old, so my mom suggested we go to the doctor to find out what the problem was. We are Jordanian, and in our culture it is particularly important that women are able to bear children——mostly because Arabic men consider childbearing to be a "wifely duty". So needless to say, my mom was pretty concerned.

We went to this rinky-dink ob/gyn near our home, which at the time was in Otisville, Michigan——just outside of Frankenmuth. During the examination, the doctor couldn't even insert a pinky into my vaginal canal and when he pressed on my abdomen he couldn't find my uterus. He told us that from what he could tell so far, my vagina was undeveloped and it was likely that I didn't have a uterus. When we got in the car my mom said, "This is ridiculous, he doesn't know what he's talking about! We'll go to the University of Michigan instead."

The doctors at U of M said the same thing. They did a laparoscopy and found that I had my ovaries and but didn't have a uterus or vagina. They called it "uterine and vaginal agenesis", but it is also known as Mayer-Rokitansky-Kuster-Hauser syndrome (MRKH).

The thing with vaginal agenesis is that the vagina appears totally normal externally, so oftentimes women with this condition don't know they have a problem. Many, like myself, find out only because they reach a certain age and still haven't gotten their periods.

I just figured I was kind of a freak. To tell you the truth, being sixteen and starting to like boys, I was actually glad I didn't have to ask my mom to help me get on birth control. I wasn't thinking of the long-term affects and the fact that I wouldn't be able to bear children. I was immature for a sixteen year old.

To correct the problem, I used a dilator to recreate my vagina. I started with a very small size and then increased the size as my vaginal canal opened up. It took about a year to get it to the size it needed to be to have intercourse comfortably. Granted, I didn't actually have intercourse for a few more years, but at least the dilators helped so that my vagina was "normal".

I had to do it in the shower because it was the only place I had privacy. My parents knew and I think my brother and sister knew—it was very embarrassing. Nobody ever talked about it openly; however, when I was first given the diagnosis my dad gave me the knowing, "I'm sorry" look.

My mom was devastated that I would never bear children and she was worried that I'd have a problem finding a man who would accept and marry me. She would say, "Well you can adopt" and occasionally add "or do surrogacy."

It was the mid 1980's and around the time the "Baby M" case was all over the media. The scandal shed a negative light on surrogacy, but it also brought the subject to the attention of the American public.

Whenever I'd go in for check-ups, the nurse would assure me, "Well you can always adopt or do surrogacy."

The doctor was adamantly against surrogacy though. I learned this during a conversation I had with him when I was seventeen, when he asked me what I was going to do about having children someday.

I told him, "Well I'm thinking about doing surrogacy."

"I don't know if I agree with that," he said, and began to list all of these reasons why it was a horrible idea. He referred to the "Baby M" case and claimed he had talked to several surrogates who had negative experiences. The funny thing is that as he was giving me this lecture, in my mind I was thinking, "I don't care what he says——I'm going to do surrogacy someday."

I figured since I still had my ovaries I might as well give myself the chance to have a biological child. I knew that adoption was an option too, and figured if surrogacy didn't work out for me that adoption would be the next step.

When I was a freshman in college, I chose surrogacy as the topic of my first big paper; specifically, I discussed the pros and cons and the issues surrounding the enforcement of surrogacy contracts. Since I wanted to be ready to pursue surrogacy myself someday, I was very interested in doing the research for this assignment.

My parents thought I might marry an Arabic man despite my problem. Our culture believes in arranged marriage, and although I was willing to consider the idea, I was also open to meeting someone on my own. But I agreed to meet this man, the son of a Jordanian couple my parents knew, with the intention of accepting a proposal to marry him if we liked each other. I figured I didn't have anything to lose.

Although my parents still follow Jordanian traditions, they have been in America since the 1970's and consider themselves Americans as well. I was comforted to know they would support my decision if I chose not to do an arranged marriage. They just wanted me to be happy.

This man and I went through the whole traditional meeting: he met my parents before he met me, and then on our second date he asked me to get engaged. I was twenty-one years old and he was thirty-one. It's customary when doing an arranged marriage to get engaged right away——on the first or second date——because then it's acceptable to continue dating without the woman having to bring a male chaperone. This way, the couple can be alone together on dates.

I said, "Before I answer, I think you should be aware of my situation," and proceeded to tell him I couldn't have children.

His response was, "Oh."

It was immediately clear that he had an issue with it. We continued with our date, but the next day he called to say he had to retract his proposal and admitted it was because I couldn't have children.

I was very glad I told him up front, because I didn't want to date someone for six months or so, get attached, and then have to break the news. That wouldn't be right.

I had no problem telling guys I dated that I was unable to have children. Most of them didn't seem to mind, which I found to be surprising. Although, it may not have been important to them because they weren't considering marriage anyway—I don't know.

Eventually, I met my first husband, Tim, who was my roommate's brother. We got married when I was almost twenty-four.

Tim had a good friend named Charlie, who happened to be an identical twin. Charlie was married to Laura, and Tim and I would get together with them once in a while. One day, Laura said to me, "You know, if you ever wanted to do surrogacy I would carry for you." A mutual friend of ours was there too and she said to Laura, "You don't know for sure that you could do something like that until you've had your own kids."

I agreed with Pam and suggested Laura wait until she had her own baby before she decided she could carry a child for someone else.

I felt that if I did go forward with surrogacy someday, it would be best to work with someone I didn't know beforehand. I didn't mind having to pay compensation if it came to that—I just didn't think I wanted a "close" relationship.

Tim and I were married for about three and a half years. After we got divorced, I ended up meeting Eddie, Charlie's twin brother. It was a little strange, given that Eddie was Charlie's brother and Charlie was still good friends with Tim, but Eddie and I started dating anyway and soon after we met he proposed. He knew about my situation from the get-go but he was fine with it.

About a year after Eddie and I were married, Laura came to me and said, "You know, if you still would consider me being a surrogate for you, I would be more than happy to do it."

I asked her, "Are you sure you want to do this?"

Laura and Charlie had recently had twin boys in addition to having two other children, so it baffled me that she'd consider being pregnant again so soon. When I questioned whether she truly understood what surrogacy entailed, she said she understood completely and still was totally on-board with carrying a baby for us.

Although Laura and I had known each other for eight years at that point, we were more like acquaintances than friends. Actually, this ended up being a good thing because I didn't want to work with someone who was a "best" friend. It really was an ideal situation given the circumstances.

When I discussed it with Eddie, he said it was a bit weird having his brother's wife carry our child, but not enough that it would prevent him going forward.

I suggested to Laura that she research extensively before doing anything. I had been researching surrogacy for years and was even on the PPS list-serv, and I felt it was important that she do some research from her end too.

Laura wasn't interested in participating on any Online support groups though—she preferred to read books and articles. So I bought her a bunch of books and we both read all the magazine articles we could find that had anything to do with surrogacy.

We talked about every different scenario: What would happen if we got in an argument? How would she feel during and after the pregnancy? What happens if we end up with multiples?

She would say, "Believe me, I have no issues. I wouldn't be jealous or want your child. I have four kids, why would I want *your* kid?"

I went to an infertility clinic about a half an hour from my house, and during our first consultation I asked the RE if she would be able to transfer our embryos into a gestational carrier. She told us that although she had done a transfer into a surrogate during her residency, this clinic had never dealt with a surrogacy situation before we approached them. She was open to the idea, however, and agreed to contact her attorney and ask him what needed to be done from a legal standpoint.

If our RE wasn't willing to do the transfer, we probably wouldn't have been able to do surrogacy. We couldn't afford to fly Laura and her family to a different state and pay for hotel and meals—plus, it would have been too much of a hassle for everyone.

The RE and I would touch base occasionally for updates on the legality end. She'd have to get information to our attorney and we'd have to get information to her attorney. By 2002 we finally had everything worked out and we each signed the papers required by all of the lawyers involved.

In Michigan, it's illegal to pay compensation to a surrogate; however, surrogacy in itself is not illegal. So we just needed to verify with the attorneys that Laura was not being paid by us and that everything was being done legally.

We started the cycle in January 2003. My egg retrieval results were excellent; I broke the clinic record with thirty-six eggs, of which twenty-three matured and twenty-one fertilized.

Laura and I wanted our RE to transfer three embryos. We were hoping for twins and we thought putting in three would increase the likelihood two would take. Eddie and Charlie thought we should only transfer two because they worried Laura would end up pregnant with triplets. Laura and I finally agreed with them and on the third day after the retrieval, two embryos were transferred.

We planned to go back to Laura and Charlie's house after the transfer. Laura was supposed to be resting so I gave her a bunch of cool gifts like Bath and Body stuff, popcorn and movies, and figured we'd all hang out and relax together while watching movies and eating popcorn. Well I had another thing coming!

With four kids, there was no way we were able to just "sit around". On top of it, Charlie and Eddie's grandmother came over with a friend from out of town, so instead of relaxing, Laura was cooking, cleaning and entertaining her guests.

We basically only had one hour of down-time after we got back to their house from the transfer. I was so worried—I was sick to my stomach.

"There is no way the embryos are going to take with her being so active immediately after the transfer," I thought to myself. I figured that if miraculously they made it, they would probably make it through anything.

I tried to do the cooking so Laura wouldn't have to stand at the stove, but then she would end up running after her kids instead. The guys tried to help, but it was so chaotic that there really wasn't much they could do.

I didn't want to act irritated in front of everyone even though I was boiling inside. It was incredibly stressful.

Four days after the transfer, Laura took a home pregnancy test and it showed a light pink line. I didn't let myself believe her because I didn't want to be disappointed if she was wrong, but she took another test on the fifth day after the transfer and the line was darker than the first time. We went in for the beta on the twelfth day and sure enough—it was positive.

At the six-week ultrasound we saw two gestational sacs and two strong heartbeats. I couldn't believe that both of the embryos made it after all.

Laura is constantly on the go with her children, picking them up and everything. I was a nervous wreck at the beginning of the pregnancy and I was starting to drive myself insane. At one point, I said to myself, "I have to give it to God. I can't worry about everything because I will make myself crazy. She's been pregnant before, she knows what she should be doing and what she shouldn't, and I just have to put my trust in that." Once I decided to give it to God, it was such a burden off my shoulders.

Even though I try not to worry about every little thing, it's difficult sometimes. They have a cat, for example, and for a long time I worried about Laura changing the litter and all of that. They also have a Jacuzzi, and she dyes her hair occasionally, and sometimes she goes to a tanning spa. She did the same things when she was pregnant with her own children, so I figure if she treats this pregnancy the same way that treated her own pregnancies, that's all we can ask.

What upsets me sometimes when I think about it, is that I wouldn't do all of those things if I were the one who was pregnant. That is the hard part about surrogacy—giving up the control.

When I first started the process, I didn't know anybody else who was in my situation besides women I had met on the Internet. I still continue to talk to other intended mothers I have met on Online support groups. We share our stories with each other and rely on each other for support and advise.

I have another friend, Deena, who is also an intended mother. Deena and I get together for dinner once in a while, and we've discussed our mutual observation many times: intended mothers tend to share certain personality traits, and one of those traits is being somewhat controlling by nature. It's quite interesting.

Surrogacy requires so much effort; there are many steps and oftentimes many hurdles to overcome. It takes a determined person to do what is required to have a child through surrogacy. Intended mothers have to have pretty thick skin.

For anyone considering surrogacy, it can seem overwhelming at first. It's like, where do you start? You have to take one step at a time. For me, the first step was convincing the clinic to work with us, even though they didn't have any surrogacy cases up until that point.

Eddie and I have both told our immediate families, but because of the Jordanian belief system, my parents asked that we don't tell other relatives that we are doing surrogacy. We don't see our extended family very often though, so keeping it hush hasn't been too difficult.

I have told my mom, however, that I'm not going to walk on eggshells for the rest of my life regarding this issue. Our children will know how they came into this world and I will raise them to be proud of this fact not ashamed of it. So if our extended family finds out later on and they disapprove, oh well!

Initially, I didn't know how I was going to approach the situation at work. I will be taking leave after the babies are born and I have no intention of hiding that I'm going to be a mom. I had to tell work because by *not* telling them it would have been like saying I was shameful of our situation. Not only am I not ashamed of how I am having children—I am very proud of it.

I've heard some pretty stupid comments though. For example, a few people have asked, "How does the mother feel?"

My response is always, "I'm feeling fine, thanks for asking."

I lot of people don't get it—the intended mother *is* the mother. It's a hard concept for some people to grasp.

One time after I responded, "I feel fine, thanks," someone said, "No really, how does the mother feel?"

I told that person, "You know, you need to be careful about your wording here because I *am* the mother." I actually don't even refer to Laura as the "surrogate mother", I refer to her as "my carrier".

She's not the mother in any way and she agrees wholeheartedly. When people ask her how she feels emotionally, she says, "I'm just the aunt, I'm not the mother here."

Another really offensive comment that I've heard is, "You are so lucky, you get to keep your figure and everything!" My response is always, "I would rather gain two hundred pounds because I could always work off the weight in time. I will *never* be able to carry a baby.

Laura and I had this conversation a while back. She said to me, "I swear, if I gain twenty pounds and you still stay skinny, I'll be so upset." I told her, "Laura, if I could be the one to gain a bunch of weight because I was pregnant, I would do that in a second!" She apologized and said she didn't mean it in "that" way.

"I know you didn't mean it that way", I said, "but I want you to understand that if I could do anything on my own to make this happen, I would. If I could do a uterine transplant, if I could go to China, whatever it was, I would do anything possible."

The downfall of working with my sister-in-law is that I have to be extra conscious of our relationship. I see her often, and while I'd love to focus primarily on the babies, I have to make sure she feels she's cared about as well. I'm concerned about how our relationship is going to be afterwards—I don't want her to think that she's only important to me now because she's pregnant with our babies. At the same time, we've been very close throughout this pregnancy and after the babies are born it will be too difficult to have the level of closeness we have now. I will simply be too busy and I hope she doesn't take offense to that.

It's hard to believe we are almost at thirty-one weeks. Laura's ob/gyn originally said we'd schedule the c-section for when we are between thirty-six and thirty-eight weeks, but now all of a sudden he's making comments suggesting she could go even longer. I'm not real happy with him to be honest—he's kind of arrogant. For example, he's decided that he's only letting one person in the room for the delivery. I work in the delivery unit once a week so I see babies born all the time, but Eddie has never seen a birth. I suggested that he be the one in the delivery room, but Eddie, Laura and Charlie all agree that it should be me.

If you think about it, it's kind of funny; our clinic had never done a transfer with a surrogate, our lawyer had never handled a surrogacy situation, our doctor has never worked with a surrogate—so we're working with all of these professionals but we are the ones teaching *them*!

This whole experience has been even more stressful because not only am I going through the pain and suffering with Laura, but we are picking up a lot of the slack of caring for her kids. I will either do her grocery shopping or go to her house and watch her children so she can go grocery shopping. It's a lot of work for me helping her with her family—not that I'm complaining—it's just very draining. At the same time, since she is our surrogate we really have no other choice. We are doing what we know is right.

Laura did offer to be our carrier, but I don't know if she *really* knew what she was getting herself into. It has not been easy for her, and it certainly hasn't been easy for Charlie and their children.

Many people have said to me, "When your twins are born you are going to be so busy."

I tell them, "You know what, bring it on. Because it will definitely be easier than taking care of a whole family!"

On top of it, I've decided to breastfeed the babies, so I'm in the middle of a protocol that will prepare me to breastfeed even though I'm not pregnant. The protocol requires that I pump for a few months before the babies are born, so I use the "Employee Breastfeeding Room" at work when I do my pumping. It's very awkward, because here I am pumping and I'm not even pregnant. I fully realize that by walking into that room I'm risking questions and strange looks, but fortunately I haven't had any negative incidences as of yet.

One benefit of knowing early on that I would never bear children is that I could plan ahead. I became a nurse anesthetist because the income is decent and I knew it would enable me to save money for surrogacy. I had many years to do the research and take the steps I had to take towards doing surrogacy someday.

Still, even though I was prepared, it has been a loss for me and I will never discount that. Sometimes when people are trying to be nice, they'll tell me that pregnancy is such a small part in the life of a child, that it "isn't that big of a deal." For me though, it *is* a big deal because even though the pregnancy is only a fraction of the life of a child, it's still an experience that I would have liked to have. Plus, going through surrogacy means you are sharing something that normally should be very intimate with everyone and their brother.

On the positive side, like my mom has said, we're fortunate we live in an era where reproductive technology is so advanced that this is even an option in the first place.

When I was seventeen and the doctor told me he didn't encourage surrogacy, I remember thinking to myself, "I don't care what he says, I know surrogacy is possible and I'm not going to let this man tell me how I'm going to have my children."

I'm just glad I listened to my intuition. In my heart I just knew that surrogacy was the way I was going to become a mom.

Postscript

Ethan and Ilana were born in September 2003, just one day short of thirty-six weeks gestation. They had to remain in the NICU for two weeks; one baby had breathing problems and the other one had blood sugar issues, but otherwise, they were healthy and everything went as well as could be expected.

Jessica and Laura had a falling out immediately after the children's birth and didn't talk to each other for about six months. It was difficult, according to Jessica, because after being totally immersed in each other's lives throughout the pregnancy, their relationship had come to an abrupt halt. Fortunately, they eventually made amends, and despite the tumultuous period after the twins' birth, both women admitted that they really just needed a break from each other.

Two years later, things are back to normal between them and their friendship is as strong as ever. Jessica says that since Laura is also her sister-in-law and they are tied together through family, they were almost forced to work things out—and she's thankful for that.

Jessica is thoroughly enjoying motherhood and she cannot imagine not having her son and daughter. Once Ilana and Ethan came home it was like they had always been there.

She laughs as she remembers people saying to her, "You're going to be so tired when the twins are born, just you wait and see." When she brought her babies home from the hospital, despite the lack of sleep and having twin newborns, she wasn't at all tired. It was quite the contrary, because she was on a natural high that gave her all the energy she needed. She describes the way she felt: "Like every day was Christmas."

Since Jessica has gone through her surrogacy journey, many others have opened up to her about their own infertility struggles. One of the things she says about going through surrogacy is that, "It can be a very fragile journey but you don't know what you are getting into until you begin. It's kind of like jumping into the water and not knowing if it's going to be ice cold or not. It's important to have a strong mate who can help you keep your eyes open—and to have strong family support."

Jessica and Eddie have nineteen frozen embryos remaining. She feels she was given the gift of her children and therefore, she should be "giving back" somehow; therefore, she is seriously considering adopting out their embryos through Snowflake Adoption Agency. Eddie isn't totally on board with the idea. He finds it contradictory, after all they went through to have their children, to "give them away." They are in no rush to make a decision regarding this matter so only time will tell.

Jessica believes their remaining embryos are souls. In fact, the pictures of her children as embryos are the first ones in their baby book. She still remembers vividly when the doctor told her they transferred #3 cell embie and #8 cell embie. And today those tiny embryos are a boy and a girl called Ethan and Ilana.

Five

Krystal
Salem, Alabama

My husband, Keith, and I were high school sweethearts. We got married when we were twenty-two years old and started trying to get pregnant when we were twenty-eight.

After a year without success, a local doctor referred us to a fertility specialist in Birmingham, Alabama. As soon as we met the doctor, Dr. H, we knew she was amazing. Her clinic runs the ART program of Alabama and she is one of the pioneers of IVF.

Over the course of two years we did about ten IUI's but we still weren't getting pregnant. Finally, we decided it was time to move onto IVF. In order to prepare for the IVF cycle, Dr. H requested that we do a Clomid Challenge Test—a test they do to check a woman's ovarian reserve. She basically wanted to make sure my body was capable of producing enough eggs.

I had done about eight cycles with Clomid with absolutely no luck at all, but I got pregnant on the cycle that we were doing the Clomid Challenge Test. We were pretty surprised because this time, we weren't counting the days or taking temperatures or anything.

We found out I was pregnant on a Thursday and I was scheduled to go to Paris on Saturday, just two days later. My friend, Lisa, is a teacher and she was taking a bunch of students—she had asked me to help her chaperone.

While I was in Paris with Lisa and her students, exactly one week after I learned I was pregnant, I began spotting. It was my thirtieth birthday.

I called a local hospital and the doctor that I spoke with advised me to go to a hospital in Paris. Of course all of this was in French, so Lisa, who is fluent, had to translate for me. One of the student's mothers also came along as a chaperone, so fortunately she was able to stay with the sixteen high school kids that day.

I had all sorts of tests done at the hospital and then a blood test showed that my beta numbers were dropping. After about eight hours in the hospital, it was painfully clear that I had miscarried.

They said I was about five or six weeks pregnant, but since we hadn't really tracked the cycle we didn't know for sure. Lisa had to translate all of their medical questions and all of my answers.

The ultrasound machine was different than the ones I had seen in the U.S., so I was hoping that maybe they just couldn't see the heartbeat—that maybe there was some kind of mistake. I was grasping at straws.

It was just a weird experience. A weird day. For the rest of my life, I'll associate my thirtieth birthday with that miscarriage.

I've talked to people who have told me that with each miscarriage it gets harder, but for me, the first time was the worst one. It was just so unexpected—I didn't have clue that it could happen to me.

Ironically, when I first found out I was pregnant I thought all of our infertility struggles were finally over. The reality was they were only beginning. What we had been through up until that point was nothing compared to what the two years to follow would be like.

When I got back home to Alabama, I had to face my mom and dad, my sisters, and Keith. I think the worst part was that we already had a doctor appointment for Monday because Dr. H wanted to see me when I came back from my trip to evaluate how things were going with the pregnancy. Instead of going to Monday's appointment to follow up on the pregnancy, we were going to discuss the miscarriage.

I told Dr. H what happened in Paris. She consoled us, then encouraged us not to give up. She believed I'd eventually get pregnant and suggested, "Let's just go forward with the plans to do IVF."

We did IVF in June and got pregnant. I thought, "It's a miracle, I'm pregnant again! This time it's going to work." We had transferred three embryos three days after the transfer. Right away we found out that I miscarried.

The first miscarriage was on March 30 and the second miscarriage was the first week of July, three months later. I guess I was naïve to think that after the first miscarriage it wouldn't happen to me again.

After the second miscarriage—from July 2000 to November 2001—it was a really dark time for me. I was very bitter and remained that way throughout the three failed frozen embryo transfers that took place during that period. I realized there was something wrong with me, physically, that was preventing me from sustaining a pregnancy, and worried that I would never experience the miracle of pregnancy and childbirth.

Aside from my sister-in-law, who is also my best friend, we didn't tell anybody about our infertility struggles. My mom knew we were having problems getting pregnant, but we didn't share all of the details with her. We figured if our family and friends knew, they would just ask questions and that would make it harder on us. It was almost like we could separate our infertility from our "regular" life.

When I found out that women I knew were pregnant, I really had a hard time dealing with it. I didn't even want to go out. I would avoid friends who were pregnant or who had babies. I didn't even want to watch birth story programs on The Discovery Channel (TLC)—I'd turn the channel when shows like that were on television. During that time in my life, I really wasn't myself. My personality wasn't even the same because I was such a bitter, angry person.

People would make really insensitive comments like, "Oh, you can have *my* kid," or ask, "Why don't you have kids yet?" Since we had been married a while, they would just expect that we should be getting pregnant and having children. It doesn't even cross people's minds that there can be problems. It made me mad. It made me not like people.

Even though I was moody most of the time and tended to take out my emotions on Keith, he understood and was completely supportive. He told me that when he married me he didn't know if we'd even end up having kids anyway.

I would say, "Just go be with someone else," and it would make him so mad because he felt I should have more faith in him. Infertility puts so much stress on a marriage.

We started thinking about adoption way back, while we were initially going through infertility. Both Keith and I had positive feelings about adoption because we have adopted kids in our family—two nieces and a nephew. It would have been normal and accepted in our family if we had decided to go that route.

Still, we decided to move forward with our last IVF cycle, which was in November 2001, as one more attempt at having our own biological child.

Something unexpected happened with my ovaries during that cycle and I ended up producing thirty-two eggs. Twenty fertilized and we transferred three embryos into me. We found out we were pregnant, but I miscarried again two weeks later. We had twelve frozen blastocysts left.

When we met with Dr. H again to do the follow-up after the miscarriage, she asked, "What are your plans?"

I told her, "We're going to do this frozen embryo transfer, and if it doesn't work we are moving on to adoption."

Her next question was, "Do you have anybody in your family who would be willing to carry these embryos?"

And the moment she said that, it was like a light bulb had suddenly turned on in my brain. It was like, hallalullah! This is the answer we've been waiting for!

We were lucky because Dr. H was more open to surrogacy than some doctors. I've talked to friends who I've met on the

Internet and their doctors encouraged them to try more times on themselves before considering surrogacy. Dr. H is just a very different doctor; she's very spiritual and very intuitive. She just gave us the option and left it up to us.

I first considered my older sister, Nicole, but she had gestational diabetes with her second son and this caused her to have some health problems. I mentioned this to Dr. H and she said Nicole wouldn't be a good candidate.

Then I thought of my cousin, Sheryl. Sheryl was in her mid-twenties, she had two boys, a ten year old and a five year old, and both of her pregnancies were very easy. Plus, she lives only fifteen minutes from our house. It took me a few days to figure out what I was going to say to her, but finally, I called her at work and told her we wanted to talk to her about something.

We went over to her house and explained what we had been through over the last couple of years. She hadn't known about the miscarriages. She was very sweet and said she was honored that we'd ask her to do something of this magnitude. She and her husband, Kurt, took a couple of weeks to talk about it. She also wanted to talk to her doctor and to do more research on IVF and surrogacy.

Kurt was supportive, but he was also concerned about her health and he wanted to make sure it was a good thing for her emotionally. They had only been married a few months at that time.

About a month later, Sheryl said, "Yes", she would be our surrogate.

Before meeting Sheryl and Kurt, Dr. H had a few concerns. After all, they had only been married for three months, and her boys were from a previous marriage so they didn't have any kids "together". Dr. H worried that Kurt would not handle the pregnancy well. She even warned us not to be disappointed if he changed his mind altogether.

But he said he would support the decision for Sheryl to be our surrogate, and once he made up his mind he was on board one hundred percent.

On June 13, 2002 we transferred two blastocysts into Sheryl. We did struggle with whether to transfer two or three embryos, because we figured if we transferred three we'd have a higher likelihood of pregnancy. But we ultimately decided to go with two and we were so lucky because we got pregnant the first time.

In the meantime, nobody in our family knew what was going on—even though our families get together on Sundays and holidays. The main reason we didn't want to tell them was that our moms would have been really disappointed if it didn't work. Also, I didn't want Sheryl to feel any pressure. I think we made it to six weeks before we told anyone.

I was at her house when Sheryl took the pregnancy test. It was a Sunday, and we were scheduled to have the beta done the next day. She went into the bathroom to pee on the pregnancy test stick while I was playing chess with her younger son.

She opened the bathroom door, and chimed, "Cousin Kryyystalll" in a very playful voice. I could tell by her tone that the test was positive. She came out of the bathroom with a smile from ear to ear and we all just started hugging and crying—me, Sheryl and Kurt.

When we had the beta test done, the number was 812. This was incredible to me since the highest beta I had ever gotten was in the high sixties. The nurses were even hinting that there could be twins. We saw one beautiful heartbeat though at our first ultrasound appointment, when we were six weeks along in the pregnancy.

We went maternity clothes and baby clothes shopping soon after that. It was a blast for me because I was able to experience everything that a pregnant woman experiences.

I never had to worry with Sheryl because I knew she was taking good care of the baby and the pregnancy. And I wasn't jealous—I was just so thankful.

I have friends I have met on the Internet who worried constantly when their surrogates were pregnant. Sheryl went out of her way to make me feel like it was *my* pregnancy too.

She would say, "We are pregnant" not "I am pregnant." She called me when the baby kicked and stuff like that. She was awesome.

On a Friday night when it was storming outside, Sheryl went into labor. We were exactly thirty-nine weeks pregnant. I went to her house and called Keith, then Sheryl, Kurt and I went to the hospital. I was driving, she was in the passenger seat, and Kurt was in the backseat.

Kurt was so nice because I was going to get into the back seat initially and he said, "I want you to drive so you can be next to her in the front seat".

We even got pulled over by a cop on the way to the hospital—I don't know if I was swerving or speeding or what. But the cop pulled us over and I just started screaming, "She's in labor! She's in labor, we're going to the hospital!"

He said, "That's a new one," and let us go.

When they did the epidural only one person was allowed in the room with Sheryl, and she chose me. I had no idea what to expect. Next thing I knew, there I was holding her leg while she delivered. This was my baby coming out of the body of another woman and it was just so surreal.

Sheryl did this for us because she wanted us to have a baby. I was so humbled that someone would go through this so that *we* could have a baby. At that moment is when it really hit me. "Wow," I kept on thinking to myself, "look what she's done for us."

I turned to my husband when Aaron's head started crowning and said, "Ya'll are crazy if you think that baby is going to come through there.

The nurses said, "Okay, when he comes out we're going to hand him to you."

The midwife pulled him out and handed him to me. It's funny, because the first words out of my mouth were, "What do I do?"

After I held him, Keith cut the cord, and then we looked at him for a few minutes before we even remembered to get the camera. Of course we were all crying with joy.

Kurt said he had so much respect for Sheryl for what she had done for us, and that the experience made him feel closer to her than ever before. You really have to have a certain kind of husband for that. He was genuinely happy for us and he kept saying, "You guys are going to be such great parents."

Aaron was born on Saturday, February 22, 2003 at 1:13 p.m. Sunday morning at 7:00 a.m., we heard a knock at our hospital room door.

There was Sheryl, dressed with make-up on, and greeting us with, "Hey Y'all!" She went home that day and she was back into a size four within a month.

Something I will always remember is what Sheryl said at the beginning, when we initially met with the counselor. The counselor asked her, "Why do you want to do this?"

She replied, "Because I'm a mom and I want Krystal to be a mom. And I'll do whatever I can to help her become a mom"

Our families have always been close, but this has made Sheryl and I good friends too. Now, we are closer than we've ever been.

When you are going through all this hard stuff you never know why, but at the end, you are able to look back and see the rhyme and reason. Even for Sheryl, I think being our surrogate has been a very positive experience for her.

I don't know. Maybe that's why it's happened this way. I do think God works in mysterious ways. I can see that now. But when I was experiencing the miscarriages—when I was in that dark place, I didn't realize that there was a "plan" for us. Now, I look back and realize that we have all have learned lessons. And everything has worked out the way it should.

Postscript

Aaron is two and a half years old now and he is the light of his parents' lives. He is a loving and sweet child who has big brown eyes and curly light brown hair. He loves animals, music, playing the drums, playing outside, and swimming with his cousins.

Krystal and Keith remain as close as ever with Sheryl; in fact, Krystal says they are best friends. They live in the same town so they are fortunately able to get together often.

There were frozen embryos remaining from the cycle that produced Aaron, so when he was about nine months old, Krystal and Keith began discussing plans to have another child.

They briefly considered asking Sheryl to be their surrogate again, but her thirteen-year-old son was having some problems at the time and they didn't want to ask her and put her in a position where she had to say, "No." They also didn't want to put her on the spot and make her feel as if she had to say, "Yes" if she wasn't really up for it.

Krystal considered her sister, Nicole, who is forty-one years old and has three children of her own, but she is a diabetic and Krystal was concerned about her health. Krystal and Keith had actually thought of approaching her when they initially went through surrogacy, but because of her condition at the time Dr. H told them it wasn't an option.

When Aaron was a little over one year old, Krystal and Nicole were at Nicole's son's basketball game. She asked Nicole if she'd be willing to be in charge of their frozen embryos in the event that something happened to Krystal and Keith, and after saying "Yes, of course," Nicole offered to be her surrogate for a sibling project—in the bleachers at the basketball game.

Since Nicole had lost a lot of weight and she was in much better shape than she was a few years ago, Dr. H gave them the okay for her to be their surrogate this time around. She had to get her blood sugar down and there were a few other things Dr. H required, but otherwise there was no reason they couldn't go forward with her.

Krystal giggles as she remembers how excited they all were at the seven-week ultrasound. The beta numbers were high and doubling quickly, and everyone was saying, "Wouldn't that be a hoot if it ended up being twins this time?" The nurse practitioner found a second heartbeat and they all roared with laughter and joy.

At the eighteen week ultrasound, they were delighted to find out they were having a boy and a girl.

Krystal wants people to know that going through surrogacy is not as overwhelming as it appears to be at first. She remembers thinking to herself, as they embarked on their first journey, "How are we ever going to get through this?" But here they are with a two-year-old son and twins on the way, and she can't imagine making any other choice. To anyone considering surrogacy, Krystal advises, "Regardless of the obstacles, it will all work out in the end. So just go for it!"

As Kumiko's story demonstrates, infertility can cause a great deal of stress on a marriage. In some instances, like in Kumiko's case for example, when one spouse already has a child and the other one does not, the desire to have a baby with assisted reproduction and/or surrogacy is not a shared goal. In their book, *How to Have a Baby: Overcoming Infertility,* Dr. Aniruddha Malpani, M.D. and Dr. Anjali Malpani, M.D. of Malpani Infertility Clinic in Bombay, state, "It is not uncommon for some marriages to break down because of the pressure which infertility subjects them to." They also point out, "It is common among infertile couples for the woman to be the much more verbal and emotional partner. This often leads to the wife thinking and talking incessantly about infertility, and her whole world now revolves around how to have a baby." In their book, Dr.'s Malpani and Malpani give advice to infertile couples dealing with stress. They say, "You will find that learning to cope with infertility allows you and your partner to grow and become closer as you share your feelings throughout this difficult time— and your marriage will become much stronger than most marriages because you have weathered a difficult time together successfully." Kumiko and her husband persevered through some rough patches in their marriage, but in spite of all of their struggles, they made it. Like Karen in Chapter Two, Kumiko's infertility experiences have inspired her to help others, and her life has taken a path that she may not have otherwise envisioned for herself.

Six

Kumiko
Los Angeles, California

I met Bob in Japan, my home country, when I was twenty-eight years old. He was twenty-three and in the Navy at the time. Six months after we met, he informed me that he was being transferred to California and asked me to come with him. We got married in Michigan, where most of his family lives, in December 1991, then we went on to Los Angeles to begin our life together.

Shortly after we were married, I informed Bob that I may have problems getting pregnant. The previous year, before we had even met, I had an ovarian cyst removed. The doctor told me that something was wrong with my fallopian tubes and said it would probably be difficult for me to get pregnant when the time came.

Bob was supportive and said if we tried to have a baby and it didn't happen, it was okay. He has a son from a previous marriage, Tommy, who was five years old when we got married, so I think having more children just wasn't a priority to him.

It was a huge priority to me though. I was almost thirty years old and I wanted a baby. A year after we moved to California, we were transferred back to Japan. We tried getting pregnant the natural way for about a year and then we finally decided it was time to see a fertility specialist. The RE in Japan reviewed my history and I told him that I had an abortion when I was very young. He suggested I have a laparoscopy because he thought excess scar tissue might be making it difficult for me to get pregnant.

The laparoscopy showed that I have a unicornate uterus, which means my uterus is one-sided and very small—about half the size of a normal uterus. He added that while I may eventually get pregnant I was at a high risk for miscarriage or having a premature baby.

When I was almost thirty-two, about a year later, Bob was transferred back to Los Angeles again. We found a new RE and ended up doing seven embryo transfers with him. None of them worked.

Meanwhile, this was causing a lot of stress on our marriage. It was costing a lot of money for the transfer attempts and the medications, plus the medications caused me to feel weepy and moody.

Bob said he couldn't take it anymore, because he felt like our whole existence centered around trying to have a baby. He didn't understand why I couldn't just accept being childless.

I told him, "You have a child so you're okay. But I don't have a child!"

We decided to get divorced. He moved out and we were separated for a year and a half before the divorce was final.

Being infertile has caused me a lot of problems, because since I cannot carry a baby I really do feel inferior to other women. I actually told Bob, when Tommy was younger, that I wished I could just adopt him. But he had his own mother, and she was raising him—he is my step-son not my son. I wanted to be a mom and I knew I would be a great one.

I really didn't want the divorce in the first place and I don't think Bob wanted it either. I just think he was having a hard time dealing with everything. We both still lived in Los Angeles, so we kept in touch throughout the divorce process. A few months after our divorce, he called me and asked me to go away with him for the weekend. We went on the trip and naturally ended up getting back together.

In fact, the day after we got home he moved back in with me again. Then we decided to buy a house, and several months later we got married again. I was thirty-six.

I felt like Bob matured in the couple of years that we were apart and it seemed that he was much more interested in trying to have a baby than he was the first time we were married. I think he was finally "ready" to be a father.

The thing is, he became a father when he was nineteen years old. He wasn't a good one at that time—I think he was just too young. Tommy is seventeen years old now, but because he lives so far away, Bob doesn't have a close relationship with him. Once in a while, he comes to visit us, but they are almost more like friends than father and son.

We still had five frozen embryos from our previous IVF attempts, so shortly after we got re-married we decided to do a frozen embryo transfer. It failed. Our RE kept saying, "You can get pregnant," but I was pretty sure it was never going to happen. One day I asked him, "Do you think we should find a surrogate? Would this would increase my chances of having a baby?"

He said, "I really think your embryos are fine and that you should be able to get pregnant yourself. You should keep trying before you consider going to surrogacy." I said, "Okay, I'll try one more time." We did one more cycle after the frozen embryo transfer and it failed.

In the meantime, Bob's job transferred us back to Toyko again, so we found a new RE in Japan.

The Japanese RE reviewed my medical records, and then announced, "I can guarantee that if you work with a surrogate, she will end up pregnant immediately." I asked her how much it would cost and she said about $40,000-$50,000. In addition to being an infertility doctor, she also owned a surrogacy agency. She told me that she currently had a surrogate in her program who lived in Hawaii. I said I would talk to Bob and get back to her.

Bob said we couldn't afford it, so I decided to turn to my mom for help.

My mom asked me if the baby would be ours biologically and I said, "Yes, the surrogate will just carry the baby."

Even though she didn't totally understand what we were going to do, my mom ended up being very supportive financially and emotionally. She knew how much I wanted a baby.

Bob and I discussed how many attempts we would try with a surrogate before we gave up. He wanted to know when we would say, "Enough is enough" whether we had a baby or not. I was almost thirty-eight years old at that point and I figured by forty my eggs would be way too old. So I told him we would try until I was forty. If we still didn't have a pregnancy or a baby by then, and we had used all of our frozen embryos, we'd be done.

We flew to Hawaii to meet Kala, the potential surrogate, and our meeting went really well. When we came back to Japan, the doctor advised us to talk to our attorney in California. Our attorney said that California is a very good state for surrogacy because the intended parents' names can go directly on the birth certificate, but if Kala were to deliver in Hawaii, we'd have to adopt our own baby. I didn't want to do an adoption procedure because I knew it could become very difficult in Japan.

I am still a Japanese citizen and my entire family—my mother, two brothers and sister—still lives in Japan. It was important to me that our future child had duo citizenship; I worried that if the Japanese government knew about the surrogacy, the baby may not be granted Japanese citizenship after all. This made choosing a surrogate who lived in Hawaii a problem for me.

We realized that the only solution was if Kala would consider moving to Japan a couple of months before she was due, so that she could deliver there. She wasn't willing to go along with this plan, so we had to tell her we couldn't work with her after all.

When we told our RE she gave us a major attitude. She kept on asking, "Do you *really* want a baby? You're talking about duo citizenship—is this more important than having a baby?" I was very offended by this and decided not to work with her anymore.

As all of this was going on, Bob and I also discussed adopting internationally, but we figured if we had a chance to have a biological child—why not try? Also, as an infertile woman, I wanted to experience going through a pregnancy, and I felt that having a surrogate would be the closest thing to going through a pregnancy myself.

Meanwhile, I did a search on the Internet and found SMO. Suddenly I thought to myself, "Hm, maybe I can find a surrogate on my own?"

Bob was skeptical and said, "You never know who you are going to find on the Internet!"

I got a little nervous about finding a stranger on my own, so I decided to contact an agency in the San Diego area that we had heard about. The agency owner, Diedre, was friendly, and she seemed very competent. We didn't even meet her in person before we signed the contract; we did everything on the phone and through emails. Shortly after we signed the contract, she said she had a candidate named Natalie who lived in California. I flew to California to meet her, and then Bob came to meet her a few days later. I liked her but Bob thought she was a little suspicious. He couldn't put his finger on it—he just said something about Natalie bothered him.

I was desperate though so I insisted we work with her anyway. I said to Bob, "Well, she seems nice, she has her own children and everything...I'm sure she's fine." We found a RE in California and did our first cycle with Natalie.

It turned out this doctor was very sloppy. He knew Natalie was a first time surrogate and this was her first time going through an IVF cycle, yet he didn't give her an organized calendar of when she was supposed to take her medications. Since she was a healthcare provider in a hospital, I figured she would be able to figure out the medications. I was wrong.

I flew from Japan to California the day before the egg retrieval and when I arrived, the RE said to me, "Natalie just got her period. She made a mistake and took progesterone instead of estrogen. Sorry, we're going to have to cancel the cycle."

Meanwhile, my ovaries were making eggs, so I should have suggested we have my husband's sperm over-nighted so that we could still create and freeze some embryos, but I was so panic-stricken that I couldn't even think straight. The doctor should have been the one to suggest this option, however, and I'll never understand why he didn't.

Since the cycle was cancelled, Bob didn't even bother flying to California. Basically, we had just thrown away the transfer fee as well as other expenses we had paid Natalie so far, the airfare, and worst of all—the money we had spent on the cycle. The doctor even collected a $600.00 cancellation fee from us.

When I talked to Natalie on the telephone she was crying and crying. Here I'm thinking to myself, "I just lost $20,000, and *she's* crying?"

This RE screwed up by not explaining the medication protocol to her, but lets face it, it was her fault too. Still, I did like her and decided we'd give it another try if she was willing. But I told her if she wanted to work with us again, we'd have to reduce her fees by $5,000.00 because we had just spent all that money on the wasted cycle. She basically said "No way", so we were back to square one.

When I contacted Deidre, she said that she didn't know anything about it. It turned out, that after Natalie and I agreed to work together and we paid the agency fee, Diedre hadn't made one phone call to Natalie to see how things were going.

What irked me even more, was that when we initially signed up with Deidre's agency and she told us we had to pay a $1,500.00 international client fee, she justified it by explaining that she and her agency would do everything we couldn't do from so far away. The reality was that she did absolutely nothing to warrant this fee.

Immediately after the bomb was dropped on me at the RE's office, I went to the agency office in San Diego, which happens to be attached to Diedre's home, and I told her how unhappy I was with the way our situation was handled.

She had just had a baby a week previous to this discussion and she said to me, "Listen, I just had a baby and I really don't have the time to deal with these complaints. It's not my fault—it just happened!"

Our lawyer said we could sue Natalie for breach of contract because she had messed up the medication protocol, but I knew she and her husband didn't have the money to pay us back and I just didn't feel right about doing that.

It boiled down to the fact that Deidre's agency didn't do their job. We went to court to sue them for the initial $5,000.00 agency fee, but the judge ruled in their favor. We couldn't get our money back because we signed a contract saying that regardless of what happened, it wasn't their responsibility or fault.

After this ordeal, I decided to find a surrogate on my own; I figured, this way I could make sure that everything was being done right. I put together a profile that included our picture as well as a letter telling our story and explaining why we were looking for a surrogate. I ended up contacting about twenty or so surrogates that I found on the classified section on SMO.

About three months later, the end of July 2001, I flew to California again to meet two potential surrogates. They both happened to be from the same town, north of the San Francisco area. I liked both of them, but chose to work with Sharon because she was married. I felt it was important that our surrogate have the physical and emotional support that a spouse could provide. Sharon and her husband, Greg, had three children; a boy and two girls.

Once we decided to work together, we didn't have any problems. She trusted us and we trusted her. In fact, she didn't even require an escrow account—she told us just to send her a check every month. I just had a good feeling about her from the beginning.

It actually worked out quite well, because coincidentally, just as we were starting our cycle for the transfer, Bob's job moved us back to California again. Because we were so unhappy with the previous RE, we decided, once again, to find a new one.

The new clinic was closer to our house in the Los Angeles area, so Sharon and her husband, Greg, stayed with us for three days after the transfer. While they were at our house she said, "I feel like I am pregnant." I told her that we shouldn't get our hopes up until we knew for sure—I was so used to disappointment.

About a week later, she called me and said, "I couldn't wait any longer so I just took a home pregnancy test. It is positive!"

I said, "Oh no, don't tell me this until you have the beta results!" I was just so worried that I'd get my hopes up only to be disappointed if the blood test came back negative. She kept saying, "I'm telling you—I know my body and I'm pregnant."

A few days later she went in for her beta and it was indeed positive.

She has been excellent from the start. A friend of hers went with her to doctor appointments and everything, so that worked out well. Otherwise, her mother-in-law or sister-in-law would accompany her to the doctor or help out with the kids so she could go herself. Her family has been very supportive.

We had the first ultrasound in the San Francisco area so she didn't have to come all the way back to Los Angeles again. Her friend was there with her also. When we heard the baby's heartbeat for the first time, all of us—including Sharon and her friend—started crying. It was a wonderful moment.

Even though I don't speak English very well, Sharon always tries to understand what I'm saying. The only stumbling block that we encountered along the way was when she told us that she was against aborting a baby unless there was something terribly wrong. She said that if it was a Downs Syndrome baby or something, that she'd have a huge problem aborting it. Bob and I had to discuss more serious questions and ultimately, we decided that if the baby had Downs, that it was meant to be. We decided that regardless of what happened, the baby would be a gift from God.

Greg called one morning at 8:00 a.m., when Sharon was thirty-nine weeks along in the pregnancy, to tell us they were on their way to the hospital. We hopped in the car immediately. It took four and a half hours to get there and she ended up delivering at 10:00 a.m., so we missed the delivery.

But Greg called our cell phone from the delivery room and we heard our son's first cry. It was just so great to *finally* hear his voice.

My mom came in from Japan to be there too. In Japanese, she said to Sharon, "Thank you so much" and gave her a hug. We spent one week at the hospital because although Brandon was fine, he had to be on oxygen for one day. Also, because he wasn't sucking on the nipple he had to stay in the NICU for almost a week.

While we were in the hospital, Sharon came every day to hold and feed Brandon. She didn't want to pump or breastfeed though because she thought it might cause her to feel attached to him.

Her whole family—her mother, her sisters, her grandma, Greg's parents—gave us gifts for our son. After our stay at the hospital, we said goodbye to Sharon and Greg and their kids. They were very sweet children; when she was pregnant they were always saying "Hello Kumiko's baby" and they'd put their hands on her belly. We are still in close contact, and as a matter of fact we are going to Disneyland together next month.

We would love to have another child, and now that our son is twenty-months old we are starting to think about what we will do in the future. If we try for a sibling someday and it doesn't work with our remaining frozen embryos, we'll have to use an egg donor or go the traditional surrogacy route. I'm forty-one now and we likely wouldn't try again for two years or so. By then, my own eggs will be too old to do another fresh cycle.

One thing that is upsetting to me is that my mother and my siblings hide the fact that my son was born via a surrogate from their friends and our relatives. They are concerned our situation won't be accepted among others on our culture and they are worried about what other people will think.

Because of this, if we do end up using an egg donor or going the traditional surrogacy route next time, I won't be able to tell my family that the baby isn't mine biologically. My mom was supportive this time only because we did gestational surrogacy with my eggs, but I'm pretty sure she wouldn't support us otherwise. It would bother me to lie to about it, plus our relatives would probably figure it out eventually.

I especially want to be honest with my son, who would be five or six by the time another child was actually born. I plan to always be honest with him about the way he was brought into the world—I feel strongly that children born through assisted reproduction deserve to know the truth about how they came to be.

I also think it's important for children to know their biological background, even if they were conceived with someone else's genetics. I don't want Brandon to be put in a position where he feels he has to lie to everyone since he would know his brother or sister had a different biological mother than he does. To be honest, I'm really not sure what to do about this dilemma.

Regardless of the struggles we have encountered throughout the years, I have to say that for us, surrogacy has been an extremely positive experience. Sharon is a wonderful person, and Greg and their children are great too.

It's just important for anybody faced with infertility to know what the options are, and what the pros and cons are of both adoption and surrogacy. I want people who are infertile, people who want a baby more than anything, to know that surrogacy can be and oftentimes is a very positive experience. It was for us, and I know it has been for many others in the United States and around the world.

Postscript

Brandon is now four years old and he has completed Kumiko and Bob's lives just as much as they anticipated he would. They still have an excellent relationship with Sharon—so good, in fact, that she stuck with her original offer to be their surrogate again. In April 2005 they did a transfer with Kumiko and Bob's frozen embryos but unfortunately, it failed.

A few years ago, Kumiko started a surrogacy and egg donation agency called KB Planning, which specifically caters to Japanese couples who come to America to do surrogacy and/or egg donation. The agency has been successful and Kumiko has helped many couples become parents. Since Sharon still desires to be a surrogate again, Kumiko may actually help her find a couple through her agency.

They would love to have a sibling for their son, but their frozen embryos are gone and at forty-three, Kumiko feels her eggs are too old to do gestational surrogacy with her eggs. Both Kumiko and Bob are comfortable with traditional surrogacy, however, so they've decided that will likely be the path they take if they eventually add to their family.

They've also considered adopting an older child from Asia or something. Kumiko has mixed feelings about the whole issue. Brandon loves babies, and when they went back to Japan recently and saw her sister-in-law's baby boy, he loved holding and taking care of him.

However, she is very busy with her business and Bob recently went back to school, so it just isn't a good time for them to embark on another surrogacy journey or venture into an adoption process. She acknowledges that the whole endeavor is very costly, time-consuming and stressful. Although she won't go as far as to say, "never," for now, they have decided they are just going to have one child. For now they are just concentrating on raising their son and giving him a good life.

Before assisted reproduction techniques were as advanced as they are today, the traditional surrogacy route was the only option for people who wanted to have a child through surrogacy. *Surrogate Mothers Online* (SMO) defines traditional surrogacy as when "the surrogate mother is artificially inseminated with the sperm of the intended father or sperm donor. The surrogate's own egg will be used, thus she will be the genetic mother of the resulting child." From an intended parent standpoint, a positive aspect of traditional surrogacy is that by eliminating the need for IVF, the costs can be considerably less than those associated with gestational surrogacy. On the negative side for many intended parents, the surrogate in this case is genetically related to the baby. Many traditional surrogates find it appealing that typically no shots or medications are necessary, as they are with gestational surrogacy. Many gestational surrogates who can easily carry and give birth to a baby who is not theirs biologically, could not envision doing so with a genetic link to the baby. Cheri and Joy, the women who are featured in the next two chapters, both suffered from agonizing gynecological problems. Cheri had an extreme case of endometriosis and Joy had a plethora of gynecologic issues which practically ruined her life for a period of several years. The ongoing and unrelenting pain that both of these women endured, eventually led them to have complete hysterectomies—which in turn forced them to come up with alternate ways of creating their families. Although traditional surrogacy is a concept that some may find difficult to grasp, Cheri and Joy certainly do not have any regrets.

Seven

Cheri
Hood River, Oregon

My husband and I will be married eighteen years in June. We really never gave having children a thought early on in our marriage. I was twenty-one and Jesse was twenty-two when we got married—we thought we had all of the time in the world.

I began thinking about having kids several years later, when I was about twenty-six, but Jesse was content with the way things were. We decided to wait a year or two and readdress the issue then.

I went off the pill when I was twenty-eight and we started trying to get pregnant, but several years went by and it still was not happening.

When I was thirty-one, we were pleasantly surprised to find out I was pregnant—but I ended up having a miscarriage twelve weeks into the pregnancy. I've never gotten over it really; losing that baby was one of the hardest things I've ever been through.

We started trying again almost immediately after the miscarriage. In the meantime, I was having some major problems with pain and really bad periods and eventually I was diagnosed with endometriosis. The doctor went in and removed a cyst and cleaned everything up as best as he could, but it got to the point that it wasn't worth trying to save everything because it was just too painful.

For about two years, we continued trying to get pregnant anyway. I took medication to suppress the endometriosis and had surgeries to remove the cysts. Dye was run through my tubes to make sure they were clear, and each time it showed they were clear. There was no reason, technically, why I wasn't getting pregnant again.

My life was miserable because I was in so much pain three out of every four weeks. We decided that I should have a hysterectomy and we would just be without children in life. I was thirty-three years old.

Friends would ask us if we were going to adopt and I'd say, "No, if I can't have my own kids it isn't meant to be." I figured my hysterectomy was a sign that I wasn't supposed to have children in life.

A few years later, we had a change of heart and decided to research adoption. We talked with the Department of Social Services to find out what we needed to do to begin the adoption process and signed up for the classes we were supposed to take before the home study.

We originally decided to try and find a three to eight year old so we could have a child close in age to a lot of our friends' kids. We also considered adopting a special needs child, but the more we learned about caring for special needs children, the more we realized that we didn't know if we were capable of handling that type of situation. We felt that an older child may come with problems that we weren't equipped to handle, so Jesse and I ultimately agreed we should adopt a newborn.

Shortly after we started the paperwork process through Holt International Adoption agency, we were invited to a Superbowl Sunday party. We hadn't told anybody, except for my mother, about our plans to adopt.

We were at the party and out of the blue my friend, JoAnn, comes up to me and says, "So when are you going to let me have that baby for you?" It was the strangest thing in the world. I just looked at her in amazement and started crying.

We've known JoAnn and Darren for about seven years. She first made this offer to us right after I had the hysterectomy but I didn't take her seriously at the time. I just thought it was kind of odd that she could do something like that, because it just didn't seem like something I could ever do myself.

Of course I was like, "You've got to be kidding me." I told her that Jesse and I had just begun the adoption process.

I was curious what gave her the impression I had that on my mind and asked her if I had a "baby glow" or something.

She said, "I don't know Bird, I just looked at you and said to myself, 'She needs a baby.'" "Bird" is my nickname. Jesse came up with it years ago because he says I look like a bird.

JoAnn added, "You are so good with our kids, you guys would be great parents. I can totally see that you are just missing out so much and I would love to help you."

She assured me, "I can seriously do this, I have such easy pregnancies." She and Darren have three kids; two that she had from a previous marriage and one that they had together.

She said she had this "feeling". She was totally content in her marriage, they didn't want to raise any more children, but there was something nagging at her—something that she felt she was *supposed* to do. She couldn't put a finger on it.

Then she had an epiphany one day. She was supposed to give Jesse and I the gift of a child. Once she realized this, she felt a tremendous sense of satisfaction and fulfillment and knew she had finally realized her calling.

When she first approached me about it, I said, "Your husband has been drinking and my husband has been drinking. Tomorrow, talk to Darren and see what he says. If he's still okay with it, I'll talk to Jesse, and we'll see what he says about the idea."

I thought for sure her husband would say it was a crazy idea, but he didn't. The next day JoAnn called me and said she talked to Darren. He told her he was so proud of her and he thought it was a great idea for her to be our surrogate.

When I told Jesse he looked at me and asked, "Really? They'd do that? And Darren would be okay with it too?" We knew that it was something we had to seriously think about.

A couple of days later, they came over to our house to discuss it. We brought up all of the issues we could potentially face and we were in agreement with everything. It was like it was meant to be. We discussed whether or not the baby would know who the biological mother was. JoAnn definitely wanted everyone to know and we agreed that honesty was the best policy.

Jesse and I didn't want our child to be the "half brother" or "half sister" to JoAnn and Darren's children. We felt that would be too weird and confusing. They agreed and said, "No, no, no, our kids will be like little aunt's and an uncle to your child."

Darren wanted to make sure that JoAnn could give the baby away, and that she wouldn't think she was entitled to parent the child. She kept on saying, "Extended family...we're going to be family..." We needed to figure out what she meant by that. Christmas with everyone? Other holidays with everyone? I said to her, "Jo, I need to know that if we go to Disney World or something, or if you are not invited to a birthday party or something, your feelings aren't hurt."

With this scenario, with it being her egg and her delivering and everything, how much is she going to think it's *her* baby? Her response was that of course she'd feel a bond with the baby, but not a maternal bond. And if we had a birthday party and she wasn't invited, she may be hurt—but it wouldn't be any different than the feelings she'd have if she wasn't our surrogate.

We looked at each other and said, "Guess we're doing this!" We were all crying. Jesse was so emotional that night.

We originally planned on going through an infertility clinic and JoAnn said she'd figure out her cycle before we scheduled the appointments. But then she ended up getting impatient and suggested we just do the inseminations at home. She kept on saying, "I'm ready to go, Bird!"

I said, "Okay, if you want to do this ourselves—if you think this is something you can do, I'm game for anything. This is totally up to you and the guys."

My poor husband had stagefright when it came time to produce his "sample". The first time, JoAnn and Darren were in the living room and Jesse and I were in the back bedroom of our house. We'd leave the cup of sperm in the bedroom and come out all red faced saying, "Okay, there it is!" JoAnn wanted Darren to be part of the experience too, so he inseminated the sperm into her.

On a Monday, she called me all upset because she got her period. She was worried that I'd be really disappointed, but I assured her that I was okay. I knew from talking to others who did home insemimations that it may take several months, so I didn't expect that it would work the first time.

We were not telling a soul at this point because we wanted to wait until we were pregnant.

The second month, they would call us when their kids went to bed and we would get busy producing the sperm sample. We realized after the first attempt that it would be more comfortable for us to do it ahead of time—instead of while JoAnn and Darren were sitting in our living room. Then we'd call them and say, "It's ready for ya!"

After they did the insemination, JoAnn and I would have a glass of red wine and the guys would have a beer. We'd talk about the future, what it was going to be like when it happened. It was very casual, very relaxed.

When it was time for her to test, I bought her two early predictor kits. I told her, "Okay Jo, these are supposed to tell you four days before it starts, so let's test tomorrow and see what happens."

I knew it was not going to be positive, but she was sure it would be.

She called me that night and said, "Darren couldn't wait, he wanted me to take the test tonight."

"Oh really?"

"Yeah, and there's a faint pink line."

"Oh my God, you're kidding me." I couldn't believe it.

"I'm not kidding you, Bird, there are two pink lines, they're really faint but they're there!"

We all started jumping up and down, crying and yelling, "It worked, it worked, she's pregnant!" After we got the news we were just in total shock.

Since day one, I haven't been at all concerned about something going wrong. I haven't worried about a miscarriage, I haven't worried about JoAnn changing her mind. We're almost at nighteen weeks and the due date is December tenth. This is it—we are finally going to be parents.

JoAnn was very sick at first and I felt so bad for her. I'd go to her house and help with the dishes and stuff, but I still felt guilty that I couldn't do more.

I'd say to her, "I wish it was me."

She'd say, "This was my decision, I'm the one that came to you."

When we initially started this whole thing, Jesse was very concerned about how I would deal with it. I told him that years ago I wouldn't have been able to handle someone else carrying my husband's child. I would have adopted. But it is truly a miracle that I'm still going to have *my husband's* baby. So it's just…this is my only choice, and I'm totally cool with that. It can't be me so JoAnn is the next best person.

It's so different for us, because it's not our own private little family. We are in a big social circle, and a lot of our mutual friends have told JoAnn that they couldn't give a baby away like she is doing. When she goes to softball games with the kids, for instance, some of the ladies will say, "I think it's wonderful what you're doing but I couldn't do it." They have been supportive but honest.

It really bothers her when people say that, so we've tried to think of what she could say in response. One lady who belongs to the PPS Online support group to which I belong, even suggested saying JoAnn's egg would have otherwise been flushed down the toilet if she hadn't donated it to us. It may be crude, but people need to realize that just because they wouldn't be comfortable with the situation, it doesn't give them the right to share their negative feelings with us.

It may be difficult for me though, because in our small town people aren't going to forget. People will inevitably say things that could be hurtful to me. I can picture comments like, "Maybe JoAnn can get the baby to settle down," or "The baby looks like her mother," and they aren't referring to me.

As long as we are open and honest with our baby from the beginning, there won't be any surprises. So I'm not going to burden myself with the worry that so many people know of our situation.

JoAnn kind of feels bad that she has no connection to the baby. She says that she doesn't have a maternal attachment to it at all, not that she doesn't love the baby—but that it's not *her* baby.

Jesse and I were away camping for the weekend when JoAnn was about eleven weeks pregnant. She had some spotting on that Friday so she went to the doctor to get an ultrasound. She wanted to make sure everything was okay.

She tried calling us but she couldn't get through on our cellphone. It turned out that everything was fine, and the doctor sent her home with four or five ultrasound pictures. She decided to find us camping so she could show us the pictures.

She said, "Don't be mad but this is what happened...." and went on to explain that she had a spotting scare. I was glad she couldn't get a hold of us before she knew the results.

It's so cool. There is a clear vision of an angel in the ultrasound pictures, off to the side of the baby. Normally I am skeptical about these types of things, but other people who see the pictures also see it immediately.

It has been an emotional whirlwind and we've all become closer because of it. I'm definitely a changed person; I have a great outlook on life now. Before, everyone thought I was a happy-go-lucky person, but anyone who really knew me *knew* there was something missing. JoAnn told me that she could sense my emptiness and knew that it was because I wanted a baby.

We help create our paths, but there is someone else looking after us too. We could have sat at the kitchen table that night and decided it was too strange, but we didn't. The fact that all four of us were up for this tells us it was meant to be. When the baby comes I know we'll feel that he or she is the baby that was meant to be ours.

Postscript

Cheri and Jesse's baby girl—their beautiful gift of love—was born in December 2003. Becca's birth was an amazing experience for Cheri and Jesse. They had wanted her for so long, and when they saw her for the first time they were instantly in love.

At that moment, Cheri was so thankful and she felt such love and appreciation for JoAnn. The doctor handed Becca directly to Cheri and she just bawled.

The other emotion she felt very strongly was relief. Cheri echos so many others when she says, "It's hard being an intended parent, with no control whatsoever of the pregnancy. Especially if you are like myself—the type of person who feels the need to have control." It was especially hard for her toward the end of the pregnancy; she wanted so much to be carrying Becca herself.

Cheri loves being a mommy and describes her daughter as the most beautiful, smart, loving, energetic little wonder. Becca is almost two years old and hard to keep up with at times, but Cheri wouldn't trade one second of it. Her daughter has blue eyes, like Cheri's, not like Jesse's brown eyes or Aunt Jo's green eyes. She also has blond hair like Cheri's. People who don't know them comment that Becca looks like Cheri—even people who *do* know Becca's genetic background say she looks like Cheri. Becca also looks a lot like her daddy and grandpa.

Cheri and Jesse recently traveled back East to visit her father and step-mom. The flight attendant came up to her and asked if she could offer some advice to a couple near the back of the plane. She said they were first time parents who were traveling with a six week old and added, "I can tell you know what you're doing, I'm sure you would be a big help to them." Cheri thought to herself, "Wow, I am being asked for advice as a mom. Who would have thought?"

She and JoAnn are closer than they were before they conjured up the idea of Becca, but not as close as they were during the pregnancy.

About three months after giving birth, there was a strange and unexpected turn of events: JoAnn left her family and moved about an hour away. She said she's always looked after everyone else and now she needed to take care of herself. Cheri has tried to be supportive, but it has been hard for her to understand how JoAnn could do this. What gnaws at the back of Cheri's mind, especially, is that she wonders if having Becca had something to do with JoAnn's need to make this drastic life-change. Cheri wonders if it changed her chemical balance in some way—like a post par tem depression that has lasted for almost two years. Darren claims the experience was a major "high" for JoAnn, and that previous to giving birth to Becca, she suffered with bouts of depression on and off. Cheri had no idea.

JoAnn says Becca *did* have something to do with it, but in a positive way. She says her surrogacy experience gave her the strength to leave her family and do what she needed to do to find herself. Cheri is sick hearted about it. JoAnn was such a good mother, she says, and one that she wanted to mentor from. Although JoAnn does see her kids, she's not there to tuck them in at night, to get them off to school in the morning, to help them with homework, or most importantly, to hug, kiss and laugh with everyday. She is missing out and Cheri finds this to be very sad.

Cheri says she loves JoAnn and wishes all the best for her. She'll never forget the sacrifices JoAnn made for Cheri and Jesse; donating an egg, being pregnant for nine months, going through birth and giving them the most beautiful little girl in the world.

Cheri admits that this may sound horrible—but that in all honesty, she was initially fearful that JoAnn would want to be too involved in Becca's life. She was afraid JoAnn would think of them all as one big happy family, not two totally separate families with a link between them.

She says, "Selfishly, I think with JoAnn away and not a part of our social circle right now, it has helped my self-esteem as Becca's mother. People don't look at Becca and compare her looks to JoAnn's—it's almost as if the fact that she was our traditional surrogate was forgotten in a way. Of course, I do hope for her children's sake especially, that JoAnn comes to her senses and moves back to our area."

In Becca's bedroom, Cheri and Jesse have photo albums filled with pictures that document the beginning of her life: Aunt Jo pregnant with Cheri and Jesse feeling her belly, Becca's birth, Aunt Jo, Uncle Darren and their three children holding her. Cheri and Jesse will tell Becca how she came into this world when it's the right time and when they feel she can understand. Becca will grow up knowing the truth, and Cheri is confident she'll be fine with it. Becca knows she is loved and she knows Cheri is her mommy.

Although she believes surrogacy is a wonderful way to create a family, she advises people not using an agency and going the traditional surrogacy route with artificial insemination, to make sure they *really* know their surrogate. She suggests that people make sure to have the psychological evaluation done. It was recommended to them initially, but JoAnn didn't want to do it and Cheri and Jesse didn't feel it was necessary. It all worked out in the long run for them; however, Cheri isn't sure it worked out so well for JoAnn.

Immediately upon bringing Becca home, Cheri says it's felt like she and Becca "were meant for each other." She says that she was never scared or worried about taking care of Becca—everything came so naturally to her as a mom. She could not love Becca anymore had she given birth herself. She believes JoAnn came into their lives for this purpose, and after being blessed with their little girl, she is convinced that God really does work in mysterious ways.

Eight

Joy
San Francisco-Bay area, California

When I was nineteen years old and away at college in Texas, I had my first ovarian cyst rupture. Although I was in the hospital for two weeks, after recovering from the surgery I went on with my life and didn't think much more about it.

After I graduated from college, I moved back home to California and got a job teaching deaf and autistic children. I was crazy about the kids and I loved teaching, but after five years I eventually got burnt out. I felt like I needed a change.

A friend of mine, Gail, lived in San Jose and she suggested I move there too. I was twenty-five years old and single so the timing was perfect. In addition to moving, I decided to sign up for some nursing courses once I got to San Jose.

Another friend who also happened to live in San Jose told me she knew a gynecologist who was looking for an office manager. I applied for and got the job. Pete, the doctor who hired me, said I could attend my nursing classes and work for him part-time. Things were really falling into place.

Three months after I started my new job, I got another massive ovarian cyst. This episode of having my second cyst removed is what started what I refer to as "my dark years". For the next several years, I would spend twelve days of every month doubled over in pain. I had chronic ovarian cysts, pelvic pain, abnormal bleeding, inflammation of my tubes, endometriosis— you name it. I'd either be doped up on meds and barely know my name or I'd be in bed, not even able to walk.

After about a year, Pete sent me to some of his colleagues for second, third and fourth opinions. They all said the same thing: "If this ovary doesn't function properly, you should have it removed."

I was like, "Fine with me!", but Pete encouraged me to keep searching for a cure before doing anything permanent. He'd say to me, "Joy, I don't want to impair your fertility." I'd respond, "My fertility? I can't even date!"

I had a diagnostic laparoscopy and the doctors took biopsies. I took Deprovera, Lupron, and tried suppression with birth control pills. Although I had to drop out of the nursing program, I was able to keep my job; since Pete was my doctor as well as my boss, he understood that I needed the time off of work. He set me up with a computer at home and the other girls in the office brought my work to me.

Finally, we scheduled the removal of my right ovary. When I woke up from surgery I felt the best I had felt in over a year. I was tap dancing out the door like, "Woo hoo! I'm a new woman!"

About six weeks later, I had my first period since the surgery and felt massive pains in my left ovary. I grew a huge cyst, started bleeding profusely, and once again I was doubled over in agony.

This is when we really started getting aggressive in our quest for a cure. We tried every therapy known to man. Pete sent me to more of his colleagues for more opinions; he sent me to an acupuncturist, an acupressurist and an herbalist. I muddled my way through the next few years and relied heavily on pain medications. I couldn't stand up straight, so in pictures taken during that time I am always hunched over. When I see those pictures I always ask, "Why didn't someone tell me how bad I looked?"

I started taking some high dosage birth control pills and this helped to slow down the bleeding. I also re-enrolled in school as an attempt to get back to my original plan and basically just accepted that I would have to live with the pain. It was incredibly taxing though because all I could do was go to work and school, then come home and get in bed.

I also got a stomach ulcer from taking the anti-flammatories. On a good day, I'd make it through the day with lots of Tylenol or Asprin, on a bad day I would stay home with Vicadin.

Finally, I sat down with Pete and said, "I can't do this anymore. I feel like I only exist to battle pain."

"Joy," he replied, "we can't take that ovary."

"Then I will find someone else who will," I told him.

He kept saying, "You are going to get married, you're going to want to have babies." I'd say, "Babies? Are you kidding me? Look at me, I'm a wreck!"

He added, "As your doctor, I can't take away your fertility in good conscience until you have gone to therapy and have done some major soul searching. What you are asking me to do will have a huge ramification on your life. I will discuss surgery again with you after you've talked to a therapist for six months—I'll even help you find someone." I agreed to go along with his plan.

I got into therapy with a wonderful counselor. He asked me, "Do you understand the implications of what you want to do?"

"Yeah, I do," I replied. "I just want to be pain-free."

His next question was, "What if they take out your ovary and you aren't pain free after all?" I had to think about that scenario too.

The counselor really made me work through the hard questions. At twenty-seven years old, I was not a functional person in society, and I realized that I had no choice but to have the hysterectomy.

After a year of therapy I sat down with my counselor and said, "I can't live my life like this. This is *not* a life. I understand the ramifications and I accept that the surgery may not cure the problem. I'm okay with it. I have to find a way to regain my life."

I scheduled my hysterectomy for Valentines Day—February 14, 1988. I was twenty-eight years old at the time. Paula, my friend from work, was with me and she was eight months pregnant with her first child.

I'll never forget her standing there in the hospital with me. There I was, registering for my surgery and she had this big ol' belly hanging out. She turned to me and said, "I'm so sorry, Joy."

"Why?", I asked.

"Because I'm pregnant and you are getting a hysterectomy."

I looked her straight in the eyes and said, "Paula, you've seen me go through pain for all of these years. Do you really think this is a problem for me?

"Well no," she said, "And I do think you're making the right decision. It just feels really weird."

"It shouldn't," I told her. "It's okay, really, please don't feel bad about this."

The one thing that became really crystallized for me in the year I spent in counseling, and it's what enabled me to make the decision to have the hysterectomy, is that I knew from the depths of my being and from the bottom of my toes, that if I decided that I wanted a family I would find a way to have one. That was my utter, absolute conviction and it gave me total peace in proceeding.

I had a total abdominal hysterectomy—removal of the left tube and ovary. I woke up in the recovery room and for the first time in four years, I didn't have *that* pain. Sure, there was pain from the incision, but it was a different kind of pain than the God awful, gut-wrenching feeling I had been experiencing for so many years. I recovered in the hospital for a couple of days, and then I was up, kicking around, walking, running, having a grand time.

The official diagnosis included some endometriosis, ovarian cysts, fibroids, pelvic adhesions, and adenomyosis, which is also endometriosis but it's on the inside of the uterus. Pete said my reproductive organs were matted down and stuck together. He said that it looked like someone threw crazy glue in there.

After the surgery, I decided it was finally time to live my life. I started dating and going out with friends and eventually I met and fell in love a guy named Bill. I had a feeling that he would have an issue about my inability to have children, but he never actually said anything about it until about a year and a half after we started dating.

When it boiled down to it and he and I were thinking of making a commitment, he said, "I can't do it. I can't adopt, I can't deal with the idea of adoption. I can't deal with the fact that you can't have my children."

It was the first slap in the face I had over my decision and it sent me into a real tailspin—I wondered, maybe this wasn't such a great plan after all?

After Bill and I broke up, I decided to get right back on the horse. I said to myself, "I'm not going to let this defeat me. I've made it this far, I've paid my dues, I've suffered for years. I deserve some happiness now."

Paula and some other friends I worked with, unbeknownst to me, put a personal ad in a singles magazine for me. At first I was livid, but they said to me, "Well you need to stop moaping! Someone in this stack of letters has to be decent."

I started getting letters from all these guys and going out on a lot of first dates. I met some really wonderful guys and I met some really weird ones too. I didn't really click with anyone in a romantic way though.

Then I got one last letter and I said to my friends, "This is the last one I'm reading." The letter was hysterical. I laughed so hard when I read it that I cried. It was total spoof on the dating scene and the funniest thing I'd ever read. At the end of the letter he wrote, "If you've read all the way till the end, you must be interested. Call me."

I met Kevin for dinner and I was just smitten. Apparently the feeling was mutual because after our date he called and asked if we could get together again. He lived about an hour from me, so we talked on the phone for several weeks before our next date.

During the fourth or fifth phone call, he asked me if I wanted to have children. I thought to myself, "Ready or not, this is the time." Since our last date I had been questioning when it would be an appropriate time to tell Kevin. I didn't want to scare him away but I also didn't want to get too attached if it was going to be another "Bill situation".

I proceeded to tell him about my hysterectomy and at the end of my speech I added, "I need you to be brutally honest with me, right here, right now. I'm not going to go through heartache someday if this is something you just can't get your arms around. This is who I am."

He was like, "Geez, you don't have to be so blunt about it," and I was like, "Yes I do."

Then we chatted for a little bit, said good night and hung up the phone. I thought to myself, "Well, might as well cross this one off the list!"

The phone rang a half an hour later and it was Kevin. He said, "I was just talking to my sisters. There is something called surrogacy—do you know anything about that? My sisters said that if you were open to surrogacy I could still have a biological child."

"Yup," I said, "that would work."

Then he asked me on a date for that Saturday night.

In 1993, before we were even married, Kevin and I started looking into surrogacy agencies. We went to an orientation at one well-known agency in Los Angeles; one of the very few that existed at that time. We almost had heart failure when they told us what it would cost.

Kevin is in banking and he's very conservative by nature. He said, "Oh no, we are not paying that much money. We'll find another way to do this."

I was upset at first because I didn't know we had any other options. It wasn't like it is today with the resources available on the Internet and everything. I didn't know where to start.

One thing I did find out in my research is that it would be must less expensive if we did traditional surrogacy instead of gestational surrogacy with an egg donor. Since I wasn't able to use my own eggs anyway, and Kevin and I were comfortable with our surrogate mother also having a biological link to the baby, we decided traditional surrogacy was a good choice for us.

Working in an ob/gyn office, I realized I had many resources at my fingertips. I'd look through the gynecology magazine articles for references to surrogacy information and I started keeping my eyes and ears open with the hopes of finding a potential surrogate.

One day, Paula brought a local Bay area parenting newspaper to the office and she said, "You have to see this."

It was an article about a surrogacy agency called, "Small Miracles" and the agency's owner who had also been a surrogate mother herself.

The way Jennifer's agency worked is that she was more like a facilitator and her agency was more like a resource center; in other words, she brought the couples and the surrogates together but the intended parents could do a lot of the leg-work if they chose. For this reason, she was able to charge a more reasonable fee than most of the other agencies.

I called Jennifer and we clicked immediately—we talked for the longest time on the telephone. Then she came to our house to meet with Kevin and I. She made us both comfortable with the idea of working with her agency, and as a former traditional surrogate she was able to give us first hand insight into the surrogate's viewpoint.

Our first meeting sealed the deal for us. Once we talked to Jennifer and realized this was an option, we said to each other, "We can do this."

Kevin and I got married in 1995, and as soon as we returned from our honeymoon we were like, "Let's kick this into gear."

Pete suggested that before we go too much futher, Kevin should probably have his sperm analyzed. It turned out that he had some serious sperm problems; he had a varicose seal and really low motility. It didn't mean he was infertile necessarily, but that it could be somewhat difficult to achieve pregnancy doing IUI with a potential surrogate.

In the meantime, we interviewed a couple of potential surrogates and chose to work with a lady named Rhonda, who was married with two children of her own.

Jennifer suggested we do six cycles of IUI's and if Rhonda wasn't pregnant by that point we re-evaluate the situation.

It was a blessing that I worked where I did because I was able to coordinate everything from a medical standpoint. Kevin would come to the office and do his thing and I would do the inseminations into Rhonda with his sperm.

We did six cycles and got six big fat negatives.

Then we found out that Rhonda wasn't ovulating properly. I said, "Wait a minute, hold on here. I'm not going to work with a surrogate who has secondary infertility."

Although we were upset that we had to move on and it wasn't like traditional surrogates were exactly lining up around the block, we knew that we had to find someone new to increase our likelihood of achieving pregnancy. Also, because of Kevin's sperm issues, we had to find someone who was "super-fertile". Rhonda was very understanding and we parted on good terms.

About two weeks later, Jennifer called me at the office and said she found a surrogate who was perfect for us. After she was done describing her, I said, "She sounds great, so what's the "but"?

"Well, this will be the second surrogacy for this woman, but she will only do it if the intended parents agree to a home birth."

My initial response was, "Oh my God, are you crazy? Of course I would never agree to that! What kind of a lunatic wouldn't want to go to a hospital to deliver?"

Jennifer said, "I know you are closed minded about this right now, but please at least think about it and call me back."

When I talked to Kevin about it, he didn't think it was that big of a deal. He said, "Is it really such a bad thing if she delivers at home? This woman has three children of her own and has already been a surrogate once. She must have easy births or something."

"Do you know what can happen?" I replied. "Babies need to be born in the hospital!"

"My father was born at home," Kevin pointed out. "Think about how many babies have been born at home throughout history."

Pete didn't think it would be a problem either. I was really surprised actually—he was the last person on earth who I thought would support a home birth.

I called Jennifer and said, "Okay, we're open to meeting her."

We met a week before Christmas, 1996. Jennifer, Leanne, Kevin and myself sat in our living room and talked for hours. I was just blown away. At the end of our meeting Jennifer said, "I think we've talked as much as we can right now, let's all sleep on this and talk more tomorrow."

As soon as they left, I said to Kevin, "As long as we have medical clearance and everything, I'm pretty sure this is a yes."

On Christmas Eve she came down and got all of her testing done. The doctor said she was good to go. That same day, we signed the contracts and from that point on it was a whirlwind.

We did our first insemination on New Years day. We were all very optimistic that it would work the first time, but Leanne took a pregnancy test a couple of weeks later it was negative. I was panic-stricken. Then we did two more cycles and they both failed.

After we found out the third cycle failed, I was *really* a basketcase. I couldn't sleep that night so I got up at 4:00 a.m. to check my email, and when I saw that Leanne emailed me, my heart sunk. I knew if it was good news she would have called us instead.

Sure enough, her email said she tested and it was negative again. I sat on the computer and cried. Then I climbed into bed and continued crying for the next five hours.

I kept thinking to myself, "Maybe I'm just not meant to be a mom. Maybe all of this has been for naught."

Leanne came to my house to comfort me and we hung out for the day. She said, "I know what an emotional toll this must be taking on you, but we can't stop now."

Leanne and I had become great friends—it was like we had known each other forever. We'd email five or six times a day and we'd talk on the phone every day.

We did our fourth insemination attempt April 1, 1997. Leanne said, "This is it! I know we are going to get pregnant this time."

Exactly two weeks later, we went out for dinner with Leanne and our midwife, Sasha. Sasha was a good friend of Leanne's and Kevin and I had become friends with her as well. After dinner, we all went back to Sasha's house and Leanne took a home pregnancy test.

I was so jaded at this point. We had done six cycles with Rhonda and this was our fourth with Leanne—a total of ten cycles. When I looked at the test I was like, "Um, there is a line here! Holy crap, this is a positive!"

Then, I started worrying.

I obsessed about everything. To be honest, I don't know how Leanne put up with me half the time.

Leanne worked full-time and her kids were three, five and seven years old. I was so worried about her exerting herself that I would drive to her house, which was in San Francisco at the time, a couple of days a week to bring her dinner. It was a sixty-mile drive each way and I was doing this after my own work day. I'd also spend most weekends up there. It was basically another full-time job for me. I felt it was my responsibility to be there for her one hundred percent of the time.

We had the most uneventful pregnancy on the earth; no problems, no scares, nothing. I think the reason I worried so much is that because of my job, I had seen what could go wrong many times. I was so happy but also so terrified.

On January 1 1998, Kevin and I were out to dinner celebrating New Year's Day. The baby was a week overdue at this point.

I told Kevin, "If this baby doesn't get here I'm going to pull it out myself!" I was so anxious and nervous—I just couldn't take waiting anymore.

When we got home from dinner there was a message on the answering machine. It was Leanne's husband and he said, "You guys, I think you are going to have a baby today. Leanne's water broke and she is on her way to Gail's house." We had all agreed ahead of time that Gail's home was the perfect setting for our baby's birth.

I remember thinking, "Oh my God, this is really happening! We are really going to be parents—tonight!"

When we arrived at Gail's house, we immediately filled up the birthing tub, played serene music in the background and lit some candles.

At 10:30 p.m., our beautiful daughter Kaley was born. And surrounding the tub were the people who had loved us and supported us throughout our journey; Paula, Gail, and Jennifer. Everything had come full-circle.

It was the most incredible night. I can't even do it justice. We all slept at Gail's house. I didn't sleep of course, I just sat there with Kaley on my chest. I couldn't do anything else.

It was phenomenal to me, the amount of love and caring— all these people ushering in this one child who was just desired and wanted so much. I still get chills talking about it.

Leanne actually pumped breast milk for us for several months. What we did with the breast milk was a good way to wind down our intense relationship. I mean, it was a wonderful relationship, so it wasn't that I didn't want her in our lives, it's just that once Kaley came, Kaley was my focus. I didn't want to offend Leanne—I didn't want to shut her out. But I needed to shift my focus to our little family.

We'd set up weekly dates where we'd meet for lunch at a half way spot. We had two coolers; she'd pack her breast milk in one of the coolers, give me the full one and I'd give her the empty one to take home and fill up again. It was great for her too because she'd get to see Kaley and she'd get to see us together as mother and daughter.

One day she said to me, "You know, the financial compensation for being a surrogate is wonderful, we were finally able to buy a house and everything like that. But seeing you with Kaley is what really brings me joy. That's the fulfillment I get from being a surrogate—to watch you and laugh at you, to see how you fuss over every burp and fart. I love to see this, I love to watch you be the mom."

After she stopped pumping for us and we stopped getting together every week for lunch, we would just email every so often and send pictures every couple of months. We have gotten together once or twice a year for the last five years. I know she will always be important and special in our lives.

I used to say to Leanne, "Wanting to be a parent so much, I cannot understand how you could enable yourself to be a biological link to a child that you aren't going to raise."

"You're right, Joy," she'd reply. "It would be hard for you to understand. You are at the opposite end of the spectrum; you just *want* the child. As difficult as this is for people to understand, I love being pregnant. I enjoy it more than anything I've ever done. Before I got married and had my own kids I read the "Baby M" story and was appalled. I decided that after I had my own family I would be a surrogate so I could prove to people that it can work. I don't think of my egg as *my* child because if it wasn't combined with Kevin's sperm to become *your* child, it would have been flushed down the toilet. There is no doubt in my mind that this is your baby; I am simply the house for it. This is something I was meant to do."

Every year on Kaley's birthday, I watch the tape of her birth. She turned five on January first and asked if she could watch the tape with me.

When it ended, Kaley turned to me and said, "Mommy, you are the lucky one—you got to take me home. I only grew in Leanne's tummy, but you got to keep me forever."

Soon after our chat, I emailed Joy to thank her for sharing her story with me. She responded and said that when we finished the interview, Kaley said, "Mommy, are you talking about that surrogacy thing again? Don't people get it? I was in Leanne's tummy and then I got to come out and be your daughter—it's really very simple!"

Postscript

Kaley will be starting second grade soon and she is growing into a delightful, funny, loving young lady. "Her baby," Joy says, "is definitely gone, and in her place is a confident, happy, outgoing big kid." She is active with art classes and piano lessons, and Joy jokes that they are single handedly keeping the "American Girl Dolls" afloat. Sleep-overs, however, currently top the list of Kaley's favorite things to do. She admits that she can laugh at herself now, but that at her daughter's first sleep-over Joy was the one who cried all night long.

It still takes her breath away each and every time she thinks of how much she loves her little girl, and how much she has completed the lives of Joy and Kevin. Kaley is so utterly nonchalant about her special start; she'll openly and happily talk about it and occasionally ask new and different questions. She still loves to look at her baby book, which is filled with pictures of Joy, Kevin and Leanne. She now ends the book by hugging Joy and saying, "I sure am glad that you are my forever mommy."

Joy says that one of the lessons she's learning is that no matter how our children come into our lives, they are only "ours" for a short time. In just a blink of an eye her daughter is almost eight years old already and growing into her own beautiful person. Joy describes raising Kaley as the "greatest job and joy of her life." She and Kevin are far past the heartache and trials of trying to have a family; however, they haven't forgotten what they went through. Something *that* painful doesn't just dissolve away. But now it's really just a distant memory, as described by Joy, a "blip on the screen."

Leanne and her family have moved out of the area, which makes it more difficult to get together, but Joy and Leanne manage to stay in touch via email, cards and pictures. "Their relationship," Joy says, "is wonderfully positive and open."

While their level of contact has changed as both of their lives have moved forward, Joy and Kevin's love for Leanne and their appreciation for the miracle she helped them create—well that will never change.

Some of the intended mothers featured in this book chose surrogacy because they simply did not want to adopt. Others were open to adoption, but their husbands were not keen on the idea. In certain instances, people choose surrogacy because it is actually easier and/or faster than it would be for them to adopt. For example, in the cases of Raquel, Dalia and Shannon, women who tell their stories later in the book, the countries in which they live have unusually long wait times for infant adoption. Hannah, the woman featured in the following chapter, would have been more than happy to adopt a baby; in fact, she and her husband even consulted with three adoption attorneys in hopes of starting the process. Their dreams were shattered when all three attorneys advised that due to Hannah's medical condition, dermatomyositis, it was unlikely they would ever be chosen by a birth mother. According to the National Institute of Neurological Disorders and Stroke, dermatomyositis is, "one of a group of acquired muscle diseases called inflammatory myopathies. The most common symptom is muscle weakness, usually affecting the muscles that are closest to the trunk of the body. Most cases of dermatomyositis respond to treatments such as steroid drugs and immunosuppressants." Hannah's situation is not all that uncommon. Many people would *like* to adopt, but for a variety of potential reasons they don't fit the requirements of certain adoption agencies. Or, like Hannah, they are convinced that even if they were to look independently, their chances of finding a birth mother would be slim to none. Hannah's condition in no way inhibits her ability to parent. Fortunately surrogacy was an option for her so that she could prove this to be true.

Nine

Hannah
Chico, California

In June of 1997, when I was twenty-six years old, I was diagnosed with an autoimmune condition called dermatomyositis. Even though it's a non-life threatening condition, it's in the same category as rheumatoid arthritis and lupus—which on all levels are a form of the body attacking itself. In my case, the connective tissue in my muscles is affected and this causes severe pain in my muscles and joints. Essentially my connective tissue is telling my body to reject its' own natural product.

At the time of my diagnosis, I had been married to Troy for almost five years. We had always planned on having children, but we were going to wait until we were in our thirties. We wanted to be established in our careers before we began our family.

In the early spring of 1997, I started feeling ill all of the time, like I constantly had the flu or something. As time went on it got worse and worse, until eventually I couldn't even get out of a chair without wincing. In March, I went on vacation with my sister and my niece to Washington D.C. and New York. At the time, I was taking four Advil every four hours. My sister finally said to me, "Don't you think you should go to the doctor or something? This isn't normal Hannah!"

Most of the pain was centered in my hands, arms and shoulders. Every morning I would take a twenty-minute shower so that the heat of the water would loosen things up a bit.

On Easter, we were at a restaurant that had a buffet and I couldn't even lift my plate to take it through the buffet line. I asked

Troy for help and he was like, "You are in that much pain that you can't even lift your plate? We need to find out what's wrong with you!" He knew I hadn't been feeling well for a while, but this was the first time he realized how serious it was.

Despite all of this, I continued coming up with reasons why I may be sick. For instance, since I was traveling a lot for work and I had a very stressful job, I figured it was probably attributed to stress. Then I developed this weird cough and I figured, "It's springtime, I must have allergies." Finally, when my hands started peeling and cracking so deeply that they would bleed, I said to myself, "Okay, I'm averaging thirty Advil a day, something isn't right here." I decided it was time to see a doctor.

I made an appointment at Stanford Medical Center, which is ten minutes from where we lived at the time. I saw an internal medicine doctor and she said, "Hm, this is weird, let's do a blood test."

I had the blood test that morning. Later that afternoon the doctor called and said, "We got the results of your blood test and I don't want you to panic, but it's showing some things that I would like you to talk to a specialist about. I want you to come in tomorrow. The rheumatologist actually had the day off but she's going to come in to talk to you."

I thought to myself, "This can't be good."

The next day, the rheumatologist explained what she thought it could be. She mentioned rheumatoid arthritis, lupus and multiple sclerosis as possibilities, but she wasn't entirely sure about a few things, so she said she'd need to do some more blood work. It wasn't too long before I received my diagnosis.

I've been with the same rheumatologist at Stanford ever since, and basically we've just been working at battling this disease. What's fortunate, if you have to have a medical condition like this, is that it does go into remission at times. When I'm in remission, I don't have to take as many medications.

Still, I take prednisone every day, along with an immunosuppressant that quiets my immune system so that it's not as overactive and as likely to destroy my connective tissue. The combination of the two meds seems to keep everything in check.

By April 2000, when I was thirty years old, the subject of children came up. It had been almost two years since I was diagnosed and things seemed to be under control. Troy and I decided to plan a trip to Sydney, Australia to go to the September 2000 Olympics and figured we'd start trying to conceive when we returned.

My doctor told me all along, "If you're in remission and you can get off your immunosuppressant, I don't see any reason why you can't have a baby. I've had plenty of patients who have carried and delivered healthy children. There is a fabulous doctor, an ob/gyn at Stanford, who happens to deal specifically with pregnant women who have autoimmune conditions."

In April 2000, soon after we had talked to my doctor about our plans to have children, I came out of remission. I had been in remission for about eighteen months by that point, when I had what they call a "flare".

The immunosuppressant didn't work like it had the first time, so we had to find a stronger immunosuppressant. I was in horrible shape; it really hit me with a vengeance. My doctor pumped me up on meds.

I brought up the kid thing again and my doctor said, "Oh Hannah, we can try and get you off of the medicine, but I think we just need to concentrate on your health right now. You are still young, you don't need to worry about having children just yet."

This only caused Troy and I to feel a stronger sense of urgency. We were like, "What does she mean we should wait? We want to start our family now!"

We discussed it and I said, "We could wait for the next eight years for me to go into remission again. Let's go ahead and start contacting adoption attorneys." I knew nothing about surrogacy at that time—I figured adoption was our only choice.

In May 2002, I decided to quit my job. I needed a break from the Silicon Valley and my high stress job, and mostly, I felt like I should take the time to focus on my health. Fortunately, Troy was able to support us on his salary alone.

Meanwhile, we contacted three adoption attorneys and they unanimously told us, in so many words: "California law requires that you disclose your medical condition to prospective birth mothers. When they learn that you have dermatomyositis they will unlikely choose you to adopt their child. Without realizing that your condition is non-life threatening, birth mothers will probably just think, 'This woman is sick. I don't want to place my child with a sick family.'"

Knowing that many birth mothers would be scared away by my condition, we decided to do some research on the Internet to see if we had any other options. Almost immediately, some information about surrogacy popped up. The only image that came to mind was the "Baby M" case. I thought to myself, "I don't want to go through that." But the more I researched and the more information I gathered, I learned the doctors could take my eggs and Troy's sperm—that it would be our biological baby. Not too long after I learned that surrogacy was a realistic possibility, I joined the PPS list-serv. It was June 2000.

I posted my introduction and said, "If there is anybody else in the Bay area out there, perhaps we could get together." A woman emailed me who was in cycle with a fertility clinic in the Bay area, and she replied, "Sure, I'd love to meet with you."

Although we were never actually able to get together until Troy and I were in cycle, she met us at the fertility clinic and then we went out for lunch. She shared her own story with us and answered some basic questions about the surrogacy process. It was very helpful.

I took the information back to my rheumatologist and asked, "Is it possible to have my eggs harvested or retrieved without them being damaged in any way?" I was concerned because I had been taking so many medications.

"You'll need to be off your immunosuppressants for two cycles, so if we can taper you off during a non-stressful time in your life, I think it's a possibility." She didn't feel it was necessary to be off of the prednisone.

Even if I could get pregnant myself, it would be a high risk pregnancy. Apparently 50% of the women who have dermatomyositis have great pregnancies, 25% do very well and actually go into remission indefinitely after being pregnant, and 25% get much sicker and then they are pregnant and can't take the medications. It can get so bad that some women can't even walk. In my situation, when it has been at its worst, I've had this awful cough and lung development. If this happened again and I was pregnant, I couldn't take the medication I needed.

We decided we just wanted a child and instead of messing around with my health and worrying about all of the potential risks involved, it would make more sense to pursue surrogacy. We talked to three fertility clinics; two of them didn't know anything about dermatomyositis but the third RE knew a lot about autoimmune illnesses. He actually knew exactly what the effects of the medications would be, he told me what the chances were that I'd produce a sufficient amount of eggs and what kind of protocol would be best suited for me. I was like, "This guy is the greatest!"

Troy and I discussed whether we should go independent or through an agency. Troy's theory was that he wouldn't buy a house without a real estate agent, so he didn't want to have a baby without an agency. We started talking to different agencies and selected one in the Sacramento area. We also found an attorney.

In September 2000, we went to the Olympics in Sydney for three weeks as planned. After our vacation, in January 2001, we decided it was time to change our lifestyle. Troy left his job, we sold our house in the Bay area and moved to Chico, where I grew up and where our families still lived. We felt the Bay area was just too hectic for us; it wasn't where we wanted to raise kids and we wanted to be settled in our life before we started our family. It was a nice change of pace.

We started meeting surrogate candidates in June 2001 and to be honest, we weren't impressed with any of the four that we met initially. We asked ourselves if maybe our expectations were unrealistic.

The first gal didn't even show up to the meeting. The second, third and fourth potentials were—I feel horrible saying this, but they were the stereotypical "white trash". Even though I am not the type of person to label people like that, I just don't know any other way to put it.

Finally, Troy and I just said to each other, "You know what, this just isn't going to work," and we called up the agency director to tell her we were done. She said, "Just wait. There is one more person that I want you to meet." This woman, Melinda, had just signed on with her agency.

We said, "Okay, we'll meet her."

For the first meeting, which was in August, we met at a Starbucks near her house. I walked in and there she was, sitting at a table with a folder and a day-timer in front of her. She was very nicely dressed, like it was a job interview or something. I thought that said a lot. At first I thought, "That can't be her," but she looked at me and said, "Hannah?" I was like, "Melinda?"

She had a list of questions and she was totally organized. I thought, "This is the person I want to work with." It was like, when you put on the dress you are going to wear on your wedding day, you just know.

Troy and I met with her again over Labor Day and we all got along just great. She was twenty-five years old and a single mom. Her daughter was seven at the time.

I just remember thinking, "This woman is raising her daughter alone and she's created this wonderful life for her." I was so impressed by that.

We asked her why she wanted to be a surrogate and she said, "I'm going to be honest with you. I'm a single mom and it's really hard for me to save enough money. I want to send my daughter to college some day and I want to give her a good life. This is one way I can help to provide for her." Both Troy and I had so much respect for that. We really appreciated her honesty.

We decided to work with Melinda in the beginning of September of 2001. And then 9/11 happened.

Melinda had been working two jobs at the time; one was for an anesthesiologist and the other one was as an airline attendant on a charter airline. On September 10, she was on a flight to Hawaii and well—the next day, she was not able to leave Hawaii for obvious reasons. She actually was stuck in Hawaii for ten days, so we had to reschedule our psyche evaluation and our initial evaluation with the RE. By the time we were finally set and ready to go it was November.

I ended up having the egg retrieval on December 17. I think they retrieved something ridiculous like forty-four eggs. Although only twenty-five of them were mature enough to actually fertilize, we ended up with seventeen viable embryos. We froze thirteen and transferred four.

According to the doctor, the eggs of women with autoimmune conditions oftentimes have a hard crust around them and it's harder for the sperm to penetrate. So we had ICSI done as the doctor suggested.

The transfer was on December 21 and ten days later we found out we were pregnant. As happy as we were, we were still very nervous. We just didn't want to get our hopes up and then have something go wrong. We held our breath for several more weeks until we found out, at eight weeks into the pregnancy, that we were having twins. It was almost too good to be true.

Then we waited for the next month or so before we finally started telling people. We didn't even tell our parents until we were around ten or so weeks into the pregnancy.

Melinda had horrible morning sickness during the first trimester and we felt so bad for her. She even had to have an I.V. for a while, and home health care would have to come out to change it. Then she'd have to take the medications for the nausea. Once she got over that hump, she was fine for the remainder of the pregnancy.

At thirty-three and a half weeks, she had an OB appointment and the doctor said, "Everything looks great. You'll probably go to thirty-eight weeks." We knew, based on our previous ultrasounds, that we were having a boy and a girl.

All of a sudden, a few days later, we got a phone call at 6:00 one morning. It was Melinda and she said, "I'm at the hospital and I'm in labor!" We didn't have anything packed, so we threw our stuff together and drove an hour and a half to Sacramento.

They rushed Melinda in and she had a c-section. The first thing the doctor said when our daughter, Tara came out was, "She's huge!" She weighed 5 lbs. 3 ½ oz. Trevor, our son, was 5 lbs. 7 oz.

The babies had to remain in the hospital for two weeks, so I stayed at the Ronald McDonald house. We decided it would be better if Troy continued working while they were in the hospital; this way, he could take a couple of weeks off when they came home.

Since the birth of Tara and Trevor, Melinda and I have stayed in touch. Mostly it's been on email because we are both so busy and it's hard to get together very often. But she was at their first birthday party and we've continued to have a good relationship. Really, I consider her a part of her family, which is funny considering I originally went into surrogacy thinking it would be a business relationship only. Once I met Melinda though, I just had so much respect for her. Both Troy and I think she is a stellar human being.

We could not have asked for a better experience, and one of the things that made it so easy is that we just had this amazing, generous, surrogate. She did everything in her pregnancy that I would have done it, so I never felt like, "Oh, I don't want her to do that." She just took wonderful care of our children.

At first, Melinda told us that although her experience with us was excellent, she never planned on being a surrogate again. When I updated the PPS list-serv that our twins had celebrated their one-year birthday on July 28, 2003, four people contacted me to ask if Melinda would be interested in doing it again. I replied to all of them that, "No, it was just a one time deal for her."

Then I emailed her because I thought she'd get a kick out of the fact that all these people had inquired about working with her, and she emailed me back to tell me, "Well, I didn't want to tell you this at Tara and Trevor's birthday party, but I'm four weeks pregnant for another couple. All of sudden I got a bug to do it again, even though I didn't think I ever would. But you and your family will never be replaced in my heart."

We have our boy and our girl, we're happy as can be, and we've known for quite sometime that we don't want anymore kids. So we ended up donating our extra embryos to a stem-cell research program.

The last year has gone by so fast in many ways. There were many times in the first year of their life when I felt so sleep deprived—I'd think to myself, "So this is why the CIA can torture people who haven't slept!"

But there is something about holding that baby in the middle of the night when the house is quiet, and you just can focus only on your little one. It's just so peaceful. I do miss that on some level, but this is a great stage too. They are laughing and smiling like crazy and they are just so darn cute.

Sometimes it seems like our surrogacy journey happened over a million years ago. We are forever grateful to Melinda for her role in bringing Tara and Trevor into our lives.

Postscript

From the moment Tara and Trevor were born three years ago, Hannah and Troy have never felt a moment of disconnect from them. They call Trevor "Mini-me" as he looks and acts exactly like his dad. Many times, Hannah actually forgets she wasn't pregnant with them.

Hannah is convinced there was a reason for her health condition, and the reason is that it caused them to travel the surrogacy path. Troy and Hannah feel blessed to have Melinda in their lives and they have learned a tremendous amount about unselfish giving from her. They don't talk to her as much as they did when she was pregnant with their babies; however, Melinda will always be an important part of their lives.

Tara and Trevor are still too young to grasp Melinda's role as the woman who carried them in her belly, but someday they will understand. Someday they will know what a special lady she truly is.

Hannah describes parenting as the happiest, hardest thing she's ever done, and says she would not change a minute of their journey—including the way Tara and Trevor came into their lives. She feels incredibly fortunate to live in a time in which there are alternative ways of becoming parents.

Cindy and Betty, the women featured in the next two chapters, have experienced the joys of both adoption and surrogacy. Cindy is what is known as a "DES Daughter"—the daughter of a woman who took diethylstilbestrol (DES). According to The United States Department of Health and Human Services Centers for Disease Control and Prevention (CDC), "Diethylstilbestrol is a synthetic estrogen that was developed to supplement a woman's natural estrogen production. During 1938-1971, U.S. physicians prescribed DES to pregnant women to prevent miscarriages and avoid other pregnancy problems. Physicians, at the time, thought DES was safe and would prevent miscarriages and pre-term (early) births. Ongoing research has confirmed health risks for DES Daughters including increased incidence of clear cell adenocarcinoma (CCA), structural abnormalities in the reproductive organs, infertility, and pregnancy complications." While Cindy has known since childhood that she may have difficulties getting pregnant, Betty, on the other hand, was not born with any gynecological defects. She did not have any problems carrying a pregnancy; in fact, by her early twenties, Betty had given birth to three healthy children. Shortly after the birth of her third son, she was diagnosed with cervical cancer, and this led to the removal of her cervix and uterus. The last thing she was worried about was the loss of her fertility. But when she divorced and remarried several years later, she had a change of heart. For different reasons and under different circumstances, Cindy and Betty had to come up with alternate ways to add to and create their families. Today, when they look at their children's faces, they cannot imagine life any different than it is.

Ten

Cindy
Atlanta, Georgia

I am a "DES daughter". Diethylstilbestrol was a synthetic form of estrogen that was prescribed to pregnant women from the early 1940's to the early 1970's. It was supposed to prevent miscarriages, and since my mother had problems maintaining pregnancies, she took it when she was pregnant with me.

I hate to complain. If my mom hadn't taken DES she may have miscarried me—and I wouldn't even be here to tell you this story. So I have to keep on remembering that.

As a direct result of being a DES daughter, I have a T-shaped uterus. Abnormally shaped uteruses are common among the female offspring of women who took DES. DES daughters also may have other problems, such as a higher likelihood of cancer of the female organs.

The doctors told me that if I ever got pregnant, I'd need a cervical cerclage and I would probably have to be put on bed rest. It bothered me on some level knowing that I'd have a hard time carrying a baby, but I never feared I wouldn't be able to bear children when the time came.

I met my husband, Don, when I was twenty-six and he was twenty-nine. I told him right away that I was a DES daughter, but that according to what the doctor's had told me I should still be able to get pregnant.

We got married in 1994, two years after we met. When I was thirty, we decided it was time to start our family, but month after month went by and we weren't getting pregnant. After about six or eight months, we went to a fertility specialist to find out what the problem was. The RE suggested we do IUI.

We did six IUI's but none of them worked. I had a laparoscopy and the RE discovered clogged water in my fallopian tube. After cleaning out my fallopian tube, he recommended that we move on to IVF. This was in 1997.

The doctor assured me that women with abnormally shaped uteruses are oftentimes still able to get pregnant. So I had a lot of hope.

The first IVF attempt ended in a chemical pregnancy but I got pregnant on the second try. I was happy as a clam, thinking I was finally pregnant—it was such a great feeling.

When we went to our six-week ultrasound appointment, however, the technician couldn't find the heartbeat. She brought the doctor in to take a look but he couldn't find a heartbeat either.

He called us into his office and told us that I had an ectopic pregnancy, which meant the embryo was in my fallopian tube. Apparently, this is more common in DES daughters because an irregular shaped uterus can cause the embryo to be pushed up into the fallopian tube.

After springing this devastating news, the next sentence out of the doctor's mouth was, "This is an emergency situation and you need to go to the hospital within the next hour. You need to get that embryo out of you or you could bleed to death."

So in addition to losing the pregnancy, I had to have my fallopian tube removed. This experience rocked our world. It was the worst thing that had happened in our journey up until that point.

We were able to recover from the failures only by moving on to the next hopeful opportunity to get pregnant, but it was still very hard not to be pessimistic at times. We couldn't help worrying that we'd never have children.

Don and I both struggled to be happy for others when we found out they were pregnant. I definitely didn't want to go to baby showers.

Don is emotional by nature, but when I got upset, he was strong for me. When he was upset, I was strong for him too. He tried to hide a lot of his emotions from me because I was so stressed out, but he told me, after the fact, how many times he would break down and cry at work because of what we were going through.

The ectopic pregnancy was so devastating, we just didn't know if we wanted to keep trying and potentially face more failures. One day, my mom said, "Maybe you should start researching adoption just in case this doesn't work out for you."

Don and I had discussed adoption several times and we both felt it would be a wonderful way to create our family, but we still hoped that I'd eventually get pregnant with the help of a fertility specialist.

Incidentally, my mom knew someone who went through surrogacy. I called the woman to get some information from her and she told me that it cost around $75,000. I was pretty daunted by our conversation and the whole thing just seemed very foreign to me. I hung up the phone thinking surrogacy was not a path we'd likely end up taking.

After the ectopic pregnancy, I would just walk into my doctor's office and start crying. Finally, I said, "There is no way I'm going back to that clinic," and we switched to another clinic.

Meanwhile, we decided that more than anything we just wanted a child, so we signed up with an adoption agency to start the process. We also did another IVF attempt in 1997, but again, I didn't get pregnant.

A week after our last failed IVF attempt, the adoption agency called. I was sitting at my desk at work and the phone rang. When I picked it up, a voice on the other end said, "Your daughter was born today." I was overwhelmed with joy! It had been only four months since we had started the adoption process.

It was a totally closed adoption. The birth parents were from Georgia, they were young, un-married, and they had a one-year-old daughter. They just couldn't afford to support another child financially. Apparently, the birth mom called the adoption agency when she was five months pregnant to inquire about putting her baby up for adoption. The next time she called was when she was on her way to the hospital to give birth.

In Georgia, birth parents have ten days to change their minds, so babies given up for adoption must go into foster care for ten days after they are born.

Within the ten days Jenna was at the foster home, the foster parents invited us to come see her as often as we wanted. They were so warm and compassionate which was very comforting to us at the time. We are actually still in touch with them to this very day.

We were afraid to get too attached to Jenna, just in case the birth parents changed their minds, but we knew it was the right thing to do. We knew we should spend time with our daughter while she was in foster care in case they *didn't* change their minds.

After Jenna was born in July 1999, we decided to take some time off from our quest to become pregnant. We figured we'd start trying for a sibling when she was about two years old.

In the beginning of 2001, we resumed our attempts at getting pregnant with the help of an infertility specialist, although we decided to go to a different RE than we had seen previously.

This clinic tried a lot of alternative medications with a focus on holistic methods. We did two IVF's and they both failed.

I had a friend who had gone to the same place. She didn't have any luck getting pregnant either, so she switched to another clinic that she was very pleased with and convinced me to do the same. I figured, heck, we've practically been to every clinic in

Atlanta, what's one more? We did another IVF cycle at the new clinic but again, I didn't get pregnant.

It's strange, because according to the embryologists the egg retrievals have always been successful. They've always told us, "Your eggs look great and your embryos are excellent quality." This is why it bothers me that nobody ever mentioned surrogacy to us as an alternative.

Don and I had discussed surrogacy before we adopted Jenna, so after the last failed IVF attempt I said to him, "You know Don, we never really explored surrogacy. Why don't we talk to an attorney and check it out."

We met with an attorney in Atlanta. In our first meeting, she told us, "A lady who is interested in being a surrogate just happened to come by today." She asked us if we'd be interested in meeting her and we said, "Sure."

A few days later, we got a bill from her for $500.00. She was actually billing us for conversations she had with the potential surrogate, before she even met us or knew of our situation. We thought that took a lot of nerve!

Don is also an attorney, and when he saw the bill he was like, "No way are we paying that."

We called her to complain, and she said, "Well I thought you were interested in working with this surrogate."

We responded, "Yeah, we wanted to interview her, not pay you $250.00 an hour to talk to her for us."

We were completely turned off by the whole idea of surrogacy after the experience with this attorney. We thought it would just be too expensive. Up until this point, the only people I'd spoken to about surrogacy were the woman who told me it cost $75,000 and the lawyer who tried ripping us off.

We decided to put surrogacy on the backburner and go forward with the adoption process again. It was the summer of 2001.

Towards the end of 2001, we did another IVF attempt and it failed.

In August 2002, a year after we had re-signed with the same agency to adopt a second child, we got a call that a baby boy was born and we were selected by his birth mother. We were ecstatic!

We arrived at the hospital to see him and were told that he was healthy and fine. But within several hours he developed breathing problems and had to be put on a ventilator.

The following day, he went into the NICU because he had hypotonia, which is basically lack of muscle strength. We spent the next four days with him while he was in the NICU. He wasn't crying or even opening his eyes. Plus, he couldn't drink any fluids because part of the muscle of his intestines didn't work. He developed a fungus infection from the surgery. Then he needed another surgery.

We were there with him on a Sunday when they finally allowed us to hold him. That day, the doctors who performed his surgeries came in and told us how severe his hypotonia was. They said he would never walk or talk. He would definitely be a special needs child, and they couldn't tell us with total certainty what would happen to him.

At that point, Don and I decided we weren't Almighty. We didn't plan on adopting a special needs child and really didn't feel we were equipped to handle the situation. Our decision not to adopt him was very painful for us; we felt like we were neglecting him, that maybe we were indeed "chosen" to take care of him and we were ignoring what fate had planned for us.

About a week later, we heard that a nurse in the NICU decided to adopt him and we were so relieved, but sadly, she ended up backing out of the adoption as well.

The baby's condition continued to worsen and he died in October, when he was about two months old.

We went from a dream adoption to a nightmare adoption experience. I don't usually tell people about it when they ask us about adoption, because what happened is so rare. Our agency had been in existence for twenty-six years and they said this type of thing had never happened before. This, by far, was the most tragic experience of our whole infertility process.

We were just torn apart by the death of that little boy. Don still hadn't recovered. If you bring it up to him he will cry, still to this very day.

We decided to take a look at surrogacy again. I found a letter from that attorney we had met with, and there were some surrogacy websites listed on it, including the TASC website which has a section where potential surrogates and potential intended parents can place ads. After about a month, I placed an ad on TASC that said we were looking for a gestational surrogate in Georgia.

We told our RE that we didn't want to do anymore IVF transfers into me anymore and that we wanted to try surrogacy instead. He wanted me to do a Clomid challenge test to see if my eggs were good. He also looked through my records and said there was no clear evidence that I couldn't carry a pregnancy.

In the meantime, Marie and I hooked up. I saw her ad to be a gestational surrogate and responded to it around the same time she had responded to my ad. I could tell immediately that she had a huge heart.

When we saw the doctor again to discuss plans for our next step, he said, "I don't like your uterus." Every time he got a new piece of information, he'd say, "I just don't like your uterus."

I said, "You know what, I *really* don't like my uterus."

I told him I found a surrogate and felt we should try IVF with her instead. He, along with the other doctors, agreed that it was a good idea for us to do our next IVF attempt with a surrogate.

While I was relieved they finally agreed with me, the point is that *I* was the one making the suggestion. I mean, if I wasn't pushing the issue, who knows how many more attempts we would have done?

We did the retrieval and transfer in November 2002 and found out, soon after, that we were pregnant. Marie, and her family live only about an hour from us, which made it very convenient to see each other. I completely trusted her with the pregnancy. I figured she has three healthy boys—ages two, four, and seven—so she must know what she's doing.

I was fine with the fact that I had no control of the pregnancy, because really, that is just something you have to accept as an intended mother.

Actually, there was one time that I was slightly concerned. Marie loves iced tea, and initially she was drinking six or seven glasses a day. The doctor told her she should cut down to two or three glasses a day, but she switched to decaf instead. I was glad that he said something to her. I didn't want to mention that I had a problem with her caffeine consumption—I didn't want to be the "bad guy".

It's just awkward, because sometimes the surrogate does things that you, as the intended mother, wouldn't do if you were the one who was pregnant.

I had an amazing surrogacy relationship, so I don't mean this to be a complaint. It's just an example of the types of situations that can come up, where you really don't feel like it's your place to tell the surrogate what to do—but at the same time you are worried about your baby.

Marie wanted to be a t-ball coach on her son's team when she was nine months pregnant. All I could envision was a bat flying through the air and hitting her smack dab in the belly. The doctor told her it was fine if that's what she wanted to do, so really, what was I going to say about it? Even though I was worried sick, I didn't want to tell her I had a problem with it and have her think I was a control freak or something. So I basically had to sit back and just pray that nothing happened.

I felt very lucky that I had Jenna to hug and love while we were going through our journey. It really helped keep my stress level down because I already was a mom. Believe me, we were very grateful that Marie was pregnant and she did an amazing job, but by the seventh month, I really just wanted the pregnancy to be over. I just wanted to fast forward the next few months so that I could finally hold our baby in my arms.

I worked full-time as a pharmaceutical sales representative while Marie was pregnant. In addition to having Jenna, working kept me from becoming totally obsessed with the pregnancy. It's a good thing, because otherwise I probably would have drove Marie nuts!

We saw each other frequently throughout the pregnancy. Not only did we all go to the doctor's appointments, but we got together socially too. We even went on vacation together to Sarasota, Florida, when Marie was in the second trimester. My parents and Don's parents are retired in Florida and have rental condominiums on the beach, so we stayed in their condos for five days.

It was somewhat difficult for Don because of what we had been through. He was afraid to get too emotionally attached to the baby because of all of the "what ifs", so in a way, he kept up his emotional guard.

Jenna was so excited that she was getting a brother or sister. Actually, at first she wanted a baby brother, then she changed her mind and wanted a baby sister because all of her friends were getting baby sisters. Every time we saw a water fountain, she wanted to throw in a penny and make a wish for a baby sister. We were all thrilled when we found out we were having a girl.

On July 24 2003, Marie called us at 3:00 a.m. and said, "I'm having labor pains and I'm on my way to the hospital!"

It was three weeks before the due date, so the doctor felt we should do an amniocentesis to make sure the baby's lungs were developed. If they were, Marie would have the c-section that day. The amniocentesis showed that Marie had placenta abruption, which means the placenta was prematurely separated from her uterus. When the doctor pulled the needle up, old blood came out instead of fluid. Talk about freaking out! It was awful—I immediately starting having flashbacks of the baby boy we almost adopted. They decided to do an emergency c-section.

Three hours after we had arrived at the hospital, Molly was born. And she was perfectly healthy.

We were in the room with Marie while they did the c-section. The doctor was just great. He set up a curtain so we could be there to watch Molly pulled out of Marie's womb without actually seeing the surgery part itself. We got to hold her immediately.

Marie had indigestion a lot when she was pregnant. She would joke all of the time that the baby must have a full head of hair and it was causing her to have the indigestion.

When she saw Molly for the first time, she yelled out, "Oh, she does have a lot of hair!" We had a good laugh about that.

We stayed in the hospital for one night. I stayed in the hospital room with Marie and her husband; they slept in Marie's hospital bed and I slept on the couch.

Don was at home with Jenna that night, but he came back to the hospital the next day. It was really neat, because not only did we get to spend time together and relish in our experience, but Marie was able to spend some time with Molly too.

A lot of people assumed it would be awkward or that it would be difficult for Marie to see Molly—but it was actually the total opposite. My mom even asked her flat out, "How do you feel when you see Molly now?" and Marie's response was, "She's just a good friend's baby!"

People are really surprised when I tell them Marie held Molly and we stayed in the same hospital room and all of that. I guess a lot of people think Marie gave Molly up, like in adoption. It's hard for people to understand that even though Marie carried Molly, she doesn't feel a maternal bond towards her.

Dealing with infertility was difficult for me, although I did feel much better once we adopted Jenna. Still, I will always look at pregnant women and envy them. What really bothers me is when I hear women complaining about being pregnant. Or people will say to me, "Oh, you had it great! You didn't have to be pregnant. You got the easy part."

I would have loved to know what it is like to be pregnant, but surrogacy is as close as you can get to pregnancy without being pregnant yourself.

Adoption is just a totally different experience. Since we've been through both adoption and surrogacy, I know what the plusses are with each option. With surrogacy, you have more control in the sense that you can choose the biology of the child, and you can choose who carries the child. Going though surrogacy, you don't have control throughout the pregnancy because that obviously falls into the hands of the surrogate, but you can at least go to the doctor appointments and have a relationship with the woman who is carrying your baby.

With adoption, oftentimes you aren't involved until the very end, so you aren't typically able to go to the ultrasound appointments and all of that. A plus with adoption, in a way, is that you aren't worrying all along if something bad will happen with the pregnancy, because you don't even know there *is* a pregnancy until the birth mom is close to delivering.

There is no difference in the way I feel about Jenna and Molly. As far as I'm concerned, Jenna's birth parents are basically an egg and sperm donor. Don't get me wrong, they are wonderful people to have given her life, but they aren't her parents.

We have even thought about having a third child eventually. If we do decide to go through surrogacy again, who knows, maybe we'll even do gender selection so we can have a boy too. Marie has offered to be a surrogate again for us, but she has also said that she may want to help a childless couple first. So we'll see.

The thing is, whether you have children through adoption or surrogacy, either way—you have to be persistent. You have to *really* want to be a parent. For people who do want kids, but are unsuccessful getting pregnant on their own, both surrogacy and adoption are such wonderful alternatives.

Postscript

Molly is now two years old and has just started school two half-days per week. She is independent and acts like a toddler in every way; she's talking, potty training, and constantly laughing and smiling.

Every time Cindy thinks about what she and Don went through to have Molly, she is so grateful to Marie. She describes herself and her husband as "the happiest parents ever." Cindy and Don have been on Atlanta's local television and radio shows talking about their experience going through surrogacy. They also speak at local conferences that their RE puts together.

They still have a nice relationship with Marie and they are in touch with her as often as possible. At first, they saw her every few months, now they get together about twice a year. Cindy always tries to make sure they see Marie and her family around Molly's birthday. Incidentally, Cindy introduced Marie to a friend of hers who was looking for a surrogate and they are now in the process of trying to get pregnant. They all went out for dinner together a few months ago.

After going through this experience, Cindy says she "loves to help other people who are having problems get pregnant." She looks at both of her daughters and feels incredibly blessed.

Eleven

Betty
Willamette Valley, Oregon

I am fifty-two years old and I have six children; three
biological boys, two adopted boys and one adopted girl. Since one
of my sons has a child, I'm also a grandmother.

I married my first husband, Rick, when I was seventeen.
We moved to California and had three boys over the course of
the next six years. When I was twenty-three, I was diagnosed
with cervical cancer and my cervix and uterus had to be removed.
Fortunately I was able to keep my ovaries.

The cancer diagnosis was definitely traumatic, but I really
didn't have any issues with the fact that I wouldn't be carrying any
more children. I was just concerned about my health and being
around for my sons.

After the hysterectomy, I went on with my life; I went to
nursing school, graduated, and got my first job as a nurse. Basically
I just worked and took care of the kids.

Rick and I divorced when I was twenty-nine and I met Rob
a few years later. We dated for quite a while before we moved to
Oregon and got married. I always told Rob that we'd be adopting
a child someday, and although he wasn't on board with the idea at
the time, in retrospect, I don't think he believed I was serious.

After we were married, I said, "It's time to adopt one of
those kids that I want," and his response was, "I've decided I don't
want any kids".

I said, "Well, I don't know what to tell you because I'm adopting." Adopting a baby was always a goal of mine. Since I already had three boys, I really wanted a daughter too. Even though he wasn't overjoyed about it, Rob decided he'd go along with my plan.

We attempted domestic adoption, but we got tired of the long wait and felt we were being given the runaround. Then a friend of mine recommended international adoption, and at the same time, coincidentally, Rob's brother and his wife adopted a little girl from India.

I decided to start looking into international adoption instead of domestic adoption. When I say, "I", I literally mean, I. We still were not united on the whole adoption issue.

The agency told us there were children in Romania available for adoption. Suddenly Rob had a change of heart and realized that he really did want a child after all. He told me, "If you want to go to Romania to the orphanage, go ahead."

I flew to Romania and picked out a two-week-old baby girl. It was really difficult because there were about nine babies available for adoption at that time. When I came home to Oregon, I could tell that Rob was really excited about adopting this baby. He was even looking at baby clothes and everything like that.

The adoption agency told us there would be a four-month wait before she could come to the United States, so I had to place her directly into foster care before heading home.

One night at 11:00, we received a phone call from the adoption agency. We were told that the attorney in Romania stole money from the fifteen sets of parents working with this adoption agency. Apparently he used the money to take his family on vacation to Greece.

The people at the adoption agency felt horrible. They said, "You know, we also have children available in Russia." I told them I'd have to talk to my husband about it.

The next day, Rob called me at work and said, "Betty, the agency called! They've got ten little boys available in Russia and I told them we'd take one of them."

"But Rob," I said, "I wanted a girl."

That night, we got a fax with a birth date list of the ten little boys. Rob's mom was at our house and she looked at the list with us.

As she was going down the list, she stopped and said, "Well this one has Dad's birthday." Rob's father had died the previous year.

Rob looked at me. "What do you think?"

"Well he is the youngest one on the list, I guess we'll take him." He was fourteen months old.

The agency processed our paperwork immediately, so we were in line to get him within the month. In the meantime, the little girl from Romania's family told the agency that they wanted $50,000 upfront before they'd release her. Before we received this news, we had still planned on adopting her too. The director said, "You can go ahead with this adoption if you want, but you will have to fly over to Romania and give the family $50,000. We can't be involved with this adoption if you go forward because it's comparable to selling a baby on the black market."

I was like, "Great, I go over there to give them $50,000 and if I get caught, I go to prison in Romania. I don't think so!"

We decided not to take her. I was absolutely heartbroken because in my mind, this little girl was my daughter. The whole thing was a nightmare.

About six months after the ordeal with the baby girl in Romania, we went to Moscow to get the fourteen-month old little boy. We had decided we would name him Robert Jr. and call him Robbie.

When we arrived in Moscow, we were supposed to go to the liaison's apartment to pick him up, but he was late coming in on a flight from Krasnadar. We were taken back to the hotel and told to wait in our room. We were disappointed and a little concerned. As we watched the hours go by on the clock, Rob and I lay on the bed in the hotel room tapping our fingers.

After four hours, there was a knock on the door. We opened the door and there was a woman holding this tiny baby.

Many of the kids in Russian orphanages were malnourished, so they were oftentimes mentally and/or physically behind other children their same age. Robbie weighed twelve pounds and he was wearing clothes for a six-month old baby. We were totally shocked that he was so small and frail. At fourteen months old we expected him to be much bigger.

He also had a very blank stare on his face. No smiling, no facial expressions, no nothing. I sat there thinking, "Something is wrong with this baby that I've insisted we adopt." When the woman handed him to me, I immediately noticed that he smelled like old milk and juice.

We laid him on the bed and he didn't move. He didn't turn his head and look at us, he didn't respond to us—he was completely lethargic. I started bawling and I got on my knees and cried out, "What have I done to us? This is a sick kid!"

Rob didn't know what to say, so he suggested "Um, let's give him a bath." As if cleaning him would make him all better.

Rob got in the bathtub with him and we washed him. Since Robbie couldn't support his weight or hold up his head, Rob propped him against his body as we gave him a bath.

It soon occurred to us that he was probably starving, so we sat him on Rob's lap with his head propped up on Rob's chest and fed him. By the time we left to go back to the U.S., about four days later, he was holding up his head on his own and keeping his body upright.

We bonded with him immediately, especially Rob. I think Rob felt a connection with him so quickly because it was his decision, initially, to get Robbie.

I was in my forties and Rob was in his thirties—my three sons were in their mid-twenties—and here we were with a new baby. After Robbie was home for about four months, he was walking and running all over the place, doing all the things that he should be doing by that age. We never had any of the bonding issues you hear about with foreign adoptions. Robbie is nine years old now and he's still a very affectionate child.

After a while, I told Rob, "I still want a little girl." He suggested we look into adopting again.

I called the adoption agency and said, "I still want a girl." About a month later, they called and said, "Betty, we found a girl. But Sonia (the Russian liaison) said they have a boy for you too."

Rob and I were like, "No way are we adopting two more children." We were adamant that we only wanted one more. But about a month later, Sonia called from Russia and said in broken English, "You have to have this boy, he looks like you." She insisted on sending us a picture—and next thing we knew we were flying to Russia to get Madison and Brian.

The adoption laws had changed in Russia since we got Robbie, so this time we had to stay there for three weeks. They wanted to make sure the biological parents weren't going to come back for the child.

First, we went to Maicop to get Brian. We had to stand before the judge and declare, "Yes, we want this little boy. Yes, we know he may have delays and we still want to adopt him."

Then we drove to Krasnador, a three-hour drive from Maicop, to go to court to adopt Madison. Rob, Robbie and I stayed in a hotel in Maicop, because since Brian was the older of the two, he was more cognitive of the fact that we were his new parents. We visited him in the orphanage every day. Brian was three years old at this time and he weighed eighteen pounds. Madison was two and she weighed nineteen pounds. We weren't really worried though since we had such a successful adoption experience with Robbie.

When the three weeks were up, we packed up the kids and came home to Oregon to raise them. And they've been just fine.

I had always felt guilty that I couldn't have a biological child for Rob. When we were first married his brothers were having children left and right and I wondered if Rob was jealous in some way. Finally, after we had been married for a while, I asked him if he ever regretted not having any biological children.

"Well no," he said, "I don't regret it. I mean, it would have been nice but..." And as soon as I heard him say the words, "It would have been nice", I realized that it was indeed something he really wanted deep down. I started thinking to myself, "Hmm, how can Rob have a biological baby?" I knew there had to be a way.

It was about five years ago when I decided I would find a way for Rob to have his own biological child—I was forty-seven at the time.

I talked to Helen, my staffing person at work, about my dilemma. "I don't have a uterus. But if I just could borrow someone's uterus I could have a baby for Rob."

At one point, she said, "My step-daughter, Dawn, would probably be a surrogate for you." I didn't think she was serious so I brushed off the idea.

Then one day, Dawn stopped by at work and introduced herself. She said, "My mom told me about your situation and I'd be happy to be a surrogate for you."

I told her that we'd pay her financial compensation and she said, "I'd even do it for free." She wasn't married and she didn't have any kids. We got to know each other for a few months before officially starting the process.

When she went in for her psychological evaluation to make sure she was stable enough to be a surrogate, she flunked. The psychologist suggested Dawn had schizophrenic tendencies. It was weird because when she and I went to see the RE, I could tell that he didn't like something about her. Rob and I made an appointment to go talk to him and he flat out told us, "I think she's going to be a problem for you."

He said, "She's overweight, she's never had a baby, we don't even know if she *can* have a baby. She isn't emotionally stable. I feel uncomfortable telling you this because I know you've bonded with her and that you really want her to be your surrogate…"

I immediately cut him off. "I want us to have a baby—I want us to have Rob's baby. I'm not bonded with Dawn, in fact, if you know of any other potential surrogates send them our way!"

We had our heart set on doing surrogacy by this point. Rob was so excited that he could hardly stand it. At thirty-seven years old, he was thrilled at the prospect of having a biological child. He loved our other children with all of his heart, so it wasn't that they weren't enough. He just wanted to see what it would be like to have a biological baby and to bring home a newborn.

I got on the Internet and found SMO. I went to the classified ad section and there was Jill's ad. She was twenty-nine and married with two daughters, ten and twelve years old. The added bonus was that she also lived in Oregon, about forty-five minutes from where we live.

Jill and I emailed back and forth for about a month before we decided to meet at a mall. As soon as I met Jill and her daughters, I knew she would be a great surrogate. She was very warm and open and so were her girls. She had been an egg donor twice before but this was her first time being a surrogate.

We really lucked out. Jill pretty much agreed with us on everything we discussed before going forward—selective reduction and all of those issues. It also turned out that she went through our clinic for her egg donations, so they already had her information on file.

I met Jill in July 2002, we did the retrieval at the end of December 2002 and transferred two blastocysts at the beginning of January 2003.

We used an egg donor because I assumed my eggs would be too old. I didn't know at the time that there is actually modern technology that makes it possible for older women's eggs to still be used. I mean, yeah, it would have been nice if we could have used my eggs, but it doesn't matter to me that much. Our clinic had an egg donor list, so we just chose an egg donor and paid a $3,500.00 fee.

The first beta was 127. I asked the nurse, "Could it be twins?" and she said, "No, your beta number is too low." I came home and told Rob what the nurse said. He told me, "I don't care what she says, it's twins and they are both boys."

I thought to myself, "Even if it is twins it's probably a boy and a girl."

The second beta, about three weeks after the transfer, was 227—which is not an especially high number for that time-frame. We were out of town when Jill was six weeks pregnant. She started spotting light brown fluid and was a little worried, so she went in first thing Monday morning to see the doctor. She didn't call us because she didn't want us to panic unnecessarily.

I was at work when she called. She said, "Betty, I have some news for you." My heart stopped. I thought for sure we lost the pregnancy.

"The doctor wanted to know if you knew you were having twins." I was like, "What?" as I screamed and laughed at the same time.

"Yeah, there are two sacs in there. The doctor wants us to come in for an ultrasound in a couple of weeks to see if there are heartbeats." She told me what happened over the weekend and that when she went in to see the doctor he did an ultrasound to see if everything was okay.

I called Rob at work to tell him the news and he was like, "I told you so!"

At our eight-week ultrasound we saw two sacs and two heartbeats. Rob and I were both there—it was pretty awesome.

In the second trimester we found out that Rob's prediction was accurate when the ultrasound technician confirmed that we were indeed having two boys.

Jill is twenty-nine weeks pregnant already. I can't believe how fast the time has gone.

Aside from the first trimester when she had horrible morning sickness, the pregnancy has been uneventful. The doctor plans on inducing when she's about thirty-seven weeks along.

I am fortunate to have been able to experience pregnancy three times, but that still doesn't take away the fact that I wish I could be the one carrying our boys right now. Every time I see Jill, I wish I was the one who was big and pregnant instead of her.

She told me that the other night, her husband was feeling them kick and I just thought how much I wished Rob was feeling them kick in my belly. Even Rob has admitted that he'd love to be able to put his hand on my belly and feel them kick at night. I've shared our feelings with Jill and she says, "I know, I wish you could be the one carrying them too."

People have said to me, "You sure got the easy route this time, you don't have to do anything but sit back!" My response is always, "Look, I'd much rather be the one carrying these babies right now if I had the choice."

To be honest, I feel the same way about my adopted children; I wish I could have carried them in my belly and given birth to them too. I hope that someday, they choose to search out their biological parents. I think that would be wonderful for them and I would be totally supportive.

The kids are so excited about the new babies coming they can hardly stand it. Even Robbie, who is really my "boy" boy— he's not normally into babies, but when I bring home baby clothes he'll say things like, "Oh Mom, that's so cute, now we have to get some little baseball hats to match."

When our three adopted kids were younger and my oldest son was twenty-six, he came over to the house one day. There were potty chairs all over the place and I was running around like a chicken with its head cut off, trying to get the kids potty trained, grabbing one as another one was peeing on the floor.

He said, "Well Mom, don't you think you've bitten off more than you can chew?"

I turned to him and said, "No, not at all!" He thought I was absolutely insane. My three older boys haven't said much about the twins on the way—I think they are just used to my crazy ideas by now.

What I want people to know about surrogacy is that it's a goal that is actually reachable. It's amazing how commonplace it's becoming. Even today, I was watching one of those maternity programs on cable, and a patient asked her doctor if she had any children. The doctor said, "Well, I was never able to have children so we had a surrogate."

With people writing books like yours and famous people like Joan Lunden being open about the fact that they are having children through surrogacy, I do think it's going to continue to become more common as an alternative to having children. At least I hope that's the case.

Postscript

In October 2003, Betty's twin boys were born via c-section at 6 lbs. 15 oz. each. Everything went smooth and both boys were born very healthy. As Jill was about to give birth, she told the nurses and the doctor, "These are not our babies. Please get the parents in here so they can finally hold their babies." Because of her request, Betty and Rob were allowed to be involved in the delivery process—and to hold their baby boys as soon as they were born.

Today they are active twenty-three month olds who look very different from each other; one has blond hair and blue eyes and the other one has brown hair and brown eyes. They love each other and miss each other when they are not together. All of their brothers and their sister are crazy about them.

Betty and her family get together with Jill as often as possible. The boys refer to Jill and her husband as "Auntie and Uncle". Jill was a surrogate for the second time shortly after giving birth to Betty's boys, and ended up having twin girls for another couple when the boys were fifteen months old. She enjoys being a surrogate so much that she decided to do it yet again—and she is now three months pregnant with a third set of twins. Her daughters enjoy the pregnancies and love staying in contact with the babies; in fact, they frequently baby-sit Betty and Rob's children.

Betty and Rob are forever grateful to Jill for the gift she has given them and happy to keep her and her wonderful family in their lives. Betty describes Jill as "a very special person who loves giving what she can to people who really want a child." Jill gets such joy out of seeing the parents with their babies for the first time. She is interested in hearing how they are doing and watching them as they grow. Betty says she knows some intended mothers call their surrogates "angels," but she calls Jill, "The Miracle Worker."

Like Betty, Sarah has been fortunate to experience pregnancy and childbirth three times. Sarah is also remarried, and like Betty, she wanted to give her husband the opportunity to have a biological child. The other commonality these two women share is a cervical cancer diagnosis at just twenty-three years old—the same age I received my own ovarian cancer diagnosis.

Of the twenty women whose stories are told in this book, Betty, Sarah and myself are the only three who had gynecological cancers. It deserves mentioning here that ovarian and cervical cancer are only two of six cancers diagnosed in the female reproductive organs; the other four include cancer of the uterus, fallopian tubes, vulva, and vagina. While ovarian cancer and cervical cancer happen to be the only gynecological cancers addressed in this book, this is not to negate the significance of the other four.

According to The Women's Cancer Network, "Cervical cancer was once the number one cause of death from cancer in women. Thanks to the Pap test, the number of women in the U.S. with cervical cancer has decreased dramatically." Cervical cancer symptoms include bleeding after intercourse, vaginal bleeding between menstrual periods, pain with menstrual periods or abnormally heavy periods. If it is advanced, symptoms can also include abdominal pain or swelling, or kidney failure due to blockage of the ureter (the tubes that connect each kidney to the bladder).

Ovarian cancer statistics are not quite as encouraging. As the United States Department of Health and Human Services Centers for Disease Control and Prevention (CDC) points out, "Ovarian cancer causes more deaths than any other cancer of the female reproductive system." Since it is a disease that oftentimes goes undetected until it is in an advanced stage, many women do not even know they have ovarian cancer. In order to catch it early and increase the odds of survival, it's important to recognize the following symptoms: abdominal pressure, bloating or discomfort, nausea, indigestion, gas, urinary frequency, constipation, diarrhea, abnormal bleeding, excessive fatigue, irregular menstrual cycle, pain during intercourse, and unexplained weight loss or gain.

In Sarah's case, she learned she had a tumor growing in her cervix during the first trimester of pregnancy with her third child. Thankfully, this did not inhibit her ability to carry and give birth to her son, but it did ultimately lead to the removal of her cervix and consequently, her inability to have more children. Although Sarah was suddenly infertile, she did not mourn this loss because she thought she was done having children. But when she met her husband, Joe, and realized she wanted to have a baby with him, surrogacy was the first alternative that came to mind. And once Sarah has something in mind, there is no stopping her.

Twelve

Sarah
Mazon, Illinois

In October 1989, when I was sixteen years old, I had my first son, Chad. I married Blake, Chad's father, when I was eighteen, but we got divorced two years later. We were just too young.

While I was a cocktail waitress about a year after the divorce, I met Tom and we started dating. Less than a year later I found out I was pregnant again. Tom and I got married in May 1995, two months before our daughter Marissa was born.

Tom was extremely jealous, physically abusive, and we basically ended up fighting throughout the entire marriage. I had enough after a year and a half, so I took Chad and Marissa with me and moved out.

We would still see each other occasionally though, so when Tom asked me to go away with him for a couple of days for Valentines Day, I said, "Okay." I ended up getting pregnant again that weekend.

Here I was, twenty-three years old and pregnant with my third child—and inevitably headed for a divorce. Since we had a baby on the way, Tom and I decided to try and make it work again and he moved back in with me. Our relationship was still as rocky as ever though.

When I went in for my six-week check up, I had a pap smear and it came back abnormal. After a repeat pap also came back abnormal, I was told that I had cervical cancer.

The doctor said I'd have to go to Northwestern Memorial Hospital in Chicago every eight weeks so that the tumor growth could be monitored, and hopefully I'd go as close to full-term as possible without the cancer spreading.

I was afraid of leaving my kids without a mom, but at the same time I had this faith that everything would be fine. Terminating the pregnancy was never an option in my eyes.

On September 5, 1997, when I was thirty-two weeks along, I went to the hospital for a stress test. It turned out the baby was under a lot of stress.

The doctor came in at 3:00 a.m. and said, "We're going to take him now," and in the early morning of September 6, Tony was born.

I had my tubes tied immediately after the delivery—I was done having kids.

When I went in for my follow-up appointment, they gave me the lab results; I had full-blown cervical cancer and I would need a hysterectomy. I told the doctor, "Really, I don't need my ovaries. Just go ahead and take them while you are in there."

He said, "You are young and I don't want you to go through menopause at such an early age. We'll only take them if we absolutely have to."

The surgery went well. They were able to remove my cervix vaginally and the cancer was contained. So aside from the follow-up appointments to make sure everything was fine, that was the end of that.

Tom and I separated for good when Tony was only two months old. It was stressful being a single mom, but I was just glad to be out of such an unhealthy relationship. I concentrated on my kids and went on with my life.

A couple of years later, in October 2000, I was at the courthouse paying a traffic ticket and this really hot guy walked by. I didn't think much about it until I saw him a few months later at the gym.

Several months went by and I saw him at the hardware store. A couple of months later, the same guy was in line at McDonalds, and then a month or so later, he was at Subway when I went there to get a sandwich one day.

It was the last straw. I said to myself, "Okay, that's it, I have to meet him." By this time it was July 2001.

I had noticed his company name on his t-shirt, so I knew it would be easy to get the phone number. I decided to give him a call.

I was a little nervous initially—I didn't want him to think I was a psycho for tracking him down. But when I told him about all of the times I had seen him around town, he thought it was really funny. We hit it off immediately and ended up on the phone for six hours.

During that first conversation, I said, "I'm going to be honest with you. I cannot have kids the normal way. If I were to ever have kids again it would be extremely difficult and expensive."

As we started getting serious I realized that if we did get married eventually, I would want to have a child with him. He said he was perfectly happy with my three children and didn't see the point of going through so much trouble to have another child. I was the one who really pushed the issue. I don't know, I think it's a natural thing—when you are in love with someone you want to have a child *together*.

I really don't even remember how I knew about surrogacy but somehow I just knew it was an option. On a whim one day, I decided to do an Internet search and I found SMO, then I started looking through the classified section and stumbled upon Maggie's ad.

Maggie lived in Michigan, which was a plus, because it wasn't too far of a drive from Illinois. I wanted to be involved in the pregnancy and attend doctor appointments.

Joe and I weren't quite ready to begin the process though. Maggie said she would stop looking for intended parents and wait until we were ready, but she wanted a retainer of $3,000.00.

I was like, "Okay, sounds good to me," and I went ahead and popped a check in the mail for $3,000.00.

After I sent the check, Maggie's emails slowed down and she stopped answering my phone calls. I sensed something was fishy.

Then in November, I got this email from her saying that her mom died in a horrible car accident. Of course I was like, "Oh my God, that's just horrible!"

I wasn't sure what was going to happen with our surrogacy arrangement at that time, but I wasn't about to ask her considering the circumstances. I gave her my condolences and left it at that.

A month later I got an email from her saying, "I'm so sorry, I know we planned on doing our transfer in a couple of months, but I am pregnant with my own child." Then she added something about how she'd be more than happy to be our surrogate in a year or so.

I said, "Great, I'm really happy for you. But no, we are not willing to wait a year, so you can go ahead and send me back the $3,000.00—okay."

Her response was, "No, I'm not going to do that..." and then she explained that she felt she was entitled to keep the retainer because we weren't willing to wait a year for her.

After talking to an attorney we found that it would have cost us more money in the long run to try and sue her, so we decided to just let it go.

I was totally frustrated and pissed off, but I knew so many people who had positive outcomes with surrogacy and I just didn't want to give up. I decided to post my own ad on SMO, and next thing I knew, between the emails I sent and the emails I received, I must have been talking to a hundred potential surrogates. I even created a file with their names and what we had talked about so I wouldn't forget who was who.

One of the women I was talking to was named Kimber. In March 2003, Joe and I drove to meet Kimber and her husband at a

Pizza Hut in northwest Illinois. I just didn't feel we clicked though; she seemed pushy or something. I thought to myself, "She doesn't seem very stable."

When we got home from dinner, I emailed her and said, "Thanks for meeting us, but I think we're going to keep looking." The nasty email she wrote back only proved that my instincts were right.

In the meantime, I was totally immersed in surrogacy. I'd be Online until 5:00 or 6:00 a.m. going through the classified section on SMO, reading and posting on the message boards.

I met another potential surrogate named Carla soon after our meeting with Kimber. Carla lived in Iowa, about a two and a half hour drive from us, so one day I drove out to meet her at a mall near her house.

Our meeting at the mall went well and we decided we wanted to work together. I was so relieved on the drive home that I finally had found someone. She seemed nice and normal, she had a child and her husband was supportive of her being a surrogate.

I don't know if it was nerves or the pizza I ate at the mall, but while I was driving back to Illinois I suddenly had to go to the bathroom. I was talking to Joe on my cell phone and I told him "My stomach is killing me! I swear I'm going to pull over on the side of the road because I cannot hold it."

There were only cornfields—no restaurants, no gas stations, no nothing.

I finally saw a Wendy's at one of the exits, so I pulled off the road and ran into the bathroom. As I turned around to sit on the toilet, I shit all over myself. It got on the wall, all over the toilet seat—it was everywhere. I threw my underwear in the garbage, but I had to wear my jeans. I mean, what was I going to do, drive home naked?

There was actually crap on the inside of the back of my jeans, so I stuck an envelope between my jeans and my back and that's how I drove home. I was miserable.

I just remember thinking to myself, "What the fuck! This sucks!"

On top of it, I got an email from Carla a few days later telling me that since she was new to surrogacy, she'd feel more comfortable going through an agency. All I could think was, "Great, I shit on myself for nothing!"

I know a lot of people choose the agency route, but personally, I just didn't feel like shelling out more money. I was confident I would eventually find someone on my own.

In addition to SMO, I belonged to another Online support group for people in the Midwest specifically. I asked the group if anyone had any recommendations for fertility clinics in Illinois, and Hilary, the moderator of the list-serv, said that she worked with Fertility Centers of Illinois (FCI) and had a great experience with them. She highly recommended their RE, Dr. L.

I wanted to see what other people who had worked with FCI had to say, so I posted the question to the group. A woman named Selena responded to my post and said she had all her screening done there when she had attempted to be a surrogate a few months earlier. Although she didn't get pregnant, she had only good things to say about the clinic.

Selena happened to be looking for new intended parents, so we started emailing each other regularly to see if perhaps we wanted to work together. After a few weeks of chatting Online, we decided we should meet in person. Joe and I met Selena and her husband at a Lone Star restaurant in Joliet and that night we all agreed it was a match.

She was my age, thirty-one, but she acted like she was sixty years old. She was such a goody-goody—it was actually kind of funny. She was very nice though, very quiet and low key. She had four children of her own and she had been an egg donor three times. Incidentally, she also lived in Michigan.

We had a consultation with Dr. L at FCI and we thought he was awesome. Plus, we were impressed with the center's statistics, we liked that they were a large and reputable, and it was comforting to us to know they have been around for a long time.

I had my egg retrieval on August 11. We got seventeen eggs and everything went as smooth as silk.

Selena came to our house on August 13, in case it was a three-day transfer, but Dr. L called in the morning of August 14 and said that it was going to be a five-day transfer. This meant Selena would be staying at our house for four more nights; two nights before the transfer and then two more nights after that so she could be on bed rest.

She emailed me a grocery list beforehand and I made sure to buy everything on the list: a specific kind of rye bread, a certain kind of cheese, and strawberry preserves, not jelly.

There was also this spinach dip she wanted me to get, but it was only sold at a store in Glenview—an hour and a half from my house. I made my own instead, but apparently she didn't like it because she didn't have one bite. She also mentioned that I got the wrong kind of rye bread.

The day before the transfer, Selena decided she wanted to go to the riverboat. I don't gamble and I had no desire whatsoever to go the riverboat, but I took her to the Empress Casino in Joliet. As soon as she got herself situated on a slot machine, I went off by myself for a while. I knew that if she saw my face she would know I was annoyed, so I figured it was better just to stay clear of her.

I have never wanted a beer so much as I did on that riverboat, but I felt stupid having a drink in front of her because she was such a goody-goody. So I went to the third level of the boat where she couldn't see me and I downed a beer. I was just so stressed out by this point.

Joe and I took Selena out for dinner that night to a restaurant in Morris called Marias.

Our transfer was the next day. Two blastocysts were transferred into Selena and everything, according to the doctor and the embryologist, went as perfect as possible.

A couple of hours after we got home, she said, "Hey, do you think we could go back to that Maria's again? I really liked that place!"

I can only imagine the look on my face. I pulled Joe aside and said, "What do we do? She wants to go out to dinner but she's supposed to be on bed-rest."

I was totally panicked. I was seriously on the verge of crying. I said to Joe, "We've spent $22,000 by this point for this attempted transfer and she wants to go to a freaking restaurant?"

Joe was calmer than I was and said, "Well, she'll be sitting in the car, sitting down to eat, I'm sure it will be okay."

Next thing I knew, there we were at Marias again—me, Joe and Selena. There I sat with a plastered fake smile on my face. I was so upset that I couldn't even eat.

Apparently, there was a power outage at her house and they didn't have electricity, so the next day, Selena announced that she was going home. I begged her to let me drive her in her car, so she could just lounge back in the passenger seat and relax. I suggested I could have Joe follow us. I also reminded her that FCI told her she should take it easy for a few days, but she said, "Oh, I'll be fine," and insisted on driving herself home.

I sent her home with three pregnancy tests. For some reason, she took the first one three days after the transfer, even though she knew the likelihood of it showing a positive that early, even if she was pregnant, was almost zero. Sure enough, the test was negative. She took the other ones a few days later, and they were also negative.

A few days after that, I asked her to go buy some more pregnancy tests and we'd reimburse her, but she said, "No, I don't want to test anymore, it's just too stressful for me."

I told Joe and he said, "You tell her to get her ass to the store and buy some more pregnancy tests!" He was like, "Hey, we are paying her to be our surrogate, so as far as I'm concerned it is a *business* relationship."

She ended up buying more pregnancy tests, but each one that she took was negative. Her beta twelve days after our transfer also came back negative.

I called her to give her the news and she said, "Yeah, they called me already. I'm really sorry, and I'll understand if you don't want to work with me again."

I said, "Well actually, I think we're going to move on." We said goodbye and that was it.

It was a devastating blow that our attempt failed, but I felt I had no choice but to get back on the horse again. I re-posted an ad on SMO and started talking to several more women.

One day, I got an email from Trish. She was from Rockford, Illinois, married to her high school sweetheart and they had two children. She seemed great. Shortly after we starting emailing each other, Joe and I went to meet Trish and her husband, Derrick, at a TGI Fridays in Rockford. Everyone seemed to get along fine so we decided we'd go forward.

On November 4th, we had our frozen embryo transfer. We all met at the clinic and she brought Derrick with her. Three blastocysts were thawed; all survived the thaw and all three were transferred. Afterwards, Trish and Derrick went back to Rockford and Joe and I went home. I was really hopeful it was going to work this time.

A few days later, Trish called me. I'll never forget it—she said, "Looks like you're going to have to add another name to your answering machine message!"

I was like, "Oh my God, really?" I couldn't believe it!

She said she had taken a home pregnancy test and she could see a very faint line. I asked her to take a picture and email it to me, but she said the line was too light and she didn't think it would show up on the computer.

I was so excited, I felt like I was going to burst! I remember driving my kids to school that day thinking, "Nothing, absolutely nothing could ruin my good mood."

Several days later, on the day Trish was going in for her beta test, my cell phone rang and it was the nurse. She called to tell us the beta results were negative.

As the day went on, I began to re-hash all we had been through up until that point. I remembered a conversation Trish and I had when I called her one morning somewhere between the transfer and the beta results.

She had said, "Oh my God, I'm freaking out—I ran out of coffee."

I was like, "Coffee?"

I recalled that the transfer instructions specifically said, "No caffeine before the beta." So before we decided to go forward and do another frozen embryo transfer, I asked her nicely if she could cut out the coffee next time.

She got defensive and said, "Well it's actually half-decaf and half-regular, so it isn't as high in caffeine as regular coffee."

"That's fine", I told her, "but the instructions said to cut out caffeine during the two week wait."

She said, "Well I guess, if it's that important to you." I could tell she was irritated.

Our second transfer attempt was January 25 and I was a total wreck this time. This was the last of our frozen embryos. Again, the doctor said the transfer went beautifully and the embryos were perfect.

Derrick couldn't drive Trish home because he was starting a new job and he had to travel out of town, but he came with her to the clinic and stayed through the transfer. We had agreed ahead of time that Trish would do the two days of bed rest at our house. She arranged for her mom to take care of her children back in Rockford.

Joe and I were renting a house at the time while our new house was being built. It wasn't a very large house, so the only place for Trish to sleep was on the couch. It was a big, comfy, cozy couch and I had it all set up with sheets and blankets, so I figured it would be fine.

After she unpacked her things, the first thing she did was plop her bag of coffee on the counter and ask, "How do I work this coffee pot?"

I was taking a real estate class to get my license and I had class that morning. I *had* to be there too—the instructor was extremely strict about attendance. Since I had to leave for the morning, my mother-in-law offered to come over so she could take care of Trish while she was on bed rest.

We got through the few days in spite of the tension between us, and two days after the transfer she went home.

Twelve days after the transfer, the nurse called on my cell phone when I was driving home from real estate class. Trish had the beta test and it was negative again. I was sad, but not at all surprised. I didn't want to talk to Trish so I asked the nurse to call her for me.

After we found out the results were negative, I realized I had not seen her take medications while she was staying with us—not even once. I didn't see so much as a syringe wrapper. I also thought it was odd that she didn't mention the shots the entire time she was at our house.

I really didn't know what to say to Trish and I didn't feel like talking to her on the phone, so I sent her an email sharing the results. I knew FCI had already called her to give her the news as well.

Then I got this bitchy email from her, ripping on me for emailing instead of calling her. And while she was at it, she told me how pissed she was that she had to sleep on the couch while she stayed with us. She complained that we didn't have enough food in the house, even though we either ordered in or took her out for every meal.

She also thought it was incredibly rude that I went to my real estate class and left her with my mother-in-law for a few hours.

The thing was, I did ask to leave the class early. I was almost in tears when I asked the instructor; I even told her what the situation was, thinking she may have mercy on me. She said "No", unless it was a life or death circumstance, and told me if I left class early she wouldn't give me the credit for it. She didn't give a crap what my situation was.

I emailed Trish back and told her how I felt, again, about the caffeine issue. How it was a slap in the face and everything like that. There was really no use going back and forth with her—we were unhappy with her and she was unhappy with us. Clearly, we were both ready to move on.

After the ordeal with Trish, we decided we needed a break. I knew I still wanted to find a surrogate, but I didn't want to find a stranger Online again. I told myself that the only way we'd go through surrogacy is if a friend or someone we knew offered to do it for us.

In the meantime, I got my real estate license in March 2004 and we moved into our new house the same month. We put surrogacy on the back burner for a while.

Then out of nowhere, in the beginning of June 2004, my friend Vicky called me and said, "Sarah, I really want to carry for you guys. I've been thinking about this for a long time, but I didn't want to say anything until I was sure."

Our daughters met in daycare when they were three years old, so I had known her for about six years.

I was totally shocked, but also very relieved because it seemed as if this was the answer we were looking for. I knew Vicky was a responsible person and a good mom, plus she lives only about five minutes from us. I told her that it would be wonderful to have her as our surrogate, and when I got off the phone I told Joe right away. We both felt that it would be the ideal situation.

We decided we'd have our transfer at the end of the summer, and in the meantime, Vicky and her husband Ken had to get all of their preliminary testing done.

I remembered reading an article in our local newspaper about a couple who had boy/girl twins via surrogacy—the lady's aunt was their surrogate. The article mentioned that this couple went through a clinic in Joliet and worked with the founder, Dr. S. It turned out that this particular clinic—The Center for Reproductive Health, was only about twenty-five minutes from our house. With all of the appointments we'd be having, we thought it would be much more convenient for us and for Vicky if we found somewhere closer to where we lived.

We met with Dr. S and he was very warm and compassionate. It initially concerned me that it was a small clinic, totally unlike FCI, but I figured they must be doing something right if that lady in the newspaper got pregnant.

Vicky and Ken got their testing done at Dr. S's clinic and we continued to get all of our ducks in a row for a transfer in early fall.

We had the retrieval in October and it went very well. Twenty-one eggs were retrieved and by day five, there were twelve blastocysts. We transferred the two best embryos on day five and froze the remaining ten.

Dr. S wanted Vicky's blood levels drawn two days after the transfer to see what her progesterone levels were, so I went with her to have her blood drawn. After the appointment we went to Applebees for lunch. David, Vicky's two and a half year old son was with us, and he was running all over the place and knocking sugars off the tables. Vicky kept on reprimanding him, putting him back in his high chair and pulling him out again. She was supposed to be taking it easy.

There I sat again with this plastered smile on my face—watching her get refill after refill of Pepsi.

About six days after the transfer, Vicky called me on my cell phone to tell me that she took a pregnancy test and it was positive. After the "Trish incident" I wanted to see it with my own eyes, so I went over to her house and sure enough, there was a line. I was still in disbelief and I didn't want to get my hopes up until we had our beta done. Three days later we had our beta and it was sixty. It more than doubled two days later, so with a sigh of relief I realized that finally, we had a baby on the way.

I was on cloud nine for a few weeks and everything seemed to be going along fine. Then one Friday, when she was five-weeks pregnant, Vicky started bleeding profusely. She described it as "coming out like Jello".

We called the doctor and he said we could come in for an ultrasound, but we wouldn't typically see anything this early anyway. So he suggested we keep the appointment we already had, which was scheduled for Monday, and advised that Vicky go on bed rest for the weekend. I was totally depressed and convinced the pregnancy was over.

We went in on Monday and the doctor showed us a fetal pole. It was still considered a viable pregnancy.

The bleeding slowed down a bit and the following Friday, at six weeks into the pregnancy, we went to get another ultrasound. There was a heartbeat. It was so faint you could barely even tell, but it was there.

I was so relieved, although I was also totally shocked. I couldn't understand how someone could bleed so much and still be pregnant. I wanted to be optimistic, I wanted to tell myself that everything would be fine from that point on, but I just couldn't. I had read about so many horror stories, so many miscarriages over the last couple of years.

That was the problem—while I was learning so much about surrogacy and meeting so many other intended mothers and surrogates, I learned how much could go wrong in a pregnancy. I had taken that for granted because all of my pregnancies were so smooth—I never worried about a miscarriage when I was pregnant with my three kids.

From that appointment on, the pregnancy itself was pretty uneventful. When I think back, I'm pretty sure the excessive blood was the other baby that didn't make it.

Unfortunately, by the second trimester, the relationship between Vicky and I went down the tubes. It all started when she was about eleven weeks along. Joe and I took Vicky and her family out to dinner, to Chilis, to celebrate her birthday. She ordered a Dr. Pepper, which of course has caffeine in it, so obviously Joe and I were annoyed. She drank the first one, then the waitress came by and asked if she wanted a refill. She said, "Yes." She drank the second one, and once again, got a refill. Joe, who is incredibly laid back, finally said, under his breath, "And that's number three."

As she sat there drinking her third Dr. Pepper, Joe and I were so tense, neither one of us could even eat.

I didn't know what to do. Joe's theory was even though she was our friend, we were paying her and therefore, it was a business relationship. For me, it was such a touchy situation because she was our friend, but also, how do you ask someone not to drink caffeine? I mean, she knew how we felt about Trish and the coffee thing—I had several in depth conversations about it with her. So you'd think she'd be more sensitive to the fact that it was an important issue to us.

After Joe and I discussed it for about a week, we decided we were going to say something to her, and if she didn't like it, too bad. So we went over to her house, sat down with her and said as nicely as we could, while very consciously trying not to seem "controlling", "Hey, think you could cut down on the caffeine a bit?"

She acted as if she didn't even know that caffeine was a bad thing for a pregnancy and claimed that she drank caffeinated pop throughout her own pregnancies.

Again, all I could think to myself was, "This sucks so bad, because I wouldn't drink caffeine if I were the pregnant one."

In order to make our case, we told Vicky that I had researched the effects that too much caffeine could have on a fetus, like premature birth and microcephaly for example.

She agreed that she'd cut down, but I could tell that she was offended by our request. It wasn't like we were asking her eliminate it completely; we just thought that three in one sitting was a bit much. Plus, if that's how much she was drinking in front of us, we could only imagine how much she was drinking when we weren't there.

Soon after this conversation, I noticed that she was avoiding my calls and emails. I tried to give her space, and even though I knew she was mad at us for telling her how we felt about the caffeine issue, I was still glad we were honest with her. I just didn't think it was right to feel like we had to keep our mouths shut about something so important to us.

About a month after we had the caffeine discussion, we stopped by her house one day. Joe was standing in the foyer, Ken and I were sitting on the couch, and Vicky was sitting on the floor. David kept on running towards her, full speed, and then pouncing onto her stomach. Each time he'd land on her she'd let out an "ugh!"

Joe and I kept on giving each other looks, and then finally I couldn't take it anymore and I blurted out, "Vicky, he's jumping on your stomach!" She responded with, "No he's not, it's my lap." I mean, what could I say at that point?

So once again, I just kept my mouth shut. All I could think about for the rest of the night was our poor little baby in there being pounced on by David. And the fact that she allowed this to go on in front of us——I didn't even want to think about what went on when we weren't around.

When she was about seventeen weeks along, it happened to be one of the worst snowstorms we had had in the Chicago area all winter. The driving conditions were so bad, the weather channel suggested, "Don't go out unless you absolutely *have* to."

Ken had a foot doctor appointment, about a 45-minute drive in normal weather from their house. For some reason, Vicky decided to go with him and bring their two kids.

Apparently they went out and had cheeseburgers afterwards; I know this because later that day she called to tell me how great the burgers were. Of course I didn't say anything. I knew she'd just get defensive instead of trying to see things from our point of view. I was totally irate though.

I thought it was bad enough that she'd put her own life on the line, and that of her children, but knowing what we had gone through to achieve this pregnancy and taking a risk to go to the damn foot doctor? I just thought it was so careless of her to put herself and the baby in such a potentially dangerous situation, especially since there was no reason Ken couldn't have just gone by himself.

A few weeks later, when she was almost twenty weeks along, she claimed she still hadn't felt the baby move. I knew by this stage of the pregnancy she should be feeling *something*, so I asked her to try using the doppler she had bought to find the heartbeat. She said that she couldn't hear anything with the doppler either, so I called the doctor to see what we should do.

He explained that Labor and Delivery will only do an ultrasound if the woman is at least twenty-weeks along in the pregnancy, so if we wanted her to have an ultrasound we'd need to go to the emergency room.

I called her and said that we wanted to go to the emergency room. She was clearly annoyed but I didn't care.

The ultrasound technician asked, "You can't feel that baby moving?", but Vicky insisted she didn't feel a thing.

The baby looked great though and the heartbeat was 150. And this is when we found out that we were having a boy!

After going to the emergency room, I told Vicky, "Whenever you feel the baby move, I don't care what time it is—even if it's in the middle of the night, please call me."

If our relationship wasn't already tense, after the emergency room incident it got even worse. I emailed her a few days after just to say, "Hi" and she never responded. I tried asking her some questions about the baby shower we were planning to have a couple of months later—I wanted to see what dates worked for her because I was planning on inviting her. When she finally responded, she never said anything about the baby shower. I brought it up several times over the next month or so, but she totally ignored my questions.

The few times that we were over at her house, she would remain sitting in a chair the entire time. It was like she didn't want us to see her stomach or something—it was so bizarre.

One day she called me and mentioned that she felt the baby move the night before. Apparently she went to Disney On Ice in Chicago with her sister, and on the way home she felt some movement. She claimed that the reason she didn't call was because it was 10:00 p.m. and she thought it would be too late. I was like, "Yeah right."

She was having a planned c-section, so the doctor said that unless she happened to go into labor before then, we should pick a day within one week before the due date, which was June 23.

We figured since we could choose the delivery date, it would be cool if the baby was born on the 17th. Joe and I were both born on January 17, one year apart. Plus, Father's Day was June 19th, so we thought it would be neat if the baby was with us on Father's Day.

We asked Vicky if this would work for her and she said, "No." She said the only day that was convenient for her was June 20th—the day after Father's Day.

She made some excuse about it having to do with Ken's work schedule, so we said, "Okay, how about the 16th then?" She claimed that wouldn't work either.

The thing is that we would have been paying Ken any lost wages for not working—and considering they had about three months notice, I'm sure he could have gotten a day or two off if he asked. In fact, when we talked to Ken about it separately, he said, "No problem."

For some reason, Vicky just wanted to make sure our baby was born when she wanted him born and she was making that decision for us no matter what.

At her next oby/gyn appointment, when she was twenty-four weeks along, Vicky had arrived a few minutes before we got there and she was called in early. The nurse finally told us to come into the room forty-five minutes later and there was Vicky, sitting up and dressed.

The doctor walked in and read us the riot act. He lectured us about the seriousness of a c-section and told us that we were stressing out Vicky. She must have been bitching about us during her appointment, probably complaining that we were trying to force her to deliver on a certain date just so the baby could be born before Father's Day or something. I'm sure she made us sound horrible.

I wanted to say, "No shit, Asshole, I've had a c-section myself!" But instead, as usual, I sat there with my mouth shut. The doctor was talking to us like we were total imbeciles, like we were children or something. I was so disgusted with the whole situation.

I called him a few days later to ask him some questions and I could sense his attitude right away. Then he said, "I'd advise you not to attend Vicky's appointments anymore."

"What if we just wait in the waiting room?", I asked, but he said he didn't think it was a good idea.

About a week later, we got a letter from the doctor's office stating that because of the HIPAA (Health Insurance Portability and Accountability Act of 1996) laws, they couldn't tell us anything about the pregnancy or about Vicky's appointments without her consent. This meant we could only rely on Vicky for information for the remainder of the pregnancy, which basically meant that we'd be getting very little information.

As we got closer to the due date, she resumed a little bit more contact with us. She'd email once in a while with doctor appointment updates, or I should say with the information she was willing to share.

By this point, I didn't really care anymore about our

relationship. I know that sounds bad, but the truth is that I was so sickened; I just felt like she was trying to be so controlling, and it was mind-boggling to me that she would shun us from the pregnancy the way she did. I just could never imagine doing that if I were a surrogate.

One good thing is that I never second-guessed whether she was taking care of herself. After we had crossed the initial hurdle in the first trimester, when she was bleeding a lot, I really didn't worry about a miscarriage or anything like that. She may have been on a power trip, but I knew she was taking care of herself and the baby.

She and Ken came over for pizza when she was thirty-seven weeks along, and for the first time she asked Joe and I if we wanted to feel the baby move. I think this was her attempt of trying to redeem herself.

To be honest, because we were not included in the pregnancy, it almost didn't feel real that we had a baby on the way. The night before he was due, when we were packing for the hospital, it finally hit me that we were having a baby. I really couldn't believe it that the day was finally here—I think I was in shock.

The delivery itself went totally smooth and the hospital staff was great. We even had our own birthing suite.

We had met with the patient care coordinator several months beforehand and given her the pre-birth order, so everyone knew it was a surrogacy situation. Illinois is a surrogacy-friendly state and there are some very concrete and specific laws that have been implemented here in the last few years. These laws state that gestational surrogacy contracts are enforceable, which ultimately means that hospitals are required by law to treat the intended parents as the "parents".

At 9:36 a.m., we were there to see our little boy pulled out of Vicky. I looked over at Joe and his neck and his face were so red—his eyes were teary. We were both pretty overwhelmed. As soon as I got a glimpse of Tyler's face, I thought he looked just like Chad, but then I saw that he had my lips and eyes and his daddy's dimpled chin.

The nurse asked if it would be okay if Vicky saw him and I said, "Sure". Then she took Tyler over to Vicky and I got a picture of her holding him.

That night, after all of our visitors had left and it was just the three of us in our birthing suite, Joe wrapped his arms around me, squeezed me tightly and said, "Thank you." I'll never forget that.

I feel bad because I'm not trying to knock Vicky or anything. We are very appreciative that Tyler was born healthy and we know she took care of herself during the pregnancy. I just thought she did a lot of stupid crap, and I probably will never forgive her for keeping us in the dark throughout the pregnancy and for being on the power trip that she was on.

I have learned a lot over the last few years. For anyone looking for a surrogate, don't base your decision strictly on distance. You can still be involved without being close-by. Believe me, there were many times when Joe and I felt like we may as well have worked with someone in California or something, even though Vicky lived only five minutes from us.

The other piece of advice I can offer, is don't make decisions based on desperation. I think so many people convince themselves that they want to work with someone even though there are red flags all over the place.

And if you do decide to work with a friend or someone you know—don't ever take for granted how "well" you know that person. You never *really* know what a potential surrogate is going to be like, friend or not, until she is pregnant.

The last few years have been rough, but I knew it was possible to have a baby through surrogacy. I just knew in my heart it could happen.

Postscript

Since the day Tyler was born, Sarah and her family have felt incredibly blessed. Tyler is such a good baby, and Sarah's other three children love him to pieces.

A lot of people told Sarah and Joe that they were crazy to want more children, that it would be so difficult to have a baby in addition to an eight, eleven and sixteen year old. Sarah finds this humorous and says that it's actually the total opposite. She enjoys watching her other kids interact with Tyler and says there has not been one ounce of jealousy from her other kids. In fact, Tony, her youngest son, has been "the baby" in the family for the last seven and a half years, and if anybody was going to be jealous it would be him. But he just eats Tyler up! He's crazy about his little brother and loves to help Sarah with him.

Chad, Marissa and Tony were all included in the surrogacy journey and Sarah was honest with them from the beginning. They know how hard it was to bring him into the world and Sarah thinks they love him even more because of that. Chad, her oldest son, will just stare at him sometimes in awe. The day they arrived home from the hospital, Sarah actually saw Chad fighting back tears when he knelt down to welcome Tyler home.

After Tyler's birth, Sarah's relationship with Vicky seemed to be okay for a while, but after about six weeks they had a falling out again. At that point, Sarah decided to cut all ties. Even though she had not included Sarah and Joe in the pregnancy for the last five months, Sarah really wanted to give Vicky another chance. But it soon became clear to her that it was going to continue to be "one thing after another" and she felt it was just not worth their energy. She plans to be honest with Tyler in the future, however, and she will share with him the details of his entry into this world. She has pictures of him with Vicky in his photo album, at his birth and while she was pregnant. It's important to Sarah that her son knows how much she and Joe wanted him.

She says she especially loves watching Joe and Tyler together. Tyler resembles his daddy so much; he has Joe's chin and forehead and he makes the same facial expressions. Sarah knew Joe would be a wonderful father since he's always been great with Chad, Marissa and Tony, even though they are his step-children. All along, Joe told Sarah that he'd be perfectly happy with her three children, but now that Tyler is here, she knows Joe is so excited that they have a son "together".

They have ten frozen embryos remaining and Sarah is pretty sure they'll try again down the road. She doesn't think they'll ever search for another surrogate—that was torture. But if someone they know and trust comes into the picture, they'll probably go for it.

It's funny, because after all they went through, and since everybody in their life knows how Tyler was born, friends left and right are offering to be their surrogate. In fact, Joe and Sarah are close with Sarah's ex-husband Blake and his wife, Holly. Holly has offered to be their surrogate after she and Blake have their second child, so if she is still on board with the idea, so are Sarah and Joe.

For now, they are loving life the way things are. And regardless of everything she had to deal with along the way, Sarah says, "without a doubt, it has all been worth it."

As exemplified by Sarah's story, relationships between intended parents and surrogates can easily go awry. Regardless of how intended parents find their surrogate—whether she is a friend, a family member, or a stranger—one of the issues that warrant discussion is the level of closeness everyone wants throughout the pregnancy and beyond. Some intended parents may prefer to keep their distance throughout the pregnancy, perhaps as a coping mechanism or maybe because there is no attachment to the baby at that point. Others would like to be involved, but because their surrogates live far away or because of some extenuating circumstance, it's difficult on a logistical level. The majority of intended parents however, do expect to be included in the pregnancy. Sarah and Linda fell into this category, but they learned when it was too late that their surrogates did not quite have the same thing in mind. Although their surrogacy journeys may not have been perfect, the end result for both of these women has been nothing short of spectacular.

Thirteen

Linda
Torrance, California

Two years after Jeff and I got married, when I was twenty-seven years old, we decided it was time to start our family. I found out I was pregnant in October 1999, the same month we moved into our new house. Everything was going according to our plan.

I started spotting six weeks into the pregnancy. By eight weeks, the fetus no longer had a heartbeat and I had to have a D&C. I was sad, but not totally devastated. Many of my friends' first pregnancies ended in miscarriage and they still went on to have children, so I figured that it would work the next time and everything would be fine.

My ob/gyn told us we would have to wait three months to try again, which we did, and on the fourth month I got pregnant for the second time.

At the six-week ultrasound there was no heartbeat. The doctor told us that sometimes the heartbeat doesn't show up that early, so even though we were alarmed, we were still somewhat optimistic. He told us to come back for another ultrasound the following week.

We went in a week later and there was still no heartbeat. It was a blighted ovum, which meant the embryo either stopped developing early on or it never developed at all. There was a gestational sac but it was empty. This time, I was devastated.

I really did not want to be put to sleep again for another D&C, so I found a doctor who would give me a general anesthesia and do the procedure in his office. It was a horribly painful experience and although it only lasted about two minutes, it was the longest two minutes of my life.

The doctor who performed the D&C offered me some advice; he suggested I take baby aspirin before we tried to conceive and progesterone suppositories during the first weeks of pregnancy. I appreciated that he was at least acknowledging that we needed some assistance. My previous ob/gyn would just quote statistics and tell me, "There's nothing you can do."

I didn't know anybody else who had two miscarriages in a row. I felt incredibly alone and emotionally lost. Finally, I went Online and found a list-serv called Multiple Marriage List-serv (MML).

When I saw that other women out there had six, seven, eight miscarriages, and still ended up having babies, I realized there was hope. I realized that I didn't have to give up, that maybe there was a chance I'd have a baby after all.

I got pregnant again in October 2000. Six or seven weeks into the pregnancy, I was at work and I started bleeding heavily. I am an elementary school teacher—I teach third grade. Fortunately, it happened at the end of the day.

As I was driving to the doctor's office, I knew there was no hope. This time there wasn't even a gestational sac; it was a chemical pregnancy. It was actually the only time I didn't need a D&C because I naturally started my period.

My ob/gyn assured me, "There is nothing wrong with you, you've just had bad luck. Maybe it's stress. You're still young. You're fine."

I thought to myself, "There is no way I'm going to just keep trying." I remembered there were several women on MML who had mentioned going through infertility clinics, so I posted to the list-serv and asked for referrals in my area.

It turned out that Reproductive Partners, a well-respected infertility clinic that also happens to be one of the best in the country—was right down the street from our house. We made an appointment and met with Dr. W a few weeks later.

One of the first things he asked me was, "What kind of tests have you had?" I was like, "Tests? What do you mean tests?"

He ran some tests to find out why I was having multiple miscarriages. One of them was an HSG, which was not very fun at all. The nurse couldn't get the dye into my uterus because my uterus was full of scar tissue. They wouldn't actually tell me what they thought the cause was, although personally, I think it was from the first D&C. The reason I say this is because I did some research after the fact and found out the doctor who performed it didn't have the best reputation.

It turned out that I had scarring on my stomach cavity and around my fallopian tubes, so really, it could have been caused by a low grade infection that I didn't even know I had.

Part of me was like, "Thank God I'll finally have an answer and I can fix this problem." But the other part of me—I'd look at all of the other people in the waiting area and think to myself, "I don't want to be a part of this group." It was just so emotionally and physically draining.

My doctor told me I have Ashermans syndrome, which basically means I have scar tissue on my uterus. He said we'd know how bad it was when we got back the pictures. I went on the Internet and found out that unless it was incredibly severe, the problem was likely repairable, so I still had some faith that I'd eventually have a successful pregnancy.

When the results came back, the doctor called me and said, "I'm going to refer you to another RE because I don't feel comfortable doing your surgery." All I could think to myself was, "You're one of the best in the country…what do you mean you're referring me to another RE? This can't be good."

He said, "Basically, two-thirds of your uterus is stuck together with scar tissue; it's actually fused together. Dr. Y works out of our office and he is pretty much the best in our field.

Because it's so severe, I'd feel more comfortable having him do the surgery."

Dr. Y turned out to be awesome. He told me, "We'll be able to fix the problem—don't you worry."

After the hysteroscopy, where they looked into the cavity of my uterus with a scope, I was bleeding profusely. I called Dr. Y at 11:00 that night and asked him what I should do. He told me to put four tampons in, leave them for an hour and then take them out. He said that should put enough pressure on my uterus to stop the bleeding.

After several hours, I went to take out the tampons and I passed out. Jeff tried to wake me up and I wouldn't wake up, so he called 911 and had me rushed to the hospital. After all was said and done I was told, "You're fine. You stopped bleeding."

When I went back for the follow-up, Dr. Y said, "The surgery went really well. The scar tissue was successfully removed and everything was cleaned out. I suggest you get pregnant as soon as possible so the scar tissue doesn't grow back."

I was pregnant a month later. I thought, "This is it! We're going to be parents!"

We went in for the five-week ultrasound and there was a gestational sac. At six weeks, there was still a sac but no heartbeat. The doctor said, "Well maybe it's just early. Come back next week." I started to panic.

I went in again at seven weeks—and still, no heartbeat. They said, "We don't know for sure until eight weeks. If there is still no heartbeat at eight weeks, we'll have to declare this pregnancy a miscarriage.

The day before the seven-week ultrasound, I had to throw a baby shower at my house. All my friends knew what was going on and they were like, "You'll be fine, don't worry!"

With the first two pregnancies I had been really open. With the third pregnancy, I didn't tell anyone because I didn't want to jinx it, but then it ended at six weeks anyway. So this time, I just figured, I'm just going to tell people. I thought, at least this way more people will be praying for us.

At eight weeks I went in for an ultrasound and once again, there was no heartbeat. That was probably one of the worst moments of my life. All I could think to myself was, "I fixed the problem and it's still not fixed." I realized that I was probably never going to become pregnant and I was an emotional basket case. It was May 2001, right before my thirtieth birthday.

I did not want a D&C again, especially because I knew it would cause more scar tissue. I asked the doctor if I could just wait and see what happens. I went in again at nine weeks and still, there was no heartbeat. Again at ten weeks, no heartbeat. At this point, the doctor said, "You are going to get an infection. You need to have the D&C." It would be my third D&C in two and a half years.

I first realized surrogacy was an option when I found the MML list-serv, but I was still hoping at that time that I would be able to carry a pregnancy. So after this third miscarriage, Jeff and I discussed surrogacy. He said, "You know, we have been going at this like crazy for three years. Let's just take a break—let's take a year off." I agreed that it was a good idea, so we planned a trip to New Zealand and just took some time off from the whole baby thing.

Almost a year later, in April 2002, I got the shingles and it lasted for two weeks. A day or so after I went back to work, I started getting really bad pains on my left side. By the time I got home, I was in so much pain that Jeff had to take me to the emergency room. I had a CAT scan and it showed that everything was fine.

I did, however, have blood in my urine, which indicated a kidney infection. The emergency room doctor gave me a prescription and suggested I see my general practitioner the next day.

The first thing my doctor asked me the next day was, "Are you sure you're not pregnant?" He didn't know anything about all of the infertility stuff we had been going through.

I told him, "I'm sure. For one, we haven't had unprotected sex." The last thing I wanted, after all we had been through over the last couple of years, was to be pregnant. He insisted on doing a pregnancy test anyway. It came back positive.

"Sorry to tell you this," he said, "but I think you have an ectopic pregnancy. You need to go to the hospital immediately." He added that he knew a really good ob/surgeon; he'd give him a call and see if he was available right away.

It turned out that he was in surgery but he was able to take me next. When the surgeon came out to meet me, I said, "I've heard there is a pill you can take that will dissolve the pregnancy. Can I just take that instead of having surgery?" I did not want to be put to sleep again.

The doctor replied, "I cannot do that. At eight weeks, this fetus is way too far along—it even has a heartbeat." That was the last thing I wanted to hear.

With ectopic pregnancies, what happens is the baby grows and grows until it bursts the fallopian tube. I even asked if they could transfer the fetus into my uterus, but of course, that was impossible.

The doctor explained that he would go through my belly button to do the surgery. He also told me that he'd try and save my tubes if he could, and that the whole thing should take about twenty minutes.

It turned out that my whole peritoneal cavity was filled with blood. In the two hours I had waited for my surgery, my tube burst and an artery burst along with it. I found out afterwards that I basically lost about a third of the blood in my body. Had I not gone to my doctor that day, I would have bled to death.

Rather than going through my belly button, the surgeon had to cut me open from one hip bone to the other. He sewed up the tube that had burst and removed the scar tissue that was in my tubes, my uterus and the rest of my abdominal cavity.

I was extremely anemic from all of the blood loss, so I had to be on bed rest for two months. Finally I said to Jeff, "Stick a fork in me. I'm done. My uterus is officially off the fertility team."

Nobody would just come out and say, "You're not going to be able to have a baby," so I felt it was up to me to decide where I was going to draw the line. Jeff totally understood of course. We just decided, at that point, it's in God's hands. If we didn't have kids it wasn't meant to be.

We discussed both domestic and international adoption, but it just seemed like it would take so long to adopt. Meanwhile, I knew surrogacy was a possibility, but it wasn't until that point that we ever seriously considered it. When we realized that with surrogacy we could have our own biological child, we thought "Wow, that would be a really great option."

In June, when I went to my RE for the follow-up, I asked him, "What do you think about us doing surrogacy?"

His response was, "I'm not going to tell you for sure that you can't have children, but if you can afford it, I think surrogacy would be a good option for you." Then he gave me the names of three surrogacy agencies.

After calling all of them, we ended up choosing the Center for Egg Options in Manhattan Beach. We liked the fact that they only work with ten or so couples at a time; we figured we would probably get more personal attention than we would with the larger surrogacy agencies. They told us it would probably be a three or four month wait before we were matched with a surrogate.

Meanwhile, my mother-in-law knew what was going on, as did all of our family members. Everyone has been incredibly supportive. When she called to see how things were going, I told her we were in the process of interviewing agencies. I expressed my concerns about the costs involved and without even pausing, she said, "I'll pay for it." She's not incredibly wealthy or anything, but she's financially stable enough that she could afford to help us. At that point, I wasn't sure exactly how much it would be—I figured probably around $40,000.

The agency's informational packet arrived in the mail and I almost fainted when I saw what the total expense would be. I thought to myself, "Well forget this." There was no way I could expect my mother-in-law to shell out $65,000.

I was too chicken to tell her on the phone, so I gathered all of the paperwork from the three agencies and mailed it to her. I figured, if she would pay $40,000, Jeff and I could come up with the other $25,000. A couple of days after I sent her the packet, I came home to a message on my answering machine. It was my mother-in-law and she said, "I got your paperwork, looks great to me. Let's go for it!"

In August, only two months after our initial consultation, Susie from the agency called us and said, "You're not going to believe this, but I think we have a match for you." She was right, I couldn't believe it—for once we were actually getting good news. Finally things seemed to be going in the right direction.

When we had our initial consultation with the agency, they asked us if we cared about race and we said, "No." The potential surrogate they were calling about happened to be African American. Angie was a nurse and a single mom with two kids. She had just been through a divorce and wanted to get back on her feet. We said, "Sure, we'd love to meet her."

We met with her about a week later and thought she was really nice. Plus, we really liked the fact that she was a nurse. We figured as someone who worked in the health industry she'd definitely take care of herself.

Then we started all of the paperwork. We met with the lawyer, did the contracts, and figured out the health insurance situation. We were ready to go.

We started the IVF protocol in January 2003 and everything went really well. I ended up having twenty-four eggs retrieved, seventeen embryos resulted and we transferred two of them. On the day we were supposed to find out what the results were, we were at Jeff's aunt and uncle's house. Our neighbor's daughter happened to be a nurse at our clinic, so she wanted to be the one to call us. When I answered the phone, I could tell immediately that she had good news. With a very chipper voice, she said, "Linda?" I started screaming—I knew that it worked.

Then I called Angie. She wasn't at all surprised because she assumed all along that she would get pregnant on the first try. When she answered the phone, I said, "Angie, I have good news!" She was like, "I told you we'd get pregnant right away!"

Apparently both of the embryos took but only one made it past the five-week ultrasound. At first, when we thought it was twins, we were really excited because we thought we wouldn't have to do this again. We knew that if we ended up with one, we'd want a sibling someday. Still, we were so happy that we had a baby on the way.

It was incredibly nerve wracking when we went in a week later to see if there was a heartbeat. At first the doctor couldn't find it and then all of a sudden he said, "Oh, there it is!" I knew at that point that everything was going to be fine. It was a great day. I was smiling from the inside out.

Since that point, everything has gone like clockwork. Getting past the eight-week ultrasound was a huge milestone for us, especially considering that I had never gotten past eight weeks with my own pregnancies.

The only "scare" we had was at twenty weeks. Angie was spotting and although everything turned out to be fine, she had to go on bed rest for a few days. At twenty-five weeks, we found out we were having a boy. That's when it became real to me. I was like, "I'm having a son!" I guess I'm kind of confident now that we're actually going to have a baby at the end of all of this.

When we originally discussed the level of relationship we wanted, we basically told her, "We'd like an open relationship with you; we want you to be a part of our child's life. But we'll let you choose the amount of involvement you want. Just know the door is wide open."

Angie's cordial and all but it's not like we are best friends or anything. We agreed at the beginning that we'd talk on the phone once a week—usually on Mondays—and see each other at doctor appointments. Truly, our relationship with Angie has mostly been professional.

It was funny, the last time she called she said, "I just wanted to let you know what is going on with our pregnancy. Our feet are swelling and we have heartburn." People will say really stupid things to her. When someone found out we were white, they asked, "What happens if the baby turns black?" She said, "Well that's what they wanted!" I thought that was hilarious.

The nice thing is that, even though we don't have a touchy-feely relationship, I know she is taking care of herself and the baby. That gives me a lot of piece of mind. It's hard though, because with another woman carrying your child, you feel such a level of responsibility and obligation to her. You know she is giving you this awesome gift and there is just no way to repay her with words alone.

Now that we are getting close to the delivery date, we are just preparing for the birth of our little boy. We've even started working on his nursery. Since we live close to the beach, we decided that it will have a beach theme. The bedding, which I'm sewing myself, will have surfboards and a Hawaiian look. It's actually turning out to be the nicest room in the house.

Recently, I was looking for something to hang in the baby's room and I stumbled upon a website that sells really cute plaques. I didn't see anything applicable to our situation, so I decided instead to make my own. On it, I put one of my favorite quotes by Ralph Waldo Emerson, "Do not follow where the path may lead, go instead where there is no path and lead the trail."

There are many different roads that can take you to the same place—it's interesting the way life works out sometimes. But once you've lived through something painful, you walk away a stronger person.

Postscript

Linda and Jeff's son, Carter, came into the world on October 13, 2003, one day before his due date. The birth went without any complications and as soon as he came out he was handed directly to Linda. Jeff cut the cord. The hospital wouldn't give Linda and Jeff a room, so they stayed in the nursery overnight instead.

Carter is a happy, healthy little guy who is now almost two years old. He has a great personality and he likes to be the center of attention. Of course his parents are overjoyed to have him in their lives. He has a lot of family that loves him very much; he was a long awaited child. Both of Carter's grandmothers are very involved in his life.

Carter and his daddy are like Frick and Frack. Jeff mows the lawn and there is Carter, right along side of him, pushing his own little lawn mower. When Jeff works in the garage with his tools, Carter is with him as his little helper.

Linda would probably have another child if she could have one the natural way, but with surrogacy being such a huge undertaking she just doesn't know if she is up for it. Her mother-in-law, however, has offered to pay the expenses to do another surrogacy if they choose to do so. Linda knows how fortunate she is. Without her mother-in-law's help, Linda says, another surrogacy journey wouldn't even be up for discussion.

It's a question they get asked a lot; in fact, many people are especially curious if they will adopt next time instead. Linda believes that it probably wouldn't be much easier going through adoption—so if they do decided to add to their family, it would likely be through surrogacy again. "The door is wide open," she says, "but I guess I'm just not emotionally ready yet to go there again." Plus, she can't imagine doing the contracts, interviewing surrogates, and going through all of the rigamarole while having a two year old. She feels so lucky to have Carter and wonders if it would just be better to quit while they're ahead.

Unfortunately their relationship with Angie was not what they hoped it would be. For example, they originally planned on talking once a week on the phone. When Linda wouldn't hear from her, she would give Angie a call and oftentimes, Angie would pick up the phone, say, "I'm busy" and hang up. Or she'd have a scheduled doctor appointment and Linda would take off from work to meet her at the doctor's office, but Angie wouldn't be there. The few times she did show up to the doctor's appointments and Linda and Jeff were in the waiting area, she wouldn't sit next to them—she'd sit across the room, read a magazine and basically ignore them.

Angie led Linda and Jeff to believe she had disability coverage, but when she was ordered by the ob/gyn to take six weeks off of work during the last trimester of the pregnancy, it turned out that she didn't have disability after all. This was something that was in the contract, so Linda and Jeff were pretty irate—especially since they ended up having to pay her eight weeks of lost wages. The reason it was eight weeks, is because since Angie worked as a nurse at the hospital, she had the doctor sign her out for eight weeks, even though she was told she only needed to be home for six weeks.

Angie's parting words, as she left the hospital, were, "Well Carter, it's been great, but you've really been holding up my life." In her mind, Linda thought to herself, "Buh bye! Don't let the door hit you in the ass."

Linda wishes things didn't turn out the way they did. She really wanted to have a continued relationship with whomever they ended up working with as their surrogate. She expected the woman to be a part of their lives, to come to birthday parties, to meet at the park, to go to lunch once in a while. She wanted Carter to know the woman who carried him in her belly. She doesn't understand why Angie was the way she was; she doesn't know if Angie regretted her decision to be a surrogate or if she was just in it for the money.

Linda says she has learned so much from her surrogacy journey. She realizes she should have asked more questions—maybe different questions, and she should have handled certain incidences differently. Her advice to anybody thinking about going through surrogacy is not to go through it alone. She adds, "Don't be discouraged by the costs or the fact that it isn't as conventional, because it may be the way that works best for you."

They worked so hard to get Carter and now they have this wonderful little boy. For this reason, Linda believes in the balance of the world after all.

Unlike most of the women featured in this book, Haley is not infertile. In fact, she gets pregnant easily and has no problem sustaining a pregnancy. As we learn from Haley's story, though, just because a woman "can" be pregnant, does not necessarily mean she "should" be pregnant. Haley suffers from a condition called, hyperemesis gravidarum, which according to the Hyperemesis Education and Research Foundation (HER) is "a severe form of nausea and vomiting in pregnancy, described as unrelenting, excessive pregnancy related nausea and/or vomiting that prevents adequate intake of food and fluids." Typically when morning sickness occurs in a pregnancy, it's just a minor annoyance. In his article, "Hyperemesis Gravidarum", Richard Chudacoff, M.D. of Women's Specialists of Houston, states "hyperemesis gravidarum, may complicate up to .3% of pregnancies, causing physiological changes that may effect the mother and fetus. Maternal weight loss, dehydration , electrolyte imbalances, acid-base disturbances leading to kidney and liver injury have all been reported in extreme cases." He adds, "prematurity, low birth weight and a slight increase of central nervous system and skin malformations have been reported in fetuses of mothers affected with hyperemesis gravidarum." Like Betty and Sarah, Haley has experienced pregnancy and childbirth—and she is thankful for this. But she also knows her limits, and carrying another pregnancy was not a realistic option for her. Fortunately, she realized, there was another way.

Fourteen

Haley
Houston, Texas

In 1991, soon after Josh graduated from law school, we got married and moved to Houston. I got a job as a legal assistant with a big law firm and then I decided to go to law school as well. A few years later, after I graduated, we moved to Minnesota and I began working as a clerk for an appellate court judge. Eventually I started a private practice doing employment defense law.

When I was thirty years old and we had been married for eight years, we decided it was time to have a baby. I got pregnant on the first try. I wanted to get a few years working under my belt before we started our family; so really, our plan was going along perfectly.

Six and a half weeks into the pregnancy, when I was in Washington D.C. for a legal conference, I suddenly got sick to my stomach. I was so nauseous—I couldn't stop vomiting.

We had to leave the conference early and Josh rushed me to Washington National Airport so that I could get back home to Minnesota. I was in almost every bathroom heaving and I even passed out in one of the airport restrooms.

Next thing I knew, I was being toted off in an ambulance to the Pentagon City Hospital. They gave me oxygen and an anti-nausea drug called Phenergan, which I was given intravenously. The doctors tried getting fluids in me because I was so severely dehydrated.

I called my boss the next day and told him, "By the way, I'm pregnant. I'm also sicker than a dog and stuck in Washington D.C."

I was finally diagnosed with Hyperemesis Gravidarum, which is a condition that causes frequent and severe vomiting during pregnancy. It hit me like a ton of bricks—I was vomiting about twenty times a day. According to my doctor, this condition hits 0.08% of the pregnant population.

I tried almost everything to take away the nausea: vitamin B1 shots, Unisom, Phenergan suppositories, and finally Zofran. The Zofran helped, but I still had to be hydrated at the hospital a few times. Home health care came out on several occasions because I had to be hooked up to an I.V. for a few weeks at a time. Of course there was no way I could continue working so I had to quit my job.

The only thing that saved me was the Zofran because even though I was totally nauseous throughout the pregnancy, Zofran at least took the edge off a bit. I was finally able to start eating small amounts of food around the twentieth week.

Josh's firm dissolved in the meantime, so we sold our house in Minnesota and moved back to Houston. I found a new ob/gyn for the remainder of the pregnancy; however, because it was the tail end she didn't realize the severity of my Hyperemesis.

Alan was delivered on his due date—January 26, 2000, and we thank God for him every day. Since I was on Zofran for the entire pregnancy, I was worried about the effects it would have, but thankfully my son was born a healthy bouncing baby. There were no complications during delivery, so after such a miserable pregnancy, we ultimately were quite grateful.

Despite the negative experience we had during the first pregnancy, we knew we'd eventually want another child. We started trying to conceive another baby when Alan was two and a half years old.

Again, I got pregnant immediately.

I really didn't think I'd be as sick as I was the first time, but I figured I should be prepared just in case. I made an appointment with my ob/gyn right away and I told her how bad things were throughout my first pregnancy. She gave me a prescription for Zofran in addition to prescribing a wristband that would send electric pulses to my central nervous system.

When I was six weeks pregnant, the same time as it kicked in during my first pregnancy, the nausea came back with a vengeance. And of course, this time I had a toddler to care for which made things even more difficult.

Josh had back-to-back trials, so he couldn't help very much. The nausea just got worse by the day. I tried to have a good mental outlook; I took the Zofran and I wore the wristband but nothing was helping.

I finally called my doctor and said, "Listen, I cannot drink a thing." She had me come in for testing and it turned out my ketone level—what they test in urine for dehydration—was sky high. I ended up in the hospital for a month.

While I was in the hospital, they tried giving me several different anti-nausea medications. They gave me Zofran in orally disintegrating tablets and in regular form, they gave me Pepsid AC, and at ten weeks, they got so desperate they tried giving me steroids. It was still kind of experimental at that time to give steroids to pregnant women with Hyperemesis, but the doctors figured we should try everything possible to stop the nausea.

It is a condition that really hasn't gotten a lot of research because the research has to be done on pregnant women and not many pregnant women are willing to be "guinea pigs" if you know what I mean. Nobody can really pinpoint why certain women get it and how it can be effectively cured, but what the medical community has learned, and what I discovered a little too late, is that women with Hyperemesis have an 80-90% chance of getting it again. To top it off, it gets worse with each pregnancy and usually peaks in the third pregnancy.

It turned out this second pregnancy *was* much worse than the first one. Finally, the doctors sent me home with an I.V., but I couldn't take care of Alan so my mom had to fly down from Wisconsin and stay with us for another three weeks. It continued to get worse and worse. I couldn't swallow my own spit, I couldn't even chew ice chips. I was despondent and didn't want any visitors. Plus, I couldn't talk because talking made me want to vomit. My mom had to bathe me.

I just lay in bed, lethargic. I went into ketosis a couple of times and even started hallucinating towards the end.

My doctors were very concerned about me so they laid out all of my options, all very bad, and one of them being termination of the pregnancy.

I try to tell people how horrible it was. I mean, I couldn't even hold my son because his smell made me want to throw up. My friends who actually saw me in the hospital understood the gravity of the situation, as did my mother and Josh.

But people who have never been around someone with Hyperemesis and who have never actually seen how sick women with this condition get, are under the illusion it's like bad morning sickness. The feeling of constantly being nauseous is hard to even explain. The only relief you ever get is if you are lucky enough to sleep.

I ended up losing the baby on September 19, 2002 at twelve weeks and five days into the pregnancy.

The best analogy I've heard was from a physician who said, "Well you know, it's like your body had an allergic reaction to your own pregnancy hormones." I'm building up more and more of a resistance as I have additional pregnancies, so I can conceive right away but I can't safely be pregnant.

Everybody has a different roadblock, a different reason they resort to surrogacy. Sometimes I look at myself in the mirror and say, "You have the equipment but you just can't carry a child." It's extremely frustrating.

Shortly after the pregnancy ended, I started thinking back to my first year in contracts in law school. Our professor had us write a contract that was based off of a fact-hypothetical between a surrogate and intended parents. As I thought back to this particular class, I started asking myself if surrogacy was, perhaps, the route for us. I was trying to re-focus—maybe it was some sort of a coping mechanism.

I called a surrogacy agency in Houston and I told the agency owner about the awful ordeal I had just been through. She had never heard of my condition before. This irritated me because I felt, personally, that anybody who owns a surrogacy agency should at least be familiar with every pregnancy or fertility ailment out there. She was sympathetic though and said it would probably be about six months to a year before we would be matched with a surrogate.

I really didn't like being told I would have to wait to start my family so I decided to start doing more research Online in the meantime. I can't imagine what it would be like without the Internet—I wonder where so many of us would be. I did key word searches for "surrogacy", "gestational surrogacy", "gestational carrier", I book-marked pages and found support groups and Online list-servs. I was like a sponge sucking in all of the information.

Josh and I started looking into adoption at the same time we were researching surrogacy and decided that we would adopt a baby from Russia. We made that choice because of the expedited timeline and also because there is a big support group here in Houston of people who have adopted from Russia.

We went to an agency meeting and we were cruising along full speed ahead, then all of a sudden we got cold feet because of all of the international unrest going on. It was the end of October 2002 and the United States was getting ready to go to war with Iraq.

We heard, originally, that some of the regions in Russia were waiving the requirement of adoptive parents to stay there for ten days and make two trips over there. But as it turned out, a lot of them were not waiving the ten-day waiting period prerequisite anymore, which meant we'd have to go to Russia twice and we'd have to stay there for ten days on one of the trips. Considering that we have a three-year-old child, the whole Russian adoption idea was starting to sound way too stressful. It got to a point where it was causing me way more worry than joy.

Also, because Josh does medical malpractice defense work, we became really concerned about fetal alcohol syndrome. We talked to several doctors and we were told that it is very hard to identify fetal alcohol syndrome. This was a major concern to us—especially since there are, supposedly, a lot of heavy drinkers in Russia.

We decided to put adoption on hold and I went back to researching surrogacy again. I was browsing through SMO one day and I came across Sandra's ad. She lived in Houston and she wanted to be a gestational surrogate. Her husband, Arty, was a city of Houston firefighter, they had two sons, and they lived about forty minutes from us in a northwest suburb.

We chatted on email for a while, then we scheduled our first telephone conversation. We immediately had good rapport. She was also talking to another couple but things fell through with them within a few days after our telephone conversation. When she told me this news, I suggested we meet in person.

A week before Christmas, Josh and I met with Sandra, Arty, and their two boys—a six year old and a two and a half year old. It was kind of surreal because we met at this restaurant and there we were talking about Sandra carrying our child. Surrogacy can be a very strange thing. As we were sitting at the restaurant talking, I was thinking to myself, "It's a good thing I'm a type-A, talkative person who is comfortable socializing with just about anyone." When intended parents and surrogates meet each other for the first time, they have to discuss things that are normally very personal and intimate.

Everyone got along well and we could tell that Arty was very supportive of Sandra's desire to be a surrogate. On the way home, Josh and I said to each other, "Well this almost seems like it was meant to be." We agreed that we liked them and wanted to go forward.

Apparently Sandra and Arty talked about it on the way home and they decided they wanted to work with us as well. We couldn't believe our luck—not only did we hit it off immediately, but we both lived in suburbs of Houston. That was very important to me since we wanted to be involved in the pregnancy and attend doctor appointments and everything.

As attorneys, we were able to do our own legal work. It's interesting, because at the time of our transfer, there was no legislation specific to surrogacy, but recently our governor signed into law really good legislation for gestational surrogacy arrangements. With the new laws in place, court approved gestational arrangements in Texas, even when the surrogate is compensated, will now be enforceable. Actually, it turns out that in terms of assisted reproduction laws, Texas is one of the best jurisdictions in the United States.

After getting several recommendations for RE's, we decided to work with Dr. M, who was coincidentally in the same building at Texas Woman's Hospital as my regular ob/gyn. When I told Sandra about him she couldn't believe it; it turned out that Dr. M was her first cousin. After our medical testing was completed, we had civil and criminal background checks done on Sandra and Arty. Then we all had our appointments with the psychologist.

We had to get lined up on birth control pills and then Sandra did a mock cycle in April. Dr. M put her on progesterone suppositories for the mock cycle but her progesterone levels weren't high enough and her uterine lining wasn't building up properly. He had her on progesterone shots and Crinone gel as additional progesterone supplementation.

My regimen started with Lupron injections, then Gonal F and Repronex. They got twenty-four eggs, twenty-one of them fertilized, and twelve made it to blastocyst stage. When Dr. M called us with the results of the egg retrieval, he was incredibly happy for us.

Josh couldn't go to the transfer, which was five days after the egg retrieval, because he had a work conflict. But I was there with Sandra and Arty. It was really nice—we had lunch beforehand and both Arty and I were in the room with her during the transfer. After transferring two blastocysts, we waited an hour and a half in the waiting room, and then I sent them home with a big care package. Sandra's mom came in from out of state to help with their children.

Five days after the transfer I called her to see how she was doing. She said, "I know you didn't want me to take a home pregnancy test, but I couldn't wait anymore. I broke down and took one and guess what—it's positive!"

Twelve days after the transfer she had her beta test done, and the number was 791. When we went in for the first ultrasound appointment at about five and a half weeks, we saw two sacs, two yolks and two heartbeats. We were beside ourselves with joy!

When Sandra was about seven weeks along in the pregnancy, she called me while Josh and I were out to dinner one evening. She said, "I'm so sorry, I don't want to upset you but I just wanted to let you know I'm spotting." She told me it was brownish and not very heavy. I asked her if she called the nurse and she said, "Yes." The nurse advised her to wait until our seven and a half week appointment a few days later. She assured Sandra that spotting is common with IVF transfers and that she shouldn't panic yet.

Our seven and a half week ultrasound appointment showed there were still two heartbeats, and both embryos measured right on track. The doctor showed us what was causing the brown blood—small subchorionic hemotoma, which, according to Dr. M, was a blood clot in the uterus that forms when the placenta is taking hold. It can cause partial separation of the placenta, which, in the worst cases, can cause an abruption and the loss of the pregnancy.

The doctor told us that the majority of the time it resolves itself over the course of the pregnancy. Apparently, as the uterus grows it can have a tourniquet affect on the hematoma—in other words, it will hopefully begin to push the hematoma against the wall so that it eventually gets reabsorbed into the endometrium.

Sandra saw Dr. M for the last time at eleven weeks and he said the hematoma appeared smaller; however, he suggested we also see a periontologist and gave us a referral. The peri said, "Even though it's small we still need to call it significant and keep a close eye on it."

In the research I've done Online, I've learned that subchorionic hemotoma is not that uncommon in pregnant women. There are even support groups totally dedicated to the subject.

Sandra hasn't experienced major bleeding, so that's a good sign I guess. In the meantime, the babies are growing perfectly—they have strong heartbeats and they are very active. Still, I'm incredibly worried and it's putting me in a funk.

The peri said that it's something we can't expect to be resolved overnight, so all we can really do is take it one day at a time. I pray every day that nothing happens to this pregnancy. I truly don't know if I'd have the gumption or the resources to do this again. It's such a big undertaking, especially after getting to this point in the pregnancy, especially after our first loss.

This development has also thrown a financial wrench into the mix that we didn't really anticipate because Sandra is on bed rest already. Obviously it's necessary and important for Sandra to do whatever needs to be done to ensure the chances the pregnancy will continue, it's just that we didn't really think we'd end up having to pay bed rest fees so early in the pregnancy.

These things do happen though, and anyone going to surrogacy has to be prepared for all types of scenarios.

Interestingly enough, many people don't consider surrogacy as an alternative form of family building because it has a reputation for being so costly. The fact of the matter is that adoption is often times more expensive than surrogacy, especially when it's an international adoption. For example, we were told that the Russian adoption, including airfare and everything, would cost us about $35,000. Our surrogacy expenses, including the IVF costs, the medications, and what we're paying Sandra, we'll probably add up to around $28,000. Surrogacy can be costly, but it doesn't have to be. There are many ways to keep the costs down.

I've met many women along the way who have gone to surrogacy to have children. Some of them have experienced pregnancy and some of them have not. For me, a woman who has been pregnant, and especially because I had such a horrible time being pregnant, I don't feel a loss because I'm not the one who is pregnant this time. I'm perfectly okay with it.

I have to admit though that I'm normally somewhat of a control freak, so at first I was worried that I'd have issues with our surrogate. I thought to myself, "Am I going to be able to trust Sandra? Will I be able to let go of that control?" She's been wonderful though—there hasn't been anything that has made me question or doubt her intent.

Despite all of the obstacles we've faced so far, we know that God has a plan for all of us. We are blessed to have Alan, and now as we begin our second trimester with the twins, I just pray that He will smile upon us again.

Postscript

Haley and Josh had a great overall experience with Sandra as their gestational surrogate. The subchorionic hematoma that was present early on disappeared by eighteen weeks and the remainder of the pregnancy was uneventful. Throughout the pregnancy, Haley talked to Sandra regularly on the telephone and joined her for every doctor's visit.

Sandra unexpectedly developed pre-eclampsia in the third trimester, so she had to deliver the twins in December of 2003— one day shy of thirty-three weeks. Although it was stressful at the time, both babies were born with good birth weights for their gestational age. Ryan was 4 lbs. 6 oz. and Kenzie was 4 lbs. 10 oz. Both came out breathing on their own and although they had to stay in the NICU for three weeks to regulate their eating, breathing, and body temperature, they've been doing fabulous ever since.

The NICU staff was very supportive and it was a pleasure to work with the hospital staff. Haley and Josh had met with the Chief Operating Officer and some other administrative personal ahead of time to take care of the paperwork and make sure everything went smoothly.

As a gift to the babies, Sandra pumped breast milk for them for two and a half months. Haley says she couldn't have asked for a more thoughtful, diligent person to carry her children. They still keep in touch with Sandra and her family, and in fact, Haley helped her find another couple to help as a gestational surrogate.

Haley thanks God every day that gestational surrogacy was an option for them, and that they found such an incredibly selfless woman to help them complete their family.

Like Vivian and Jessica who were featured earlier, Monica and Raquel, the women who tell their stories in the next two chapters, were also born with MRKH. Raquel knew early on that she wanted children and just like Vivian and Jessica, she began researching and planning even before she was married. Monica, on the other hand, did not do any planning. Her husband was not interested in adoption and they did not realize they had other alternatives, so they opted to remain childless in life instead. But when she was in her late thirties, Monica became active on the Internet and learned they could have a child through gestational surrogacy. Presumably as a result of her age, Monica's egg quality was poor; therefore, unlike the other MRKH women featured in this book, if Monica and her husband wanted to have a child through gestational surrogacy they would need an egg donor. In his article, "Egg Donation: Why and how women decide to donate", Dr. Mark Bush, M.D. of Conceptions Reproductive Associates, a Denver, Colorado infertility clinic, states, "Egg donation has become a mainstay of infertility therapy in the United States. According to the most recent CDC statistics, slightly more than 11% of all IVF cycles in this country involved donor eggs or embryos. With women delaying childbearing for professional, financial, educational, or personal reasons—or a combination of all of these—many women who are ready to start a family find out that their eggs have a poor prognosis in establishing a pregnancy." Once Monica and her husband realized they had options, regardless of her MRKH or egg quality issues, they took all the necessary steps in reaching their goal. And the rest is history.

Fifteen

Monica
Berks County, Pennsylvania

In 1978, when I was seventeen years old, I was diagnosed with Mayer-Rokitansky-Kuster-Hauser syndrome (MRKH). Since I hadn't gotten my period yet, my doctor suggested that I have exploratory surgery and sent me to a hospital in Philadelphia. I awoke from the surgery to learn I didn't have a uterus or a left kidney. This is when I found out that I would never bear children.

It was totally devastating to receive this news, but since I was getting ready to finish high school and go to college it wasn't like marriage and children were in my immediate future anyway. So I figured, I would just deal with it and move on. I'm not going to say it was easy for me because it wasn't—it was just something I had to overcome.

My mother felt very guilty and wondered if she did something wrong during the pregnancy. The doctors assured her that as far as they knew, it was a syndrome that occurs in a small percentage of women, without anything that necessarily causes it to happen. It's just one of those things.

I didn't know anybody else with MRKH. The doctors I saw at the time didn't know much about it either, so they weren't of much help. I didn't have a support group or anything and I felt completely alone.

I met my husband, Phil, during my last year of college. It was really hard for me to tell him initially about my inability to have children. I felt it was important to be upfront, but at the same time, I worried that he wouldn't want to be with me anymore. Fortunately, it was never an issue with him.

We dated for ten years and got married when I was thirty-two and he was thirty-three. I was comfortable with adoption but Phil was not, so we just decided we would remain childless in life.

Despite the fact that I couldn't have children, I was never really jealous of others who were pregnant or who had babies. I realize some infertile women have major issues with this, but I refused to let myself become bitter. I figured that it was something I had to accept about myself and there wasn't anything I could do about it, so I just didn't let it get the best of me. I think, as a defense mechanism, I almost became callous.

People were constantly asking, "So when are you and Phil going to have a baby?" I'd just say, "We're still working on it." Only our immediate family knew that I couldn't have children.

When I was thirty-seven and the Internet was becoming widespread, I decided to search for some information Online and came across an MRKH support group. I learned there were many degrees and variations of MRKH and felt fortunate that my case was actually considered somewhat mild. I also felt fortunate that my problem was internal because for many women with this syndrome, there are external defects. I also found out that since my ovaries were still functioning, I could have children with the help of a carrier.

I thought, "This is amazing!"

I was excited about the prospect of having a baby through surrogacy, but I was also irritated because the option was never suggested to me. In the course of twenty years, even knowing that I had functioning ovaries, not one doctor ever suggested surrogacy as an option.

Since my husband wasn't interested in adopting, I had accepted that we were going to be childless—but deep down I really did want to have children.

I made an appointment with my gynecologist and asked him if he worked with surrogates. He said, "No, but I have a friend in

Philadelphia who works at Pennsylvania Reproductive Associates (PRA), and I'm pretty sure they handle surrogacy arrangements."

Shortly thereafter, Phil and I had a consultation at PRA, which is an hour from where we live, and things just spiraled from there. It was kind of difficult for Phil at first, because for over seven years we had planned on remaining childless. And then all of a sudden, there we were discussing plans to have a child through surrogacy.

At thirty-nine years old, the RE told us the age of my eggs was going to be a big issue. He had me do a Clomid challenge test to check my ovarian reserve and since I don't get a period, he also did blood work to determine where I was in my cycle.

In May 2000, we officially entered the IVF and gestational carrier program at PRA. We had to pay a fee to meet with the psychologist and the nurses; however, the costs of the program didn't include finding a carrier for us. That was our responsibility.

We started by asking my sister who has two boys of her own, but at thirty-eight, she felt she was too old to carry another pregnancy. Phil's sisters are not married and they don't have any children, so they would not have been good candidates. PRA required that all surrogates who go through their clinic already have children of their own.

I went onto the Internet again, found TASC, and posted an ad looking for a gestational surrogate. Three months went by and I hadn't gotten any replies. I was starting to lose hope.

Finally, I saw an ad that intrigued me. The woman's name was Beth; she was married and had three children who were eight, six and one years old. She lived in Northeast Pennsylvania, which was perfect for us. Phil and I agreed that it was important to find someone who was in driving distance so we could attend the doctor appointments and everything.

We emailed for about a week and then we had our first phone conversation. We clicked immediately and ended up talking for an hour. It turned out that we had very similar backgrounds.

In May of 2001, Phil and I went to meet Beth for the first time. We were nervous as we drove to her house, but as soon as we met her and her family, it was like it was meant to be. We were immediately comfortable with them.

When we were getting ready to leave, her eight-year-old son gave me a hug and said, "I hope my mommy can have a baby for you and Phil." I thought that was so sweet! She was very upfront with her kids from the beginning about being a surrogate.

By July, Beth had all of her screening done. I'm a teacher, and I wanted to have my retrieval done in the summertime so I could avoid taking time from work. Since we didn't have the contracts signed in time for Beth to be prepared for the cycle, we figured we'd do the retrieval and freeze the embryos for a transfer a few months later.

Our retrieval took place in June 2001. We ended up with eight eggs, but sadly, none of them fertilized. The doctor called with this devastating news and we were like, "Oh my gosh, after all of this?"

He said, "We're really sorry, we had no incline that this would happen."

When we asked him what he thought the cause was, he told us he believed it was the age of my eggs. He said, "With forty year old women, such as yourself, sometimes the shell of the egg hardens. We often do ICSI with older patients—my suggestion is that you do another cycle with ICSI."

Of course my response was, "Well why didn't you just do ICSI *this* time?" He just reiterated that they really had no indication that there was a problem with the egg or the sperm quality.

So it was a wasted cycle.

Two months later, in the middle of August, I had another retrieval. We still didn't have the contract signed, so we did the cycle knowing we'd have to freeze the embryos.

This time, the retrieval produced six eggs and with ICSI, five fertilized and four were good enough quality to freeze.

In September, we signed the contracts and Beth was prepared for the transfer.

Three of four embryos made the thaw—a three-cell and two four-celled embryos. We knew they weren't great quality, but we were still hoping for the best. The transfer was in November, right around Thanksgiving, and it went as smooth as could be expected.

Beth took a home pregnancy test the day before the beta and it was negative. Although we still held onto the hope that we'd have good news the next day, the beta came back negative too.

After the first wasted cycle and now this, Phil and I were like, "Can we even do this again?"

The clinic encouraged us to try again, so in January 2002, we did a fresh cycle. I realized that I couldn't just do the retrievals during my breaks; I would inevitably have to take a week off of work.

We got six eggs, but only three fertilized; a three-cell, a four-cell and a five-cell. We knew it was unlikely the three or four-cell embryos would take, but figured that maybe the five-cell would make it.

Two weeks later, we got the call that the beta was negative again. We were devastated. By this point, I was forty-one and Phil was forty-two. We realized that my eggs were likely the problem. We were paying for it out of pocket—our insurance wasn't covering a penny. And we are not wealthy by any means.

We discussed our situation and said to each other, "Do we want to do this one more time?" Phil asked, "Can we even afford to do this again?"

My response was, "We'll find a way. If it's meant to be it will work. Let's just try this one more time."

This time we opted to use an egg donor. Whether or not I was biologically connected to a child was a non-issue for me, so I didn't have a problem with it. Shortly after we informed the clinic of our decision, they emailed us a biography of a potential egg donor.

When we looked at the profile, it was like it was almost too good to be true. This woman was so similar to me. She had the same physical features, the same blood type—everything. It was crazy!

She had been an egg donor five times previous and all five times had resulted in a pregnancy. Phil and I said to each other, "Let's go for it." We figured we'd give it one last shot and if it didn't work, it wasn't meant to be.

Beth told us she'd stick with us no matter what—that she would go through as many transfers as we wanted. She was incredibly supportive.

The egg retrieval and transfer were in October. We got fifteen eggs and ten of them fertilized. The clinic suggested that since our egg donor produced such good quality eggs we freeze some just in case, so we decided to freeze three right off the bat.

By day three, two embryos were starting to compact; one was a seven-cell and the rest were six-celled. We transferred the two that were compacting in addition to the seven-cell.

Beth called about ten days later to tell us the good news— her beta was 581. We were pregnant!

The first ultrasound at six weeks showed one sac and one heartbeat. Beth was spotting at eight weeks and this scared us a bit, but an ultrasound showed that everything was fine. We actually found out later that the second embryo had taken but that it never developed. I'm pretty sure this is what caused the spotting. We had another ultrasound at nine and a half weeks and everything looked great.

Our next ultrasound was at nineteen weeks into the pregnancy and that is when we found out we were having a girl.

Initially, Beth and I talked on the phone every other week but as the pregnancy progressed we began to talk more frequently. I think when I wasn't talking to her as often at first, it was some sort of defense mechanism for me. I didn't want to be too close to the pregnancy at first because I was afraid something would go wrong. Phil and I went to every ultrasound though and we were with Beth the first time she met with her new ob/gyn.

Her previous ob/gyn, the one that delivered her three children, wouldn't take her as a patient because she was a surrogate. Apparently, they had a bad experience, a lawsuit or something, and just didn't want to get involved in anything outside of the norm.

Aside from our parents and immediate family, we actually didn't tell anybody we had a baby on the way until Beth was fourteen weeks along. It was hard to believe that it was happening really, so we just kept it very quiet.

Beth came to my baby shower, which was wonderful. I had taken a picture of Beth's belly with my digital camera and my sister, who planned the baby shower for me, put the picture in the invitations. Everybody thought that was so special. My family and friends were really impressed with Beth and what she was doing for us.

By the time she was thirty-five weeks along, it was summer again and the school year had ended. At thirty-eight weeks the doctor said, "Let's do another ultrasound to make sure everything is okay." At that point, the baby measured 7 lbs. and 10 oz., so we knew we were going to have a big baby.

On July 1, when Beth was almost thirty-eight weeks along, but measuring at forty-three weeks, she asked the doctor if she could be induced. He said, "Yes" and she was admitted to the hospital the next day. Nothing happened that night, but at 8:45 a.m., after she had been going through hard labor for over four hours, Kaitlyn, was born.

I watched her little head come out and everything, which if you think about it, how many mothers can see their children being born from this view?

The entire pregnancy went really well. Actually, the doctor said he wished he could clone Beth because she was the "perfect pregnant woman".

We consider Beth a part of our extended family. She was recently here with her kids and they stayed for the weekend. Kaitlyn will know early on that her Aunt Beth did this because her mommy couldn't—so it isn't going to be anything we hide from her.

It was a long struggle. From the time we entered the program until the time we had Kaitlyn it was over three years. All total we did four egg retrievals and three transfers. It was really hard going through all of this, but I guess I just realized that no matter how much I complained or how much pity I had on myself, it wouldn't change the outcome.

Now that we have Kaitlyn, Phil and I know how lucky we are to have her. We are enjoying each and every moment with our little girl.

Postscript

Kaitlyn is now two years old. She is extremely active, very tall like both of her parents, and a lefty like her mommy. Monica says that every day when she looks at her daughter, she still can't believe it all worked out for them. Monica believes that as a result of their experience, they appreciate having a child more so than some couples who take their children for granted.

Monica realizes that most people don't have a clue how much time, money and emotion is involved with surrogacy. When she shares her story with other women, it is not unusual for their eyes to well up with tears. Monica is very open about their journey, however, and feels it is important to shed positive light on surrogacy. She notes that in the past two years, surrogacy has become more common as it will in the years to come with the advancement of reproductive technology.

They consider Beth a part of their extended family and try to get together with her every few months. When Kaitlyn is old enough to understand, she'll be told, "Aunt Beth carried her in her belly because Mommy could not." Monica feels that they have a unique and special relationship with Beth; in fact, Beth has offered to be their surrogate again if they decide to try for a sibling.

They aren't sure at this point whether or not they are going to tell their daughter about the egg donor part yet. They're still kind of on the fence about that part of the story.

Monica and Phil have three frozen embryos, but at this time they do not have the money to go through another surrogacy so they aren't sure what they are going to do. They are so grateful to have their little girl and they just don't know if they want to push their luck.

Raquel, Dalia and Shannon live in different countries, but they worked with infertility clinics, attorneys, and surrogates in California. Raquel lives in Argentina where surrogacy is not illegal, but the laws regarding surrogacy are still undefined. In France, where Dalia lives, surrogacy is legal but payment to a surrogate is not. Dalia wishes so much that this would change; she believes many women in her country would benefit if surrogacy became legal. Shannon lives in England, where surrogacy is legal as is paying a surrogate "reasonable expenses" but according to the Childlessness Overcome Through Surrogacy (COTS) organization UK, "there is very little the intended parents can do to secure their position prior to the birth, even in the case of gestational surrogacy." Thomas M. Pinkerton, Esq., a California based third party reproduction attorney, writes in an article titled, *Surrogacy and Egg Donation Law in California*, "Infertile couples around the world have found California to be a favorable legal forum for a surrogacy and egg donation. California courts have taken the lead of all U.S. jurisdictions by favorably extending existing California Family Law statutes to protect all parties to surrogacy and egg donation pregnancies. Prospective parents, surrogates and egg donors can be reasonably certain that their intentions, as expressed by their agreement, will be upheld in California." Infertile couples from other countries are coming to the United States in droves to pursue their baby dreams. Raquel, Dalia and Shannon coordinated their futures from many miles away, all the time keeping sight of their goal. It was a long road to motherhood for these three women—both literally and figuratively.

Sixteen

Raquel
Buenos Aires, Argentina

I learned at sixteen years old that I have Mayer-Rokitansky-Kuster-Hauser syndrome (MRKH). Like many young women who are diagnosed with this condition, I hadn't gotten my period so my mom took me to the doctor to find out if something was wrong with me. In fact, we went to many doctors in Argentina before I was finally told that I was born with an extremely small uterus and the absence of a cervix and vagina. Fortunately, it turned out that my ovaries and fallopian tubes were fine.

As is the case with most MRKH girls, my vagina looked totally normal on the outside, but it was not completely developed on the inside. I had reconstructive surgery in 1988 and although the surgery itself was painful, my sex life has been perfectly normal ever since. My doctor actually advised that I should have intercourse at least occasionally; otherwise, the results of the surgery might not be as successful.

My husband, Juan, was my high school sweetheart. We broke up when I was nineteen; I was just starting law school and he was going away to college in Europe. We remained friends though and when I was twenty-three years old we started dating again.

Looking back, I remember wondering if my infertility had something to do with our four year break up. I always questioned whether Juan was uncertain he wanted to marry a woman who couldn't have children. He never said anything along those lines—it's just a theory I had at the time.

During the four years Juan and I weren't together, I dated other guys. I always wondered how I would have children someday, but in my early twenties I was more concerned with hiding my flaw. I was embarrassed that I wasn't like "normal" women.

I believe this is a universal fear shared by infertile women, based not only from my own experience, but also from speaking to many others in my shoes. It's interesting because no matter where they live, no matter how rich or how poor, women who are infertile always say the same thing.

About a year after Juan and I got back together, I became interested in speaking to other women in my situation. I did some research on the Internet and found an MRKH Online support group. It was wonderful to find women from all over the world who were there to support and inform each other. Many women on the message boards either already had children through surrogacy or were considering surrogacy as a way to have children.

Juan and I both wanted kids, so we'd occasionally discuss how we would create our family when the time came. While we were engaged, I wasn't overly focused on the baby issue because I was busy finishing law school, we were buying a new home, and we just had a lot of other things going on. But after we got married, when I was twenty-eight, I started to take it much more seriously.

I eventually joined the PPS Online support group. Soon after introducing myself to the other members, someone suggested I read the book, *A Matter of Trust*, by Gail Dutton. This book was actually the very first step in our surrogacy journey because after reading this book I said to myself, "This is something I want to do."

I know several lawyers who arrange adoptions, so while I was researching surrogacy I was consecutively looking into adoption. I went to the government office that handles adoptions and they said it would take three years to go through the process. The waiting lists here are very long and there is a lot of red tape involved.

I should clarify—this is if everything is done "legally." Many people who don't want to wait three or four years to adopt a baby directly approach the families of pregnant girls instead. This is considered illegal in our country, and since I am a lawyer I didn't feel right breaking the law. To be honest, in a way it was just easier to go through surrogacy.

In August 2001, a year after we got married, I told my gynecologist we were interested in pursuing surrogacy. She referred me to an infertility clinic in Pasadena, California and mentioned an agency in San Diego. There aren't any surrogacy laws in Argentina; it's not that it's "illegal", it's just something that isn't regulated. This is why we had to do everything in California.

A month after I talked to my doctor, Juan and I flew to Pasadena for our consultation at the clinic. The clinic worked with surrogacy agencies and one of them happened to be the same one my gynecologist in Argentina had suggested.

When we got back to Argentina, we immediately wrote a letter to the agency to request an interview. We originally planned to meet with the owner, Barb, in December 2001. But we had to put off our plans temporarily because of a major economic crisis here in Argentina that spiraled our country into a recession. Juan and I had no choice but to put off our plans temporarily. We had to wait until we felt comfortable spending *that* kind of money.

Finally, in June 2002, we went back to California to meet with Barb and to see the RE again. Barb suggested she'd meet us at the clinic, and this way we could have our interview after Juan and I met with the doctor. She knew we were coming all the way from Argentina and she wanted everything to be as convenient as possible for us.

Our appointment with the RE went well and I was told my ovaries and everything looked fine. Afterwards, we had our interview with Barb as planned, and ended up talking to her for five hours. We signed the contract to work with her agency and she told us she'd contact us when she had someone for us to meet. During that same trip, we also met with our attorney.

A few months later, Barb called to tell us that she found a potential surrogate named Mary who lived in California. We talked to her on the phone shortly thereafter, and although she was shy at first, we found her to be very nice and genuine. She had been a surrogate one time previous so we felt comfortable knowing she was experienced. She also spoke Spanish, which I thought was a huge bonus.

Juan and I hadn't met Mary in person yet, but after reviewing her profile and talking to her on the phone several times, we felt totally comfortable moving forward. We all signed the contracts in October 2002.

We planned a cycle for the beginning of December. I had to be monitored here in Argentina and this was very nerve wracking to me. My gynecologist had never monitored an IVF cycle before so I was worried she would mess up the medication protocol.

We went to California about a week before the retrieval so that I could continue to be monitored at the clinic. It turned out that my follicles weren't developing well, so I had to continue the medications for a few days longer than originally planned. This not only delayed the egg retrieval but the transfer date as well.

I ended up having the egg retrieval on December 9. They only got three eggs but all of them fertilized, and on the day of the transfer, which was December 12, there were two eight-cell embryos and one four-cell embryo remaining. We had only planned on staying in California until December 11 and we couldn't change our flight, so we had to leave the day before the transfer. It was really disappointing because we wanted to be there for the whole thing.

About twelve days later, the clinic called to tell us Mary's beta results were negative. Needless to say, we were extremely upset.

The RE explained that oftentimes, the first transfer doesn't succeed. He told us there was a higher likelihood the following attempts would work because the medication protocol would be changed accordingly. They would determine where things went wrong with the first cycle, make the adjustments, and then hopefully we'd have better results next time around.

We agreed with Mary beforehand that we would try at least three transfer attempts. Neither of us wanted to wait too long to start up again, but we had to wait a month after the failed transfer to start the next cycle.

We begun our next protocol in February 2003; Juan and I flew to California on February 21 and the retrieval was on March fifth. This time we were prepared to stay longer—we learned from our previous experience that sometimes things don't go as planned. It was a good thing we allowed enough time, because although the egg retrieval was originally scheduled for March 2, my follicles weren't responding rapidly enough and we had to prolong the protocol for another three days.

They changed my protocol in order to increase the egg retrieval results, so this time I was taking much higher dosages of the medications. Apparently it helped, because eight eggs were retrieved. Of the eight, six fertilized, but only five—two eight cell, one six cell and two four cell— were good enough quality to transfer.

The RE asked us if we wanted to put all of them in, or just the eight and six celled embryos. He explained that the two eight-cell and the one six-cell embryo had a chance of taking, but that the four-cell embryos probably wouldn't survive the freezing and thawing process.

On the third day after the retrieval, we transferred all five remaining embryos. Juan stayed in the waiting area because he thought Mary would be uncomfortable with him in there too, especially since her legs would be in stirrups and everything like that. But I was in the room with her, and I have to say that watching the embryos going in on the monitor was the most unbelievable thing I've ever seen.

After the transfer, we went out for breakfast and then Mary went home. We went back to Argentina the next day.

Almost two weeks after the transfer, Juan and I went out for dinner and we were on our way home when my cell phone rang. The agency told us that if Mary's beta results were negative the clinic would call us and let us know, but if the beta results were positive, Mary would be the one to call. The caller ID on my cell phone showed Mary's phone number. I answered the phone, "Hello" and her voice on the other end said, "We're pregnant!"

Juan actually had to stop the car because he was so shocked that he couldn't drive. I asked Mary if she was sure, and she said, "I am sure!" I remember pieces of that day—the whole thing was a blur.

Mary's next appointment was two weeks later. Since I couldn't be there, they arranged it so that I would be on the telephone with her during the appointment. I could hear everyone speaking to each other, and then the doctor said, "We have one heartbeat," and he let me hear the heartbeat on the telephone. It felt like I was in a dream.

The next ultrasound appointment was approximately five weeks later when Mary was eleven weeks along. From the time of the first ultrasound to the next one, I was a total nervous wreck. I couldn't eat, I couldn't sleep, I couldn't do anything.

Juan and I had a mini-celebration after I heard the heartbeat, but the next day I woke up and started thinking, "Oh my God, what if something happens to this pregnancy?"

Whenever my telephone rang late at night and I didn't recognize the number on caller I.D., I'd think to myself, "Oh no, something has happened."

The first twelve weeks were awful. I don't know if it's a cultural thing or what, but here in Argentina it is very common to do CVS. All my friends, regardless of their age, have CVS done to make sure the baby is okay.

Once we did CVS and it showed that the baby was fine, it was a huge relief. The other reason I worried constantly during the first trimester is because there is a higher likelihood of miscarriage during the first thirteen weeks of pregnancy. I had heard so many horror stories where woman had miscarriages and I couldn't imagine going through something so horrible.

The reality, however, is that most women who have miscarriages, as awful as it is, can at least just have sex and try and get pregnant again. Women in this situation can just keep trying, over and over again, to get pregnant. For me, someone who had to go through so much to achieve pregnancy, it's a much different story.

Mary was bleeding a lot after the CVS. She was concerned that something was wrong, but when she went to the doctor it turned out that everything was perfectly fine. It's a good thing she didn't contact us until after she knew everything was okay. I probably would have flipped out if she told us about the bleeding before she met with the doctor.

Aside from worrying about the results of the CVS, we did find out some exciting news—we're having a boy! It wouldn't have mattered to us either way, but once we found out the gender of our baby it felt more real to us.

Juan and I actually turned to each other and said, "Okay, it's time to celebrate. Now we can enjoy the pregnancy."

To be honest, we haven't been able to completely let go of our fears. There is a constant element of worry in the back of our minds.

Fortunately, we are approaching an important benchmark. We are almost at twenty-four weeks, the time at which a baby is considered viable if God forbid he came this early.

Mary and I have a nice relationship; we talk on the phone and email several times a week. She had a bad experience with her former intended parents. Apparently the intended mother was very close with her during the pregnancy, she'd visit Mary and her daughters all the time, they'd talk on the phone, email, the whole nine yards. Then, the baby came and the intended mother wouldn't let her see the baby or anything. From that point forward, Mary never heard from her intended parents again. They don't even send her pictures.

She has mentioned to me that sometimes she worries that we could do the same thing to her. The only thing I can say to assure her is that I would never do something to hurt her like that when she's done something so wonderful for us.

Juan and I will be going to California around October 17 for the baby's birth and we are so excited that we can hardly contain ourselves. Time just seems to be going by so slow right now.

It isn't easy to go through surrogacy to have a child. You have to have the resources, financially and otherwise. You have to be willing to cross a lot of hurdles, because inevitably, there are some. I'm sure there are so many people around the world who would love to do surrogacy but it simply isn't an option for them. To have the opportunity, the access to the medical resources, the computer technology and everything, Juan and I know how fortunate we are.

Even though medical reasons brought me up to this point—and believe me, I would have never wished for MRKH, I would never change a thing. Actually, all my life I've gone to therapy because of my issues associated with having MRKH. Learning I would never have children has been very, very difficult for me. Women who are infertile, whether it's a sudden diagnosis or something they learn throughout the years, oftentimes go through a lot of pain and anguish.

A lot of people don't realize how difficult it is, mentally, for women in our situation. I feel it's very important for those facing this problem to turn to others who are in their same shoes for support. I also think it's important to find a good therapist if need be. It's just important to talk about your feelings and to meet other people who truly understand your pain.

Frankly, I never thought I'd be able to have a child through surrogacy. But once I realized that it was something that I could do, and something that I *wanted* to do, I told myself, "Raquel, whatever you have to do, no matter what." If it boiled down to it, literally if we had to be broke, if we had to live without anything but food and shelter—I'd spend everything we have if it came down to it.

We are expecting the baby to be born around November 25, 2003. I just can't stop thinking about what it's going to be like on that day. I can't stop envisioning what it's going to be like to finally hold him in my arms.

Postscript

Raquel and Juan's son is almost two years old and has brought more joy to their lives than they could have ever possibly imagined. Luka has a calm personality and always has a smile on his precious little face. He enjoys being outside in the garden, running and jumping, and playing with his many friends in the neighborhood. He loves books and music; when he hears his favorite songs he instantly starts dancing. Raquel and Juan play classical music for their son all of the time, especially when he's going to sleep. He is growing up in a peaceful atmosphere, surrounded by trees and birds and all of the love of his grandparents, aunts, uncles and cousins.

Sometimes Raquel feels like she's in paradise. When she watches him laughing, she says, "It's the only thing I need to be the happiest person in the world." He is the sunshine in her life, and she can't imagine what life would have been like without him.

She has learned a lot in the last two years. In addition to learning how to be a mom, which she admits, is a difficult job sometimes, she feels she is now a completely different human being. Luka teaches her every day how to be patient, how to enjoy life, and how to appreciate that in some ways she has been re-born.

Most of the time, Raquel doesn't even remember the process she went through to have her son. She has forgotten about a lot of the pain and emptiness that she felt for so long. Now she is just like all of the other moms, taking him to birthday parties, to the theatre, to play with his friends, to the beach, and to the doctor when he is sick.

Raquel is still in contact with Mary, although it's only by email and not very often. She sends Mary pictures via email and gives her updates on what Luka is doing. She feels that it's important to do this as a thank you to her for what she has done for Raquel and Juan. Mary is appreciative of Raquel's continued updates and pictures—she always comments how precious Luka is.

Raquel and Juan do want another baby, but it's not a desperate wish like it was before their son was born. They would love to give Luka a brother or sister though. Finances of course, play a big role in whether or not adding to their family through surrogacy is an option. They just cannot afford it right now. If in the future, they can come up with the money, they will probably go forward with a sibling attempt someday. If not, they will still feel forever grateful that they have Luka.

She realizes that surrogacy is not an option for everyone and offers some advice for anybody considering going this route to have children: "You have to be a very strong person mentally and you must be able to deal with some very complicated issues. It's absolutely crucial to have a strong relationship with your spouse or partner. So if you think you are ready—fight for it, but be patient. Going through infertility can be hard at times, it can seem like the pain will never end. But trust me, it will. It can be a long road with a lot of obstacles, but the day you have your baby in your arms, all of the heartache you've endured along the way will vanish."

Seventeen

Dalia
Paris, France

We started wanting a baby when we got married in 1990. As a matter of fact, Georges and I went to Santa Fe, New Mexico on our honeymoon and I found out I was pregnant when we returned home. It was a really a wonderful surprise! But I ended up having a miscarriage when I was six weeks along in the pregnancy. I was thirty years old at the time.

We continued trying after the miscarriage and four years later I finally got pregnant again. Unfortunately it was a tubal pregnancy. I woke up in the middle of the night in so much pain that my husband, mother and sister took me to the emergency room. It was a good thing they did, even though my doctor told me it was okay to wait until the morning, because I later found out that if I didn't go to the hospital immediately I probably would have died. It turned out that I had to have one of my fallopian tubes removed.

For the next two years, we continued trying to get pregnant the natural way, but we were repeatedly disappointed when I got my period each month. Finally, we decided it was time to see an infertility specialist.

During our first appointment, the RE discovered that my remaining tube was totally blocked and suggested, "We either open up this tube or you can just go straight to IVF."

We ended up doing a total of ten IVF's over the course of four years, from the time I was thirty-seven until the time I was forty-one. After every negative result, I was totally devastated and would be depressed for a couple of days. Luckily, my depression wouldn't last for too long—I would just get back on the saddle and think to myself, "What else am I going to do? I don't really have too many other options, right?"

Normally I'm not a jealous person at all. The gift of life is so beautiful, that how can you be jealous of somebody having this joy in life? But all of a sudden it seemed that so many of my friends and relatives were getting pregnant, one after the other, and I have to admit it was difficult for me.

We went all the way to New York for one of our IVF treatments; one of the infertility clinics there had particularly high pregnancy statistics so we felt it was worth a try. When my brother found out he said, "You know what, we are going to try at the same time so we can make cousins." They ended up pregnant and we did not.

We are a big family, a kids oriented family, and I did not want to spend my life without a child. I kind of started late, yes. I studied, and then I modeled in Milan, Paris and New York. I had never met anyone with fertility problems before beginning our surrogacy journey so I just assumed I'd get pregnant like everyone else.

I figured it would be difficult to have a child via IVF and there was the age issue with my eggs, so we decided to try adoption. However, adoption here in France is virtually impossible because they want you to be very young—like twenty to twenty-five years old—if you want to adopt a newborn. My husband was not too keen on adopting an older child. So we were going to start the adoption process in the United States, where the chances of adopting a newborn are higher. This was in 2000 and I was forty years old.

We signed up with an adoption agency in Texas and they gave me a time frame of between one and two years. They said they'd find a birth mother for us and this birth mother would choose the family she wanted for her baby. I just thought, "Okay, we'll wait for our baby." While waiting we did another one or two IVF treatments.

And then, all of a sudden I read about surrogacy on an American website. I thought to myself, "Hmm, this sounds like a really great idea."

I started researching surrogacy Online and found a ton of information. Then, one day, I found a classified ad on one of the surrogacy websites that sounded very interesting to me. This woman, April, was offering to be a traditional surrogate—and she lived in Europe too.

We started emailing each other and hit it off immediately. I thought, "I can't believe my good fortune!"

She was twenty-eight years old, married and had two daughters. I was impressed with how knowledgeable she was about cycling and coordinating the prime times for inseminating my husband's sperm. She explained to me that we could either do IUI's at an infertility clinic or we could do the inseminations ourselves at home. I thought she was the angel to help us to fulfill our dreams.

Eventually, Georges and I went to meet April, her husband and their children. Her daughters were beautiful; the baby was only six months old at the time.

We all agreed that she'd deliver the baby in California because it is one of the states that allows the intended parents to get pre-birth orders. This way, the intended parents' names go directly on the birth certificate so that they don't have to adopt their own child after he or she is born.

April planned on moving back to the States in a year or so anyway, so this would have worked out well. We found a lawyer in California, signed the contract, and everything seemed to be great.

She got pregnant on the very first try of inseminations and I couldn't believe my good fortune. One day, when she was about three months pregnant, her husband called. He asked to speak to Georges. I said, "Sure, but what's wrong?"

We learned that she had a D&C. I could have asked for written proof from the doctor but I didn't. I'll never really know what happened, but I have a feeling that this was not a normal miscarriage.

At this time, she had received her first payment because we agreed to pay her on a trimester basis. I had already told everyone that we had a baby on the way.

I called her right away and she was crying. Of course I cried too. She assured me, "Whatever it takes for you to have this baby, I will do whatever it takes, trust me." In retrospect, I am pretty sure she didn't even try to maintain the pregnancy—something just didn't sit right with me. But I ignored my intuition and asked April if she would be willing to try again.

Instead of meeting at a hotel for the following inseminations, we decided to have her come to our house. She was unhappy with her husband and wanted to leave him anyway, so it was an excuse for her to get away from him for a while. Plus, it was difficult for Georges to leave every month to go do the inseminations.

It turned out that she was the laziest, I mean, by far the laziest person I've ever met. Every month she'd come stay for a week. Where we live is a popular place to live, a nice place to live, so it was basically a little vacation for her. I believed I had to put up with her if we were going to continue trying to have a baby.

We tried seven times—she came to our house for seven months in a row and stayed for a week each time. I was so sick and tired of her and I'd be so relieved when she left. I've never met anyone who would take such advantage like she did.

On a typical day, Mrs. Lazy would get up at 12:30 or 1:00 just in time to have lunch with us. She'd come downstairs in her pajamas, and then after lunch she'd go back into her room and go to sleep or she'd sit on my computer for hours.

She never used a hanger or put anything in the closet. Her underwear and everything was all over the place. One time, she came with both of her daughters and her seven year old took care of the baby more than April did. Georges finally snapped and told her, "This is not a hotel service, you can help out with something too."

Usually I'm the type of person who will move on if I'm in a situation I don't like. But I didn't think I had any other options than to try and achieve pregnancy with April. We were also trying to avoid starting up another search for a surrogate because we had already invested so much money in her.

After seven months she left her husband and went back to the United States where she was from originally. She said we could still work together and I thought to myself, "Yeah right, like we're going to fly her in from the States every month." Plus, I was so irritated with her that I didn't want to see her face anymore.

I started looking for another surrogate on the Online classified ads. It was January 2002 and I was forty-two years old. This is when things began to go uphill.

There was no way I was going to do traditional surrogacy again; instead I decided to look into egg donation and gestational surrogacy.

After a while, I finally met both a surrogate and an egg donor Online. I found our surrogate, Michelle, on the TASC website and our egg donor, Tami, on SMO. Coincidentally, they both lived in California, so going through a clinic there would be convenient for everyone.

I began talking to and getting to know Michelle and Tami and I tried organizing when they would see the RE for their preliminary testing. Both women told me, "Don't worry, we'll take care of everything." I couldn't believe that I found these wonderful women who were two real partners.

While we were waiting for the transfer, we emailed daily and talked to each other on the phone quite frequently. I was thrilled to have met these two, but trying to stay in contact with both of them was incredibly time consuming. It was also tricky because of the time difference between California and France.

This time I really wanted to be sure. It was really important to me that I see photos of their husbands, their children, pictures of "normal" families. Good faces, real faces…it's hard for me to explain. I go by intuition. It was probably dangerous living in Europe and finding a surrogate and an egg donor in the U.S., but I had to hang onto the faith that everything would work itself out.

Georges thought I was crazy. But I wanted things to progress, I didn't want to wait year after year. I'm the type of person that if I want to do something I go for it.

Our trip to California for the egg retrieval and transfer was the first time Georges and I met Michelle and Tami. Both women were as wonderful in person as they were on email and the telephone—we had a great time together.

Tami's egg retrieval produced eight eggs and all eight fertilized when they were combined with Georges' sperm. Five were good quality and three were excellent quality, so we transferred the best three embryos on day three and froze the rest.

I said to Michelle, "Please don't take any home pregnancy tests, I don't want to know anything about them." Pregnancy tests aren't always accurate and I didn't want to be unnecessarily disappointed.

"Let's just wait for the first beta," I suggested.

I called her the day before the beta to set up a time to call her to find out the results. She said, "You can call me tomorrow, but you know what, I did a home pregnancy test."

"What?"

"I did a home pregnancy test and it was positive!"

And then she told me that she had been doing home pregnancy tests for several days already and they were all positive. I felt like I was living in a dream.

There were some spotting scares, but she was fantastic throughout the entire pregnancy. I wasn't able to go to any appointments so she would send me the ultrasound pictures. She was very informing; she called me with everything I wanted to know. We come from different countries but we have become very good friends.

Michelle knew that I was hoping we'd have a girl. She found out the sex around the eighteenth week and of course called me immediately. I was so surprised because in my family, everyone has boys. Then all of a sudden this miracle news came that we were having a girl. I could not believe my good fortune.

Once or twice a month she would send me all types of things for the baby: powder, oil, clothes, and all sorts of other baby stuff. I liked to spoil her but she spoiled me just as much.

The delivery was as easy as the pregnancy was. I was in the room, but my husband was lying outside of the waiting room because he had an upset stomach.

The room I shared with Michelle had a curtain running down the middle. It was so funny because at one point, I stood up to check on her and at the same time she was getting up to check on Jasmine and me. We stayed up late talking that night. It was kind of like a slumber party.

I was so happy and fulfilled. Once I held Jasmine in my arms, I felt a sense of peace and serenity come over me that's hard to even describe.

Michelle often says that our journey—the way our daughter came into our lives—was simply meant to be. And I definitely agree.

Postscript

Dalia says she and her family couldn't be any happier. Jasmine is two and a half years old now and advanced both mentally and physically; in fact, she already speaks both French and English with ease. "This may seem shallow to some people out there," Dalia says, "but to be honest, the dream of my life came true the moment our daughter was born."

She is still in regular contact with Michelle and Tami. She feels very lucky that she found both of them and knows she made the perfect choice in a surrogate and an egg donor. She acknowledges, as she knows first hand, that it isn't always easy to find a good match.

If intended parents stick together and help each other along the way, Dalia believes succeeding in surrogacy is entirely realistic. She recommends that anyone considering surrogacy be patient, strong, and persistent and suggests that it's better to wait for the right person then to rush into things. While in the process of choosing a surrogate, she adds, it's important to go with your intuition. Once you find a surrogate, stay in contact with her and make sure to pay attention to her needs too. Dalia points out that it isn't always easy for the surrogate either.

She is very grateful that she had the option to do surrogacy in the United States, because she never would have had the option in France. She says that many women in France are against surrogacy—even hostile towards the subject. From what Dalia observes, most women who are opposed to surrogacy do not have a clue what they are talking about. She is convinced they are lacking both information and compassion. She mentions, as an example, that successful career women oftentimes wait until they are over forty to begin their families, but once they decide they are "ready" to have children, they are dismayed to discover they have fertility problems. If surrogacy was not tabu as it is, Dalia believes it could be a solution for many women in her country.

Personally speaking, she says she cannot be thankful enough for the opportunity to have a child via surrogacy. She remembers vividly the moment Jasmine was born, and how she reacted immediately to the first sounds of her mommy's voice. Dalia only hopes that all potential intended parents out there will be able to experience the same level of joy.

Eighteen

Shannon
London, England

I always assumed I would have children. It wasn't even a conscious decision really. So when we started trying and it wasn't happening, I was truly surprised. In fact, it wasn't until we were unsuccessful getting pregnant that I felt, for the first time in my life, desperate to have a baby.

Michael and I have been married for seventeen and a half years and we are both forty-four years old. We started trying to get pregnant ten years ago. For the first seven years that we were married, we didn't feel it was the right time to have a baby. We wanted to wait until we felt stable and grounded. We wanted to be "ready".

We were so confident that we'd get pregnant immediately, that we'd say things to each other like, "Let's wait to get pregnant until next month so the baby will be born in the spring." It's kind of funny now when I think about it.

After a year passed and we still weren't pregnant, we even considered that maybe we just wouldn't have children. We asked ourselves if, perhaps, God didn't mean for us to be parents.

When we finally went to see a doctor, he suggested running some hormone tests. After about six months, he told me I needed more tests. Michael and I used the National Healthcare System (NHS), which is free to the public—well, not totally free because we pay for it in our taxes—and since there is a lot of red tape involved with the NHS, things tend to take a long time. People end up on waiting lists and files shift from one person to another. At the time, I didn't think it was necessary to be proactive, even though I was thirty-six years old.

Meanwhile, I was also doing holistic things like focusing on my diet and going to an acupuncturist. Most people advised me to just get super healthy and it would happen on it's own.

I was aware that IVF existed, but I was afraid of the needles and the medications. It all seemed so unnatural to me. Also, I met a woman who had done IVF and by the time I was done talking to her my head was spinning. She had become so obsessed that her life ceased to exist until she got pregnant. I didn't want that to happen to me. I realized I may never get pregnant and I didn't want to feel like I had no purpose to live if I couldn't have children. I was trying to keep things balanced.

It wasn't until I was almost thirty-seven that I finally got a laparoscopy, which shows whether or not a woman's uterus, ovaries and fallopian tubes are normal. Everything appeared to be fine with my reproductive organs. Michael's sperm was analyzed and found to be fine too, so we were classified as having "unexplained infertility."

After the laparoscopy, I was in excruciating pain, crying and screaming from the agony. When Michael called the hospital in the middle of the night, they told us we could come to the emergency room but it would be a four to five hour wait. I couldn't even get out of bed let alone sit in a hospital waiting room for that long. We didn't go.

The next day, the doctor came to my house and gave me antibiotics. She said, "Good thing you called me, because this could have ended up making you infertile." At the time, I was so naïve——I didn't have a clue what she was talking about and didn't ask. All I could think about was the pain.

I had told the doctor immediately after the laparoscopy that I was in agony, but she dismissed it as being a normal reaction. It never occurred to me that I had an infection or that anything could be wrong.

Another year or so went by and we were still not pregnant. Since the laparoscopy showed everything was fine, there was no reason why we weren't getting pregnant on our own.

In addition to all of the alternative stuff I had been doing already, I started seeing a Chinese holistic doctor who was excellent—probably the best Chinese medicine doctor in England. I was getting acupuncture twice a week and taking herbs every day. I felt really healthy but I wasn't getting pregnant.

Two years later, we decided that perhaps we should try IVF after all. We agreed to do three IVF attempts, and if we weren't pregnant by the third time we would be done.

We went to the Lister Hospital in London; they have an Assisted Conception Department. The doctors encouraged me to continue with the acupuncture and they were very supportive of the holistic life-style I was leading. Despite my initial opposition to IVF, once I met the nurses and doctors at the clinic I felt like we had a team behind us. They were just so supportive.

We got thirteen eggs from the egg retrieval and ten fertilized. According to the embryologist they all looked really good, but we only transferred three. I was freaking out that we were going to end up with triplets.

The infertility clinics here typically tell women to take a home pregnancy test, and if it shows a positive they schedule an ultrasound. They don't necessarily draw blood to confirm a beta number as they do in the States. Following their instruction, I took a home pregnancy test a couple of weeks later. It was negative.

I called the nurse and she said, "That's a shame. Well, call us after your next period." And that was it!

The entire process went so well that I was absolutely convinced it would work. I was crushed when I found out it didn't. Looking back, I realize that I probably had a bunch of questions to ask her, but I was basically in such shock that I just said "Okay," and hung up the phone.

We were going to do another IVF attempt right away, but the Chinese doctor suggested waiting a few months to let my body rest. I thought that made sense. In the meantime, I started researching other clinics.

One day, Michael brought home an article about a clinic that had excellent pregnancy results. It was more expensive than the clinic we had been working with for the previous year. Still, we needed to maximize our IVF attempts since, according to our plan, we only had two tries left.

Michael and I met with Dr. T, the RE at the new clinic and we were very impressed. We decided to have our frozen embryos transferred and do our next attempt with this doctor instead. We were certain it would work, but the frozen embryo transfer—we transferred three embryos—was unsuccessful.

We decided to try again the following month. There were four frozen embryos left; three survived the thaw and we transferred all three. Again, I didn't get pregnant.

Michael and I decided to scratch our original plans to only do three IVF attempts and try the following month with a fresh transfer.

Before the cycle, Dr. T checked my hormones. I got a call from his nurse and she said, "The doctor isn't happy with your hormone levels, so he wants you to wait an extra month."

When I started asking questions she actually had the nerve to say, "Oh, you Americans. You always have so many questions!"

I wanted to yell out, "Hey, I'm the customer here!"

I'm the type of person who normally speaks up for myself but I kept my mouth shut. I felt they had so much control over whether our not we got pregnant—I didn't want to piss anybody off.

We waited another month, but Dr. T wasn't happy with my hormone levels and he cancelled the cycle again.

I finally said to his nurse, "I don't understand this," and began asking her a few questions.

She made some comment suggesting I ask too many questions and I said, "You know, I have to say, you said this to me before and since I am a customer of your office, I believe I should be able to ask as many questions as I want. I'll stop asking questions when I feel satisfied with the answers I'm receiving!"

All of a sudden, she responded, "Oh no, that's not what I meant. Of course you can ask as many questions as you want. The doctor just wants to give you the best possible chance of getting pregnant, and that means your hormones have to be at the most optimal level."

We decided to try another cycle the next month, but it was cancelled because of my hormone level results. Dr. T suggested trying again the following month.

Suddenly, I was like, "Ah ha! I know what's going on!" It finally clicked.

I called my gynecologist to get his opinion. He was never too thrilled with my decision to switch clinics in the first place. I told him, "I'm starting to think the reason this guy's results are better than everyone else, is that he's so selective about who he decides to stimulate for the egg retrieval." It made total sense. If he only let women start cycling who have perfect hormone levels, they would have a higher likelihood of getting pregnant.

I asked my gynecologist if he could possibly refer me back to the Lister, and if he thought they would take me back.

"Of course they will," he said.

There are about six doctors in the Lister's Assisted Conception Department. I didn't really click well with the doctor we had worked with the first time, so my gynecologist said he could get me an appointment with the head doctor. The day we went in for our appointment, he happened to be out on a family emergency, so we were told we could see another doctor if we didn't want to reschedule.

I asked the nurse, "Who would you see if you were in my shoes?", and she replied, without hesitation, "Dr. O."

Dr. O is from Nigeria, and he is the most wonderful man. Our first conversation lasted two hours—he actually spends that much time with *all* of his patients. He is very down to earth and he made us feel comfortable asking him questions. We began preparing for another cycle. It was 1999 and I was forty-one years old.

Again, everything went really well, until I had an HSG. The HSG showed I had a hydrosalpinx, meaning my fallopian tube was blocked and filled with fluid.

I talked to Dr. O about it, and he told me there was some research showing that this condition could prevent women from getting pregnant—even if the embryo quality is excellent. He mentioned that sometimes, in this type of a situation, fluid spills into the uterus and causes an environment not conducive for pregnancy. The embryos, in this case, can have a difficult time attaching and thriving. He added that with treatment many women with hydrosalpinx's still can become pregnant.

Again, my cycle went like clockwork. We got ten eggs and all of them fertilized, and they transferred the best three embryos. I didn't get pregnant.

Both Dr. O and the embryologist agreed that it didn't make much sense to freeze the remaining seven. They said that based on our ages they just didn't think the embryos would survive a thaw.

Michael and I discussed it and we said to each other, "Yeah, it's expensive to freeze them, but we're willing to incur those costs just in case they do end up surviving the thaw after all." They froze the only four that were freezable.

Two weeks later, we found out that I wasn't pregnant.

Dr. O suggested that since I had hydrosalpinx, I should consider having my tubes removed. I set the date for the surgery. I figured, I didn't need my tubes anyway. It's not like I'd ever get pregnant without assisted reproduction.

Two nights before the surgery, Michael told me he wasn't thrilled with the idea of my tubes being removed. He thought it was too invasive. I agreed that I was not so comfortable with the idea either. We started doing research on the Internet and found out that when women get their tubes removed or tied for sterilization purposes, blood flow to the ovaries is reduced. This can affect the woman's hormones. Because my mother had breast cancer four years ago, I am acutely aware of the connection "messing" with hormones has with the female body.

I was almost forty-two at this point and Michael and I decided we really needed to figure out what we wanted to do. We asked each other, given my age and infertility history, what the chances were that I would ever get pregnant?

When we sat down with Dr. O to discuss the situation, he explained that there are a few ways tubes become blocked. One is from infection. The first thing that came to mind was the laparoscopy I had five years previous, when the doctor had to come to my house to give me antibiotics. There isn't any way to prove it, but I have a feeling that could have had something to do with why I wasn't getting pregnant.

In my research Online, I came across a doctor who was renowned for repairing fallopian tubes. Coincidentally, he practiced in Chapel Hill, North Carolina—where my mother lives and where I'm from originally. I called his office and was told to send in my most recent x-rays, and then I called my mother and announced, "I'm coming to visit!"

During my initial consultation with the doctor in North Carolina, we talked in depth about the surgery. Then, I had another appointment with him to discuss the side effects and I found out that tubal surgery might increase the chances of ectopic pregnancy by up to sixty percent. I didn't know what to do.

After the visit to North Carolina and the consultations with the doctor there, I went to visit my sister who lives in Switzerland.

We were horse back riding and I told her what the doctor said about the ectopic pregnancy statistics with tubal repair.

She turned to me and said, "You know, Shannon, you could go have this surgery and you can keep going down this road. But it just doesn't feel right to me. Maybe you should stop all of this and look into adoption?"

I just burst into tears. It was the most perfect place to be having this conversation too; there we were, walking along with these two horses in the countryside. It was so beautiful. My sister and her husband don't have any kids, just horses and dogs.

She was verbalizing what I was thinking. At this very moment I realized that we needed to let go of the fertility stuff. I still had to talk to Michael about it, but I felt in my gut that she was right. We needed to start considering other alternatives.

After the conversation with my sister, Michael and I had a heart to heart and decided to give up on the fertility treatment. It was actually a huge relief, we felt like a weight was lifted off our shoulders.

On that walk, my sister had mentioned Elise, a woman she knew who had adopted and had an excellent experience. I told Michael about this and we decided that we didn't know if we wanted to adopt. We didn't know what we wanted to do. We just wanted to let it go for a while.

All of a sudden the phone rang and it was my sister. She said, "I just heard from Elise and she wants to talk to you."

I said, "How weird that you just called, because Michael and I have just made the decision to stop infertility treatment."

I called Elise and we had a great chat. She told me her story and I just felt so much more informed after talking to her.

The more Michael and I talked about it, the more we realized that we wouldn't have a problem bonding with a child that wasn't related to us genetically. Sure, we would have to process and grieve not having our own biological child, but we just wanted to be parents and passing on our genetics wasn't that important to us.

A few weeks later, we happened to be out to dinner with our closest friends, a gay couple who live in Boston. They told us about a German couple they knew who ended up adopting twice within two years. They worked with a lawyer from New Jersey who handled the whole adoption process; she helped the couple find the birth mothers and everything.

Michael called the couple and they said wonderful things about this attorney, so we gave her a call. We decided that during Christmastime, when we went to visit my family in North Carolina, we'd fly to New Jersey to meet with her.

When we did eventually have our meeting, we were very impressed. We were so anxious to begin the adoption process after we came home to England, that I started putting together our profile and everything. It was my new project and I felt great about it.

The way it worked in the United Kingdom, up until about a year before we were going to start the adoption process, is that a social worker would come to the home of the adopting parents and do an interview. Then, there would be a home-study process that would take about three months or so. When I called a social worker to start the process I was told about the *new* laws.

There were these twin babies born in Wales not too long ago who were adopted by a couple in the States. Apparently, there were two potential couples that were both told they could adopt the babies. The whole thing went awry and the government here in the United Kingdom was all over it. It was a huge outrage—the media focused on whether or not anyone can just "buy" a baby over the Internet.

The government decided there should be stricter rules on adopting and that instead of contacting a social worker directly, potential adoptive parents would have to go to the local council instead. The new laws meant it would take anywhere from eighteen months to two years to complete the home study, simply because of these new steps. Basically, it's just a bunch of paper pushing; paper sitting on some bureaucrats desk. These aren't even adoption specialists.

It was February 2002 when I was told it would realistically take almost two years to get the home study done. I slumped into a huge depression. I thought to myself, "I just cannot do this anymore."

The day after I learned of the realistic time frame for adoption, we went to visit some friends for the weekend, Stephanie and Paul. Stephanie told me she recently met a woman who had a child with the help of a surrogate mother. A few people had mentioned surrogacy to me, but I just brushed it aside. I guess I thought it was too farfetched, too crazy.

When we got home, I called Stephanie's friend and she told me about her surrogacy experience. She explained how it all worked and it was such a contrast to what we had been dealing with in the adoption world. The bonus, I thought, is that at least Michael could be biologically related to the baby. Not that a genetic connection was crucial, I just thought it would be neat.

I went on the Internet again and found the PPS Online support group. I also found a bunch of other great websites pertaining to surrogacy. I knew that if we were going to pursue surrogacy we'd have to do it in the States because even though it's legal in the United Kingdom, there are no laws to protect intended parents.

After some suggestions from various people I met Online, I contacted a surrogacy agency in Southern California. They are a smaller agency and they only work with surrogates in the Southern California area so they can attend the doctor's appointments and such. We signed with them in April 2002. The agency owner said it would take four to six months to find a surrogate. We also decided to use donor eggs since we knew the chances of achieving pregnancy with my eggs were very slim.

In August, we got a call that they found a surrogate for us. We would have to meet her first, of course, and she would have to go through all of the necessary screening. We were going to see my family during Christmas, so we figured that after our visit to North Carolina we'd fly out to San Diego to meet with everyone.

Meanwhile, I started looking for an egg donor. After searching through egg donor agency websites for several months, I finally found someone who I thought was a great match.

One night, I was looking at one of the agency's profiles and decided to sort the potential egg donors by hair color, which I had never done before. Previously, I had been looking at women with black, brown or blond hair—I had not considered women with auburn hair for some reason, which is strange because I have red in my own hair.

I happened to click on "auburn"—it was the first option— and then I clicked on the first woman who came up. I looked at her picture and just knew she was our egg donor. Physically, she was attractive, but that isn't necessarily what drew me to her. We had so much in common; we both do yoga, we're both avid skiers, we're both interested in travel, and we're both creative.

Pat and I decided we wanted to work with her, so we signed a contract with the egg donor agency and sent in the deposit.

As planned, we spent Christmas with my family in North Carolina and then flew to San Diego on a Friday for our appointments with the RE, the psychologist, and the attorney. The RE suggested that while we were there, Michael should produce a sperm sample for analysis.

After all of our meetings, we were exhausted, so we went out for a nice dinner and then went back to our hotel room. Suddenly, our cell phone rang and it was the embryologist with some bad news. Michael's sperm count was zero; literally, there was not one living sperm. The embryologist asked if Michael had been in an accident or had a major illness.

The whole night, I tossed and turned, wondering if something was wrong with Michael—if he was dying or something. Then I started wondering if it had something to do with the Chinese herbs he was taking. Michael has a liver condition and no doctor could ever seem to figure it out. The Chinese herbs had seemed to be helping him.

The next morning, we told the RE about the herbs and he suggested Michael stop taking them and get another sperm sample taken in three months.

Later that day, we went to the agency to meet Terri and her husband, Scott. Even though we were devastated about the information we had received about Scott's sperm count, we still had to put on happy faces. It was incredibly stressful.

During our meeting, we discussed all of our expectations and the complicated issues we could encounter along the way. Then, we all went out to dinner. It went really well actually—I was surprised because I was so nervous previous to our meeting.

Meanwhile, we had already called Michael's brother to ask him if he'd donate his sperm if we needed a donor. We totally caught him off guard, the poor guy, but he and his wife were so supportive and without hesitation, he said, "Absolutely."

We told Terri about our dilemma and she was wonderful. She and Scott are very spiritual. They are unscathed by things that would bother most people because their theory is "God will take care of everything."

Her response to the news was simply, "Okay, if it isn't Michael, it will be his brother." And that was it.

Dr. O arranged for us to see one of the top urologists in the United Kingdom to find out if something was wrong with Michael. When his sperm results came back, it showed that only about 1% sperm was viable. Dr. O said that even though it was only 1%, it was still enough to do ICSI. He pointed out that 1% of millions and millions was still a lot of viable sperm.

Michael called the Chinese doctor to ask if the herbs could have caused his sperm count to be so low. The doctor said "Yes", the herbs could have affected his sperm, but if he stopped the herbs, his sperm could return to normal. The next month, Michael had his sperm analyzed again and this time forty percent were good quality.

We decided we'd aim for a March transfer. We also thought it would be a good idea to have Michael's brother come with us, just in case there weren't any viable sperm in Michael's sample. A week before we were scheduled to go to Los Angeles, he called us to tell us he developed a horrible infection from having his tonsils removed and that he wouldn't be able to come to the transfer after all. In the meantime, the egg donor was being stimulated and Terri was taking the medications to prepare her for the transfer. We didn't want to cancel the cycle, so we just crossed our fingers that we'd have at least *some* viable sperm.

It was the end of March 2003. We arrived in California on a Monday and went to Terri and Scott's house to meet their kids for the first time. We were jet lagged and exhausted.

Suddenly Michael's cell phone rang. It was the doctor calling to tell us that the egg donor wasn't doing very well with the stimulation process and her estrogen levels were plummeting. He asked us again if we wanted to cancel the cycle. I wanted to freak out and scream out a few four-letter cuss words, but I had to maintain my composure. I didn't want to make a bad impression on Terri and her family.

When I got off the phone to discuss things with Michael and Terri, she said, "Look, it only takes one egg. Of course we're going to continue plans for the transfer."

We called the doctor from our cell phone on the car ride back to the hotel and told him, "Yes, we want to go forward." After all, we had come this far.

Our egg retrieval was on Wednesday. We were given the choice whether or not we wanted to meet the egg donor, who had flown in from Chicago, but we decided it wasn't a good idea. We didn't want to meet her, see some small flaw and be unnecessarily disappointed. We were also afraid that we'd meet her, love her, and end up having to find another egg donor if things didn't go well with the retrieval.

Instead, I wrote her a nice note and we gave her a bracelet. While we were waiting for the egg retrieval results, all of the nurses came up to us to tell us how wonderful she was—so that was comforting. We could see for ourselves in the letter she wrote us. She thanked us for the bracelet and note that we gave her, and said if we ever wanted to meet her that would be great, but if we preferred not to she'd totally understand. I'm not sure if we will ever take her up on the offer—but it was thoughtful of her to put it out there nonetheless.

They retrieved seven eggs, which really isn't very good considering our egg donor was only twenty-four years old. We were hopeful, but fearful at the same time.

The next day they called to tell us six eggs fertilized, and of the six, five made it to the six-cell stage. At this particular clinic, they do their transfers on day two, so on the second day after the transfer they transferred three embryos into Terri.

After ten years of going from one failure to another, I really didn't think it was going to work. Michael was convinced we'd end up with triplets or something. Terri was certain it was twins.

About twelve days after the transfer, Terri called to tell us she got her beta results—she was pregnant! It took about twenty-four hours for it to sink in.

We are already twenty-two weeks along in the pregnancy and the baby is due on Christmas Eve. I speak to Terri every week, usually on Wednesdays, and things are going very well with her.

I've only recently started getting excited about the baby. It took me a while though; I didn't want to jinx anything. I'm superstitious like that sometimes. But I actually let my best friend buy me a little outfit the other day—a big step for me! I'm even starting to look at strollers and all of that stuff.

We are planning the baby's birth, working things out with the hospital, and figuring out where we are going to stay when we are in California. No doubt, it's a happy project, but it's still stressful and a lot to think about and plan.

Actually, when I was in the States not too long ago, I spent a week with her and stayed in a motel near where they live. I hung out with Terri and their kids and we all went to Sea World. I also met their friends and people from their church—there are so many people who are excited for Terri and also so happy for Michael and I.

The only thing that bothers me a bit—it's not a huge deal, but it does concern me slightly—is that she eats a lot of fast food. I know that a lot of pregnant women eat fast food and the babies are born fine, it's just because of my belief system and our way of life in regards to healthful eating that this is important to me. I don't want Terri to think I'm being a control freak, so I'm going to mention something to the doctor and see if he'll nonchalantly give her some nutritional advice.

It's such a touchy situation, but as intended mothers we sometimes have to sit and watch our surrogates do things that we wouldn't do if we were carrying the baby ourselves. At the same time, it's hard to do that without seeming neurotic or controlling.

It isn't Terri's fault really, it's the agency's fault. When we signed up with the agency, I was very clear that we wanted to work with a surrogate who would be conscious about the foods she ate while pregnant. We really should have put it in the contract. I guess the agency just didn't think it was important enough to mention to Terri.

Maybe she can take some supplements or something. I feel silly for even mentioning this because she is truly an excellent surrogate. Her kids are healthy and they are great kids. I feel blessed that we found someone so spiritual, so fun, who is such a good mother and who has a good relationship with her spouse. She doesn't drink, doesn't smoke—there are so many positives.

A friend of mine who is a nutritionist made a great point. She said, "Look Shannon, there are so many great things about her. If her diet isn't totally perfect, it isn't the end of the world. The baby is much better off being carried by someone who is a calm, spiritual, and happy person."

I'm going to be forty-five years old when the baby is born, but in spite of everything we have been through I wouldn't change a thing. Whatever has happened to get us to this point—it got us to this point. Now we have a baby on the way that is going to be so loved and have such a wonderful home.

One thing about surrogacy is that you realize how little control you have with anything in life. But I definitely see things that other people miss just because they take them for granted. I see people with their kids who complain, "They're driving me crazy!" I think to myself, "If only you knew how blessed you are."

Postscript

The last trimester of the pregnancy was a stressful time. Terri and her family were wonderful, but it was difficult for Shannon to relinquish control of the process—especially being so far away. The agency they hired was supposed to be "managing" the surrogacy, but for various reasons, Shannon and Michael didn't have a lot of confidence in their agency.

As they got closer to the delivery date, Terri began to experience high blood pressure and her oby/gyn said she thought it would be best if Terri were induced. This was something that neither Shannon or Terri wanted. It turned out their doctor was going away for Christmas, so they decided to take their chances with the doctor on call.

Terri's blood pressure worsened, so they ended up in the hospital a couple of days before the due date. The doctor who happened to be on call was, according to Shannon, "Straight out of the 1950's—very patronizing and prone to scare-mongering." This doctor immediately told Terri they had to do a c-section, otherwise, she could die.

They got a second opinion from another doctor who felt it would be okay to induce Terri and let nature take its course. About an hour after she was induced, Shannon and Michael's beautiful baby boy, Alex, safely came into the world.

They spent a lot of time with Terri and her family during the ten days they stayed in California after Alex's birth. On the last night, Shannon and Michael had Terri and her family over to their hotel room for a farewell dinner. Shannon describes it as "very bittersweet", because on one hand, they were excited to be leaving to see Shannon's family in North Carolina for a visit en route to London, but at the same time, it was sad in a way that their intense joint endeavor was coming to an end.

Their entire experience in the United States was a whirlwind. After visiting family in North Carolina as planned, they went back home to London. This is when reality set in. Michael works long hours and travels frequently, so Shannon suddenly found herself alone with Alex. She felt overwhelmed and lonely. The highly developed skills she had developed to get her son here were no longer needed and her expectations of a "happily ever after" once the baby came were not being met. Over the next couple of months, Shannon developed anxiety and insomnia and this led to depression. Finally, she sought help from her doctor and was referred to a psychiatrist. She started treatment with anti-depressants and therapy and within a short amount of time she relaxed and slowly began to enjoy her new life.

Shannon points out that there were several factors that led to her depression. One, she has a history of depression in her family. She also realizes that she's had some mild depression in the past, but it has not been treated previously. Mainly, Shannon thinks it was a mental collapse of sorts, after all she had been through to have a baby.

The other issue she was having, was that she wasn't feeling totally bonded with her son. She has decided since, that one of motherhood's biggest myths is that all women instantly bond with their babies. But especially in her case, since they used an egg donor and all, she worried that because she hadn't carried or given birth to her son that she would never bond. Because she wasn't experiencing this initial bliss, she was very hard on herself for not feeling more overjoyed about Alex being here. She felt she should be more grateful. She really beat herself up about it.

Now, she cannot imagine life without her little boy. As difficult as her years going through infertility were, and as stressful as the first months were after her son's birth, it was, without a doubt, one hundred percent worth it. Shannon believes that her journey enriched her life and made her a better mother.

She reminds other potential intended parents to be very clear from the beginning about what they want their surrogate to do or not do. Shannon wishes, in her own case, that she had been more honest about what she expected during her surrogacy journey. In retrospect, she realizes that knowing Terri, she probably would have obliged and Shannon could have avoided a lot of unnecessary stress.

She also advises intended mothers, specifically, to monitor their expectations. After a long struggle with infertility it's easy to believe that once the baby comes, everything will be perfect. In most ways it is, but having a baby is a huge change and when you are putting all of your energy into getting him/her here, you don't always have time to settle into preparing emotionally like you would if you are carrying the baby yourself.

Shannon and Terri stay in touch, but not consistently and not very often. Shannon thinks, more than anything else, the lack of communication is more of a function of different and busy lives. Nevertheless, Shannon says, "The feelings of love and closeness are still there." Shannon, Michael and Alex plan to visit Terri in California within the next year or so. They consider Terri and her family a part of their lives and they want Alex to know and understand the role she had in getting him here.

We are very fortunate to live in an age where reproductive technology is possible, but sometimes when reproductive assistance should work, it doesn't. Peggy and Dana, the women who share their stories in the remaining two chapters, were faced with different medical circumstances that made their chances of getting pregnant "the normal way" virtually zero. Their doctors advised that they go straight to IVF. Many IVF cycles and many tears later, neither were pregnant, and it became clear that IVF was not the solution. But that did not mean something else could not be done. For various reasons, some women are not particularly affected by their infertility. Peggy and Dana, however, are like most infertile women who, like myself, experience some level of mental anguish as a direct result of their infertility. Perhaps it is stated best in the Resolve fact sheet, *The Emotional Aspects of Infertility,* in the section titled, "Shame: The Dark Shadow of Infertility", by Carol Munschauer Pearson, Ph.D. Dr. Munschauer Pearson points out, "The process of coming to terms with infertility is long and gradual, but it is possible to transform the sense of failure into an empathy with yourself, an affirmation of your strength, an acceptance of your limits, a pride in your endurance, and maybe most of all, an empathy with others who, as partners in the human condition, also face defeats. In time, the shadow cast upon your life can fade and the light can shine through again." For Peggy and Dana, along with the eighteen women featured in the previous chapters, that light is now shining through indeed.

Nineteen

Peggy
Thompson, Connecticut

In 1990, when I was twenty-nine years old, I felt a lump on my stomach while I was getting dressed one day. I went to see my gynecologist and he immediately did an ultrasound. It turned out that I had fibroid tumors on the inside and the outside of my uterus and I would need surgery to remove them.

Before going into surgery my doctor said, "I will try and keep your uterus, but I can't make any promises." I woke up from the surgery and the first thing I asked the nurse was, "Do I still have my uterus?" I did.

When I married my husband, Kal, my gynecologist told us we'd have to go straight to IVF to get pregnant because of the scarring on my uterus. We still held onto the hope that we'd get pregnant on our own, but despite our efforts we were not having any success. We tried using the ovulation prediction kits and everything, but nothing worked.

I went back to see my doctor and he did laproscopic surgery to check things out. Sure enough, the tumors had come back and there also was severe scarring on my fallopian tubes and ovaries. We decided it was time to take the doctor's advice and try IVF.

Our first IVF cycle was in January 1995. The success rates weren't as high as they are now because when we started doing IVF they weren't transferring blastocysts. Still, I was convinced it would work on the first attempt and I was totally crushed when the pregnancy test came back negative.

We did another IVF cycle in March 1995 and this time we used frozen embryos. Again, it failed.

Over the course of the next four years we ended up doing seven more rounds of IVF. It was like being on a roller coaster; every time we did another cycle we'd have the hope that we'd get pregnant, then it wouldn't work and we'd be depressed.

Throughout our infertility struggles, however, we were very fortunate about one thing. Since we lived in Massachusetts and had Massachusetts insurance, we didn't have to pay for any of the infertility treatment. Massachusetts law requires health insurance companies to cover infertility, including the IVF cycles and the medications. It's the only reason we were able to try IVF so many times.

I was so focused on getting pregnant that it was all I could think about. In the meantime, I was eating and eating because of all of the stress, and then I gained a bunch of weight from the drugs. I ended up putting on about twenty-five pounds and I was totally disgusted with myself. It seemed like I was always waiting for the phone to ring, waiting for the clinic to call with the pregnancy test results. I would drive myself crazy waiting.

I was working so hard to get pregnant with IVF and it just seemed like everyone else was getting pregnant when the wind blew. It was hard to hear about other women getting pregnant—I was very resentful.

At first, I didn't know anyone else doing IVF. Eventually though, I learned that two other women that I worked with were also going through IVF. One of them got pregnant with twins and the other friend got pregnant with triplets after several tries. I was genuinely happy for them, especially because they had similar circumstances to mine.

In the meantime, Kal and I continued getting negative pregnancy results after each IVF attempt. Kal was distraught because he wanted a child just as much as I did, but it also really bothered him to see me so unhappy all of the time.

I finally got pregnant in 1999, on the sixth cycle. The night before the pregnancy test I was bleeding a little bit so I naturally assumed it didn't work again. The next day, I was in a horrible mood and nasty to everyone at work. Then the doctor's office called to say I was pregnant. We were so thrilled, we couldn't believe it!

We went in for our five-week ultrasound and saw a sac, but there was no heartbeat. The doctor said it was early and that we should come back in ten days. We went back ten days later, but there was no heartbeat.

We were told I could either have a D&C or let the miscarriage happen naturally. I was like, "No way am I going to wait around for this to happen!" I had the D&C.

I was crushed. We wanted children so desperately—we didn't know what to do. The RE suggested we consider surrogacy or adoption, but I wasn't ready to give up on getting pregnant myself yet. He said, "Well you do produce a lot of eggs, so if you are on board let's try again."

Since our doctor was encouraging, we decided to do one more fresh cycle. I didn't get pregnant. At that point, Kal and I sat down and had a discussion about what we were going to do. Kal said, "I'm happy the way things are, and if we don't have children I'm fine with that." I told him, "I'm *not* happy. I have always wanted children. There is more to life than just going out on the weekends with our friends—it's a waste of life. I'm getting old, I'm tired of the way things are. I want more!"

I started looking into adoption, but Kal really didn't want to adopt. So we started talking about surrogacy.

My sister had offered throughout the years to carry for us, but when it came down to it her husband wasn't supportive of the idea. He was afraid that something bad could happen to her, physically, during the pregnancy or delivery. I was a little ticked off for a while and I wouldn't talk to him.

My neighbor had also offered several times, so one day I asked her if she was serious about being our surrogate and she said, "Let me think about it and I'll let you know." After two weeks, I finally approached her and asked her if she had made a decision. She said, "No I really don't want to Peggy. I'm so sorry, but we have two teenagers and it's just not good timing for me to be pregnant right now."

I told her, "It's fine, really." I knew she felt bad about it though.

I decided it was time to start looking Online. It was crazy, the first time I clicked on SMO I thought, "This is like a whole new world!" There was so much more out there than I knew about. Once I started answering classified ads, things just started rolling.

I answered this ad for a girl named Denise who lived in western Massachusetts. We started emailing each other and seemed to get along great, so we decided I would drive out to meet her a couple of weeks later.

The day before we were supposed to get together, I called Denise to confirm our plans. She wasn't home so I left a message.

I finally got an email from her saying, "I'm so sorry, something came up." Again, I planned on driving up to see her and tried calling her before hand to confirm our plans. She never answered my calls—it was as if she fell of the face of the earth.

I went Online to look for another surrogate and met Lana, who lived in North Carolina. She was twenty-three years old and had four kids. We emailed back and forth but she couldn't decide if she wanted to work with us or another couple with whom she was corresponding.

She kept telling me she'd call me to tell me her choice, but a few days went by and she still hadn't called. Finally, I called her and asked, "Who are you going to pick?" She said, "I think I'm going to choose the other couple."

I had already planned to fly out and meet her if she would have told me she chose us. My friends were like, "Are you insane? You are going to take a plane to North Carolina to meet someone?" I told them, "I'll be fine!"

I started plunging deeper into depression and eating more and more. I was crying all the time and totally miserable.

I kept on thinking, "Maybe a miracle will happen and I'll just get pregnant on my own. I'm such a nice person, I deserve to get pregnant." But I didn't get pregnant. I became more depressed and continued to eat excessively.

Finally, I said to Kal, "Lets take a break."

In March of 2000, we decided to take a vacation to Jamaica. In the meantime, I was still corresponding with potential surrogates Online.

I had posted my own ad and started getting a few replies. One day, I got an email from this woman in Florida named Ann. She was thirty-seven years old, married with two children, and she said she had always wanted to be a surrogate.

I emailed her my story and we started chatting back and forth. Kal and I decided we wanted to work with her, but she insisted she wanted to work with an agency. If we went through her agency, we'd have to pay additional fees that we wouldn't pay if we worked together independently.

I talked to Kal about it and he said, "Honey, that's a lot of money to pay an agency." But I really wanted Ann to be our surrogate, so Kal agreed that he'd consider working with the agency since it was important to me.

We flew to Florida in June 2000 so that we could all meet each other. First, we met the lady from the surrogacy agency for breakfast. She explained the contracts, how the escrow worked, and everything else that we needed to know. Then we met Ann and her husband, Dave, and thought they seemed really nice. Looking back, I remember how careful I was to not say anything stupid. But the meeting went very well and afterwards we all went out for dinner.

I was so worried on the way back to the airport that we had done everything wrong. It is so much easier to communicate on the computer sometimes. When we got home, I sent her an email apologizing and told her I was sorry if she got the wrong impression of us. She didn't think we acted strangely and said she totally understood if we were nervous. Soon after our visit, we decided we would go for it.

A month later I met with the RE at our infertility clinic in Boston, and shortly thereafter, Ann came up so that we could both meet with the IVF coordinator.

Three days after the egg retrieval, which was in September 2000, three embryos were transferred into Ann. She stayed at our house for a few days before going back home to Florida.

She emailed me a picture of a pregnancy test about a week and a half later and I couldn't believe my eyes—it was positive! I was so convinced it wouldn't work that I was crying on the phone with joy when I found out I was wrong.

The lab drew her blood that day and her beta was 106. After all we had been through we finally had a pregnancy.

Even before we officially decided to work together, Ann and I felt as if we knew each other already. On 9/11, I called my mom, and then the next person I called was Ann. She and I were on the phone for an hour watching the whole thing on television.

Kal and I flew down to Florida every month for the entire pregnancy. In between our visits, Ann would take pictures of her belly and email them to us. I also tape-recorded my voice so she could hold it to her belly for the baby to hear.

People at work would ask me if I was nervous that she wasn't taking care of herself and I'd reply, "No, I'm not nervous in the least, I know Ann takes care of herself."

They'd ask, "Aren't you afraid she's going to try and keep the baby?"

"No," I'd say, "because she doesn't want *this* baby—she has her own children." And then I'd usually add that the baby was created with my egg and Kal's sperm, so Ann didn't have a biological connection to it.

I'm a nurse in the intensive care unit. I've been working at this hospital for eighteen years and we are a pretty close-knit group.

But because my eggs were thirty-nine years old and we planned on doing an amniocentesis, I didn't want to tell too many people in case there was a problem. After we found out at eighteen weeks that the amnio results were good, I finally told everyone at work.

I got a photo album with palm trees on the front and I filled it with pictures of our visits to Florida to see Ann. I also included the ultrasound pictures. When I told my friends at work, I showed them the album so they could see us with Ann and see her pregnant belly. They were all so happy for me. Actually, everybody had only positive comments to say, except for one woman who said, "I noticed you were getting a little heavy lately." I replied, "Um, I'm not the one who is pregnant!"

I found out after the amnio that we were having a girl. I always knew it was going to be a girl—I don't know why, I just had a feeling.

Finally, in June 2001, I flew down to Florida to await the arrival of our baby. Kal flew down several days later.

The staff at the hospital was very accommodating. Ann wanted a doula, which we thought was a fabulous idea. We were all in the room while she labored; Ann, myself, and our husbands.

We had planned a head of time that when Alexa was born, she'd be handed to me first and then to the nurse. When she came out though, she was totally purple and didn't appear to be breathing. Immediately I panicked, because I had seen many babies like that at work and it often times resulted in tragedy. The nurse suctioned fluid from Alexa's throat and then, thank goodness, she was fine.

We were discharged July 4. Ann's sister and her friend planned a little party for all of us—it was very sweet. We stayed in Florida until Alexa was three days old and then we flew home. Alexa slept for the entire flight.

Ann and I went shopping the day before we had our transfer. We heard that yellow is a good luck color for fertility, so we bought these little yellow bracelets. We wore them for the longest time. I still have that bracelet; I keep it with the palm tree photo album that's filled with pictures of Ann's growing belly.

Eventually, we will tell Alexa the whole story. We will tell her, "The doctors took an egg from mommy and sperm from daddy and put them into Ann's belly for ten months." We'll always be honest with her about the way she was conceived.

When I'm asked about our surrogacy experience, I'm always happy to talk about it. Most people only hear the bad stuff, like the "Baby M" story from years ago. I always tell people, "There are so many wonderful surrogacy stories out there…and ours is definitely one of them."

Postscript

When Peggy looks at Alexa she can't believe she's already four years old. She's determined, fiercely independent, and such a little adult now. She is the perfect combination of Peggy and Kal; she loves dresses and girlie things and playing dress-up, but she also likes to go fishing with her daddy. She grabs the worms, her fishing rod, and off they go.

Peggy wishes they could have another sibling for her, but they don't have any remaining frozen embryos. In the last three years, Peggy has had surgery twice—once for removal of her uterus and one ovary, and the second time to remove the remaining ovary. She realizes they could go the egg donor route, but she just doesn't have the drive anymore that she had when they went through surrogacy the first time.

Their surrogacy journey was incredible and she proudly tells everybody who asks about it. Alexa and Peggy try to fly down to Florida to see Ann and her family twice a year. Peggy sends Ann pictures of Alexa whenever she has a roll developed. They talk on the phone about once a week and they exchange gifts at

Christmas and birthdays. When their children are older, Peggy and Ann plan to escape for a girls' weekend in New York City. She wishes all intended parents and surrogates could experience the special friendship they share.

Going through infertility was long and exhausting but Peggy and Kal were determined to become parents. They love their roles as Mommy and Daddy and can't imagine their lives any other way.

Twenty

Dana
Marietta, Georgia

Back in 1987, when I was twenty-one years old, I had a ruptured ectopic pregnancy. One day I was having severe abdominal pain, and the next thing I knew I was in the emergency room having one of my fallopian tubes removed. I didn't even know I was pregnant.

I married my husband Pat when I was twenty-seven and eight months after our wedding I found out I was pregnant. Even though we weren't exactly "trying", we weren't making any efforts to prevent pregnancy either, so we were really quite excited.

Pat is Canadian, and at the time we were living in Toronto. When I saw my ob/gyn, he said, "Since you have a previous history of an ectopic pregnancy, we should get you in for an ultrasound."

When this was happening, and also with the way the medical system is in Canada—they had to schedule my ultrasound two weeks out. I started experiencing severe abdominal pain about a week before the ultrasound appointment, so I immediately went to the emergency room. It turned out to be another ruptured ectopic pregnancy.

My doctor was encouraging and he told me, "You are a great candidate for IVF. I have no doubt you will be able to get pregnant with IVF."

Shortly thereafter, we moved to Georgia and Pat and I both started law school. I had been practicing law for about a year when we said to each other, "Okay, let's do IVF—we're ready to have a baby." I was thirty-two, and it had been over five years since the ectopic pregnancy in Toronto.

We went to an infertility clinic in Atlanta and met with the RE. Just as my doctor in Canada had told us, he said: "You are a perfect candidate for IVF. If you do IVF, you will probably get pregnant right away. Your FSH tests are fine, all of your tests are fine. You just have a plumbing problem."

The cycle went well—we even had embryos to freeze. But I didn't get pregnant.

The next time we did IVF, we did a fresh cycle and got pregnant, but at the eleven-week ultrasound the doctor couldn't detect a heartbeat. We had lost the baby.

He suggested it was probably a fluke, perhaps a chromosome problem with the baby or something. We were obviously both devastated but we just went on with our lives. We tried to be optimistic that we would get pregnant eventually and everything would be fine.

At this point we had six frozen embryos left, so we did two more cycles with the frozen embryos. They both failed. We did another fresh cycle and that one failed too.

The doctor said, "Even though it looks like your embryos are great, I think this may be an egg quality issue. Perhaps you should consider using donor eggs."

Pat and I were both fine with the idea, so I began researching like crazy. I was on the Internet constantly. In the meantime, we decided we needed a second opinion, so we began researching clinics all over the country.

We had phone consultations with The Institute for Reproductive Medicine and Science (IRMS) of St. Barnabas Medical Center in New Jersey, Reproductive Medicine Associates (RMA) in New Jersey, The Colorado Center for Reproductive Medicine (CCRM), and finally, Cornell's Center for Reproductive Medicine and Infertility (CRMI). We ended up choosing Cornell.

They required that we did a pre-op and a biopsy two months before the transfer date and they insisted we do all of our monitoring at their center. So in August 2001, we went to New York and rented an apartment in Manhattan for three weeks.

When we had our initial consult with Dr. S at Cornell, he looked at our records and said, "You know, it's possible this is an egg issue, but it doesn't look like it to me. It looks like an implantation problem because your eggs are perfect, your bloodwork is fine, and you make good embryos.

Meanwhile, for the IVF cycling, I'd go in the morning to get monitored and then I'd be done for the day. We were very impressed with Cornell—there's no doubt they knew what they were doing. The only problem was that since they had such a good reputation, so many people went there and the waiting room was incredibly crowded every morning. There would literally be between fifty and seventy women in the waiting room on any given morning. It's easy to get lost at a place like that—so it's important to be your own advocate.

The cycle went totally smooth, but the day the transfer was supposed to take place, the embryologist called and said, "Sorry, we can't do your transfer because your sample was contaminated in the lab."

Cornell is a teaching hospital, and there was a fellow in the operating room during the retrieval process. I immediately thought they must have let her do the retrieval and she wasn't careful enough or something. Although we'll never know for sure what really happened.

They felt terrible, apologized up and down and told us they wouldn't charge us for the next cycle. Of course that didn't make up for the $1,500 worth of medications plus money we had spent to stay in Manhattan for three weeks—which was not cheap. Not to mention the three weeks I had to take off of work. But, there wasn't anything we could do about it, so we went home to Atlanta to wait for the next cycle.

We went back to Cornell for our next cycle in October 2001, about a month after 9/11. While we were there they had the

New York marathon, with teams of fireman and everything like that. It was a very patriotic time.

I have to say, that even though we were extremely upset that we had to return to do another cycle, and we certainly weren't happy that our embryos were contaminated, being in Manhattan at that time was a very interesting experience and one I will never forget.

The cycle went well and I ended up getting pregnant. But at eight weeks along in the pregnancy I miscarried again. It happened between Christmas 2001 and New Years 2002.

Right before our first trip to Cornell, I started becoming very depressed about our situation, but after this miscarriage I really felt like we were living under a black cloud. I was losing time at work and everything; it was just starting to really wear on me. I saw a therapist and that was very helpful—but this whole ordeal was really taking its toll. I don't think you can go through something like this without going through emotional struggles. I even had to stop going to baby showers for a while. I was happy for my friends, but it made me feel sad for myself.

It would especially bother me to hear about teenage mothers leaving their babies in dumpsters and things like that. All these people were getting pregnant without thinking twice about it—and there we were, the nicest people in the world, totally prepared to be parents, and we couldn't have a baby. It wasn't fair.

I turned to the Internet for support and found the INCIID website, which was incredibly helpful. There are doctors who answer questions through the site and they have a support forum for people going through IVF or for people who have experienced a miscarriage. I ended up meeting some women who are now really good friends instead of random people on the Internet. They were a huge source of support during this time in my life.

Since Dr. S said that it may be an egg issue and had suggested we look into donor eggs, we decided to go to Reproductive Biology Associates (RBA) in Atlanta to discuss our plans to find an egg donor.

We ended up meeting with Dr. T at RBA and we were quite impressed. Even though he's very busy, he spends a lot of time talking with his patients. Dr. T looked at my records and said, "I can put you in our donor program, but in my opinion it doesn't look like you have an egg problem. It appears to me that you have an implantation problem instead. I'd just hate for you to go through all of the effort and expense of getting an egg donor, doing a transfer, and then not getting pregnant or miscarrying again. I'm going to re-run every test and see if we get different results."

All the tests came back fine. Then Dr. T did an endometrial biopsy and sent it to Dr. K at Yale to do an Endometrial Function Test® (EFT®).

The tests came back abnormal. They showed that I don't produce a type of endometrial protein——or I don't produce it at the right time. The whole thing was at the study phase, so they couldn't pinpoint the causation; however, research had determined that certain things are connected to this problem——mainly extreme stress, obesity and endometriosis. I didn't have any symptoms of endometriosis and I wasn't obese, although after going through infertility for five years I undoubtedly was stressed.

Dr. T decided we should do a laparascopy to see if there was any endometriosis, and it turned out there was actually a little bit of scarring leftover from my ectopic pregnancies. He cleaned it all out and then we waited a month and tested again, but the results were even worse than the first time. Although this was unfortunate news, I was just glad to finally have a diagnosis. I was actually relieved to know I wouldn't be doing another wasted IVF cycle.

He then suggested, "Maybe you should look into getting a gestational carrier, because even though you are thirty-seven, your eggs are good quality and you and Pat make good embryos together."

I was not interested in doing one more major project that was going to take a couple of years. I didn't want to try something else that was just going to fail and then end up trying to adopt at forty years old or something. I just wanted a baby and I was getting sick of waiting. I suggested we start the adoption process instead.

Pat and I began to discuss whether we would adopt or attempt surrogacy. Pat is the type of person who will say, "Yeah, let's do this," and it really means, "Let's do it at some point down the road." He has no sense of urgency about certain things. I'm the type of person who will say, "Yeah, let's do this," and it means I'm ready to get stated *now*. It means I'm ready to start doing research and get the ball rolling.

I had to say to Pat, "Honey, you need to understand that while this is an open issue for us, I am going to obsess about it twenty-four hours a day. I can't go another year of 'let's work on this.' We need to make a decision, either way, on whether we really want to pursue surrogacy or if we want to go the adoption route. We need to set a timeline and I need your help."

Pat has been very supportive, but I'm the one who has researched everything and told him, "Here are the options, what do you want to do?" But this time, I simply didn't have it in me anymore.

Our friend Marty, who happens to work right across the street from my office, is one of three or four lawyers in the Atlanta area who is truly an expert in surrogacy situations. He actually handled one of the first surrogacy cases in Georgia.

Pat said he would call Marty to ask him what would be entailed if we did go the surrogacy route. The thing is, he still had the dream of having a biological child, whereas for myself, I really didn't care about the genetic link anymore. I just wanted a baby.

This was in the late summer/early fall of 2002. We agreed that if we hadn't found a surrogate and we weren't well on our way to getting pregnant by the first of the year of 2003, we'd sign up with an adoption agency and begin working on plans to adopt.

When Pat called Marty, he said, "This has never happened before, but ironically, a woman who is a computer consultant in my office called me the other day to see what she needed to do to be a surrogate. Apparently it has always been a dream of hers. I'm not a facilitator or anything, but if you want I can give her your email address and you can start corresponding with each other."

Lynn and I spent several weeks emailing back and forth and then I met her for lunch one day at the end of August 2002. She was thirty-eight, a year older than I was, and had six children. We hit it off instantly.

In December 2002, we did the cycle and transferred three embryos on the third day after the egg retrieval. We found out she was pregnant between Christmas and New Years—we couldn't believe it actually worked on the first try. Actually, from the moment we found out Lynn was pregnant everything has fallen into place.

Since the beginning, Lynn and I have had lunch together once a week. She has been wonderful, and so has her family.

We are grateful we found Lynn and we know how lucky we are to have a baby on the way. Still, it is really hard sometimes. Surrogacy is a solution to the problem of not having a baby but it's not a cure for infertility. You never totally lose all of those feelings—the sadness, the jealousy that oftentimes accompanies infertility.

We have friends in our neighborhood who were classmates of mine when I was in law school and they just had a baby three weeks ago. If we weren't expecting our own baby, to be honest, it probably would have been emotionally painful for me in a lot of ways. Knowing our little one is going to be here soon makes it much easier for me to deal with these types of situations.

Now that we are so close to the delivery, the focus has shifted from the pregnancy to the baby. All I can do is envision what it is going to be like to finally be a mom—and I can hardly wait.

Postscript

Dana and Pat ended up having a boy and they named him Adam. They have enjoyed parenthood so much that almost immediately after his birth, they decided they'd try for a sibling when the time was right. Lynn enthusiastically offered to be their surrogate again when they were ready.

This past summer, they went through another transfer and as it turns out, Lynn is now pregnant with Dana and Pat's twins. Dana says that she and Lynn have a great relationship, and although they aren't "best friends" per se, it is a very nice friendship. Adam absolutely loves Lynn's children and the two families get together often.

Things have been great and Adam is the joy of their lives. He has a sunny, easy-going personality, he is very bright and with his ever-expanding vocabulary he is constantly talking. They are actually in the middle of potty training—just typical two-year old stuff. As Dana puts it, "Regardless of how it all started, a toddler is a toddler and a mom is a mom."

Acronyms & Abbreviations

AI – Artificial Insemination - Introduction of semen into the vagina or uterus without sexual contact (answers.com)

ART - Assisted Reproductive Technology - includes oocyte (or egg) donation, embryo donation, in vitro fertilization, artificial insemination and sperm donation. Within each of these areas there are several different medical procedures that are used. (Adoption. com)

CVS - Chorionic Villus Sampling - Biopsy of the chorion frondosum through the abdominal wall or by way of the vagina and uterine cervix at nine to twelve weeks of gestation to obtain fetal cells for the prenatal diagnosis of genetic disorder (MedlinePlus.com)

D&C - Dilation and curettage - a gynecological procedure performed on the female reproductive system. The procedure involves dilating the cervix and inserting instruments to clean out the lining of the uterus while the woman is under an anesthetic. D&Cs are most commonly performed for the purposes of abortion or miscarriage. (Answers.com)

DES - Diethylstilbestrol - A synthetic form of the hormone estrogen that was prescribed to pregnant women between about 1940 and 1971 because it was thought to prevent miscarriages. DES may increase the risk of uterine, ovarian, or breast cancer in women who took it. DES also has been linked to an increased risk of clear cell carcinoma of the vagina or cervix in daughters exposed to DES before birth. (Thehealthencyclopedia.com)

FSH - Follicle Stimulating Hormone - A naturally occurring female hormone. In the infertility workup, this hormone is usually measured on Cycle Day 3 (Day 1 is the first day of bleeding). The FSH level in the blood gives the doctor information about ovarian reserve. FSH levels on Day 3 should be less than 13 miu/ml. A high Day 3 FSH level may indicate decreased ovarian reserve (FirstvisitIVF.org)

hCG - Human Chorionic Gonadotripin - A glycoprotein hormone similar in structure to luteinizing hormone that is secreted by the placenta during early pregnancy to maintain corpus luteum function and stimulate placental progesterone production, is found in the urine and blood serum of pregnant women, is commonly tested for as an indicator of pregnancy, is used medically to induce ovulation and to treat male hypogonadism and cryptorchidism, and is produced in certain cancers (as of the testes) – MedlinePlus.com)

HSG - Hysterosalpingogram - A type of x-ray test in which dye is inserted into through cervix into the uterus and fallopian tubes. The x-ray is examined for any abnormalities, such as blocked fallopian tubes. This test may cause cramping. If abnormalities exist, the cramping may be severe. (FirstvisitIVF.org)

ICSI - Intracytoplasmic Sperm Injection - A procedure in which a single sperm is injected directly into an egg. (Fertility-docs.com)

INCIID - The InterNational Council on Infertility Information Dissemination, Inc. (inciid.org)

IUI - Intrauterine Insemination - the introduction of specially prepared and washed semen into the uterus through a very small catheter. (About.com)

IVF - In Vitro Fertilization - An ART procedure that involves removing eggs from a woman's ovaries and fertilizing them outside her body. The resulting embryos are then transferred into the woman's uterus through the cervix. (Fertility-docs.com)

MMPI - Minnesota Multiphasic Personality Inventory - A series of questions with yes-or-no answers. It was designed several decades ago to provide psychologists with an overview of the personality style and emotional symptoms of the person taking it. There are several scales measuring things like depression, anxiety, etc. There are also subscales that assess whether the person appears to be answering the questions randomly or is trying to appear either better off or worse off than they really are. (iVillage.com)

PPS - Parents Pursuing Surrogacy (Online Support Group)

RE - Reproductive endocrinologist - A sub-specialist doctor who is dedicated to the treatment of infertility. An RE has gone through advanced training to understand female hormones, the causes of infertility, and the latest infertility treatments. An RE is capable of handling very complex infertility cases. (FirstvisitIVF.org)

SCSA - Sperm Chromatin Structures Assay - A test that measures the level of DNA fragmentation in the sperm, to enhance the diagnosis of and treatment for male infertility (Infertilityspecialist. com)

SMO - Surrogate Mothers Online (surromomsonline.com)

TASC - The American Surrogacy Center, Inc. (surrogacy.com)

Glossary

Amniocentesis - The surgical insertion of a hollow needle through the abdominal wall and into the uterus of a pregnant female to obtain amniotic fluid especially to examine the fetal chromosomes for an abnormality and for the determination of sex. (MedlinePlus. com)

"Baby M" Case - This case involved a custody dispute between a father and a mother. The father, William Stern, had contracted with the mother, Mary Beth Whitehead, to bear him a child through artificial insemination. The contract, in part, provided that she would receive a fee of $10,000 upon terminating her parental rights and giving up the child to him. A lower court held that the contract was enforceable and that the custody of the child, known as Baby M, should be awarded to Mr. Stern on the basis of the child's best interests. Mrs. Whitehead appealed, asking the court to determine "surrogacy contracts" unenforceable and void, to reinstate her parental rights and to grant her custody of Baby M. The Supreme Court ruled: 1) that giving money to a woman to induce her to surrender her child for adoption was unconstitutional; 2) that the state's adoption laws permit irrevocable surrender of a child only after birth; and 3) that the law requires proof of abandonment or unfitness prior to termination of parental rights or adoption without consent. [Source: *In Re* Baby M, 217 N.J. Super. 313 (1987).] (ascensionhealth.org)

Beta - Alternate name for HCG test (see definition for human chorionic gonadotropin)

Blastocyst - The stage of embryonic development following the morula. There are two layers at this stage, the outer layer or trophoblast and the inner cell mass. Implantation occurs during this phase. (About.com)

Chemical pregnancy - Very early pregnancy that is indicated through a positive pregnancy test only. When applied to IVF, a chemical pregnancy may not be a pregnancy at all, but rather the result of the hCG injection creating a false-positive pregnancy test. This term may also refer to a true chemical pregnancy that may or may not progress to a clinical pregnancy. (FirstVisitIVF.org)

Cycle (IVF Cycle)* - Treatment cycles are typically started on the third day of menses and consist of a regimen of fertility medications to stimulate the development of multiple follicles of the ovaries. In most patients injectable gonadotropins are used under close monitoring. Such monitoring checks frequently the estradiol level and, by means of gynecologic ultrasonograpy, follicular growth. Typically approximately 10 days of injections will be necessary. Endogenous ovulation is blocked by the use of GnRH agonists or GnRH antagonists. When follicular maturation is judged to be adequate, hCG is given. This agent would lead to ovulation about 42 hours after injection, but just before that time a retrieval procedure will take place to recover the egg cells from the ovary. (Answers.com)
*This definition includes only the steps leading up to egg retrieval and transfer: also see egg retrieval and transfer definitions)

Egg donor - A woman who provides usually several eggs (ova, oocytes) for another person or couple who want to have a child. Egg donation involves the process of in vitro fertilization as the eggs are fertilized in the laboratory. The role of the egg donor is completed after the eggs have been obtained. Egg donation is part of the process of third party reproduction. (About.com)

Egg retrieval - A procedure to collect the eggs contained in the ovarian follicles. (Fertility-docs.com)

Embryologist - A scientist who is highly trained in embryo growth and development. (FirstvisitIVF.org)

Endometrial biopsy - An outpatient procedure in which the doctor removes a small amount of tissue from the uterine lining (called the endometrium) to examine it for abnormalities. To control pain, local anaesthesia may be injected into the cervix. Bleeding or cramping may occur after this procedure. (FirstvisitIVF.org)

Endometrial function test - A test to determine whether a woman's endometrium (uterine lining) is healthy and ready for embryo implantation. An abnormal EFT is associated with pregnancy failure, while a normal EFT is associated with pregnancy success. (Eurekalert.org)

Endometriosis - A disease in which tissue similar to the uterine lining implants and grows outside the uterus. Endometrial growths are often found on the ovaries, bowel, fallopian tubes, or vagina, but may also grow in other areas of the body. Endometriosis can cause a variety of symptoms, including pelvic pain, bowel changes, heavy menstrual bleeding, bloating, fatigue, and infertility. (FirstvisitIVF. org)

Endometrium - The glandular mucous membrane comprising the inner layer of the uterine wall. (Answers.com)

Escrow account - Money put into the custody of a third party for delivery to a grantee only after the fulfillment of the conditions specified. (Answers.com)

Estradiol level - An estrogenic hormone, $C_{18}H_{24}O_2$, produced by the ovaries and used in treating estrogen deficiency. (Answers. com)

Ectopic pregnancy - A pregnancy that occurs outside the uterus, most often in the fallopian tube. Ectopic pregnancies are usually resolved by medication that dissolves the pregnancy. In some instances, surgery is required. (FirstvisitIVF.org)

Fibroid - A benign tumor especially of the uterine wall that consists of fibrous and muscular tissue (Medline Plus)

Follicles - Fluid-filled sacs in the ovaries that contain the eggs (FirstvisitIVF.org)

Fresh cycle - Embryos from fertilized eggs from the same menstrual cycle are transferred. (also see definition of "Cycle") (Answers. com)

Frozen cycle - A cycle in which embryos are preserved through freezing (cryopreservation) for transfer at a later date. (Fertility-docs.com)

Frozen embryo - Embryos that have been generated in a preceding cyle, cryopreserved, and are thawn just prior to the transfer. (Answers.com)

Frozen embryo transfer (FET) - The frozen embryo(s) is/are thawed and transferred to the uterus in the same process as in a fresh IVF cycle. (Fertility Stories.com)

Gestational surrogacy - The surrogate mother is not genetically related to the child. Eggs are extracted from the intended mother or egg donor and mixed with sperm from the intended father or sperm donor in vitro. The embryos are then transferred into the surrogate's uterus. Embryos which are not transferred may be frozen and used for transfer at a later time if the first transfer does not result in pregnancy. (surromomsonline.com)

Gestational Sac - The only available intrauterine structure that can be used to determine if an intrauterine pregnancy (IUP) exists, until the embryo is identified. On ultrasound, it is an anechoic (dark) space surrounded by a hyperchoic (white) rim. It is spherical in shape, and usually located in the upper uterine fundus. The mean gestational sac diameter (MGD) is an effective estimate of gestational age between 5 and 6 weeks, with an accuracy of about +/- 5 days. (Answers.com)

Gonadotropins - A hormone that stimulates the growth and activity of the gonads, especially any of several pituitary hormones that stimulate the function of the ovaries and testes. (Answers.com)

Gynecologic ultrasonography - The application of medical ultrasonography to the female pelvic organs, specifically the uterus, the ovaries, the Fallopian tubes, as well as the bladder, the culdesac, and any findings in the pelvis of relevance outsite of pregnancy. The examination can be performed transabdominally, usually with a full bladder to achieve better visualization, or transvaginally with a special vaginal transducer. Generally transvaginal imaging gives better resolution, however lesions reaching into the addomen are better seen transabdominally. The procedure is painless, noninvasive, and safe. (Answers.com)

Human chorionic gonadotropin (hCG) - A glycoprotein hormone similar in structure to luteinizing hormone that is secreted by the placenta during early pregnancy to maintain corpus luteum function and stimulate placental progesterone production, is found in the urine and blood serum of pregnant women, is commonly tested for as an indicator of pregnancy, is used medically to induce ovulation and to treat male hypogonadism and cryptorchidism, and is produced in certain cancers (as of the testes) – MedlinePlus.com)

Hysteroscopy - Visual inspection of the uterine cavity with an endoscope.. (Answers.com)

Intended parents - The parents to be in a surrogacy arrangement.

Ketones - The end-product of rapid or excessive fatty acid breakdown, and they are present in the urine when the blood levels surpass a certain threshold. (Allrefer.com)

Ketosis - An abnormal increase of ketone bodies in the body in conditions of reduced or disturbed carbohydrate metabolism (MedlinePlus.com)

Laparoscopy - A surgical procedure (usually outpatient) in which a small instrument called a laparoscope is inserted into the abdomen through a very small incision, often just above or below the naval. The laparoscope sends pictures to a TV monitor in the operating room, giving the doctor a clear view of the inside of the abdomen. During this procedure, the doctor looks for any abnormalities that might be causing infertility. (FirstvisitIVF.org)

Mock cycle - When a woman's uterine lining is prepared through medication to accept the donated embryo, and once this is ascertained to be successful, the actual donor cycle is carefully timed for the most optimum window of receptiveness. (Diamond Institute.com)

Ovarian cyst - A fluid-filled sac inside the ovary. It may be completely normal (a functional cyst) that will disappear within a few cycles – or it may be the result of ovulation disorders or other conditions. (FirstvisitIVF.org)

Ovarian Hyperstimulation Syndrome (OHSS) - When an IVF patient becomes seriously ill after being stimulated with injectable fertility medications. Signs of OHSS may include hemoconcentration, weight gain, severe abdominal distension, ovarian enlargement and in severe cases even renal failure. (FertileThoughts.com, Courtesy of Christo Zouves, MD)

Progesterone - A naturally-occurring hormone that is essential for normal reproductive function. During an IVF cycle, Progesterone is administered by injections or vaginal suppositories to prepare the uterine lining for implantation (pregnancy). (FirstvisitIVF.org)

Spotting - Light bleeding at anytime except menstruation. (Preconception.com)

Traditional surrogacy - The surrogate mother is artificially inseminated with the sperm of the intended father or sperm donor. The surrogate's own egg will be used, thus she will be the genetic mother of the resulting child. (Surrogate Mothers Online)

Transfer (embryo transfer) - The process in which an egg that has been fertilized in vitro is transferred into a recipient's uterus (Answers.com)

Tubal pregnancy - Ectopic pregnancy in a fallopian tube (Medline Plus.com)

Unicornate Uterus - An abnormality in which the uterus is one sided and smaller than usual (Reproductive Health Center.com)

Varicocele - A varicose vein of the testicles, sometimes a cause of male infertility. It is a dilation of the veins that carry blood out of the scrotum. The resulting swollen vessels surrounding the testicles create a pool of stagnant blood, which elevates the scrotal temperature. It is a major cause of male infertility. (Reproductive Health Center.com)

Surrogacy and Infertility Resources

National Infertility Organizations

AFA (The American Fertility Association)
www.theafa.org
MISSION STATEMENT: The American Fertility Association is a national organization dedicated to educating, supporting and advocating for men and women concerned with reproductive health, fertility preservation, infertility and all forms of family building.

APA (American Pregnancy Association)
www.americanpregnancy.org
MISSION STATEMENT: The American Pregnancy Association is a national health organization committed to promoting reproductive and pregnancy wellness through education, research, advocacy, and community awareness.

ASRM (American Society of Reproductive Medicine)
www.asrm.org
ASRM is a multidisciplinary organization for the advancement of the art, science, and practice of reproductive medicine. The Society accomplishes its mission through the pursuit of excellence in education and research and through advocacy on behalf of patients, physicians, and affiliated health care providers.

INCIID (The InterNational Council on Infertility Information Dissemination)
www.inciid.org
MISSION STATEMENT: INCIID provides current information and immediate support regarding the diagnosis, treatment, and prevention of infertility and pregnancy loss, and offers guidance to those considering adoption or childfree lifestyles.

RESOLVE (The National Infertility Association)
www.resolve.org
MISSION STATEMENT: The mission of RESOLVE is to provide timely, compassionate support and information to people who are experiencing infertility and to increase awareness of infertility issues through public education and advocacy.

SART (Society for Assisted Reproductive Technology)
www.sart.org
MISSION STATEMENT: The Society for Assisted Reproductive Technology promotes and advances the standards for the practice of assisted reproductive technology to the benefit of our patients, members and society at large.

SOCREI (Society for Reproductive Endocrinology and Infertilitiy)
www.socrei.org
[In association with the American Society of Reproductive Medicine (ASRM)]. Members of SREI are dedicated to providing excellence in Reproductive Health through Research, Education, and the Care of their Patients.

Online Surrogacy Support Groups and List Servs

All About Surrogacy
www.allaboutsurrogacy.com
An online community of Surrogate Mothers, Intended Parents and Egg Donors that is built by the members, for the members.

COTS - Childlessness Overcome Through
Surrogacy
www.surrogacy.org.uk
A voluntary surrogacy organization working in
the UK

Everything Surrogacy
www.everythingsurrogacy.com
An unbiased surrogacy education resource
which seeks to promote safety in the surrogacy
community through education as well as
promote a more realistic and positive public
perception of surrogacy.

Intended Parents Inc.
www.intendedparents.com
Created by intended parents for intended
parents.

Parents Pursuing Surrogacy list-serv (PPS)
Moderator email: owner-pps-l@surrogacy.org
For people who are considering surrogacy,
going through surrogacy, or parents through
surrogacy.

Proud Parenting
www.proudparenting.com
An online portal for gay, lesbian, bisexual
and transgender parents and their families
worldwide.

Surrogacy in Canada Online
www.surrogacy.ca
A resource for Canadians involved with
surrogacy providing free information, referrals
and support to Canadians involved with
surrogacy.

Surrogacy Mentoring
www.surrogacymentoring.com
Mission statement: Support intended parents
emotionally through their journey and
relationship with their surrogate, making it
a rewarding and enjoyable journey for all
involved.

Surrogacy Online Support
www.surrogacysupport.com
Provides information and support to individuals
who are interested in pursuing surrogacy or
egg/sperm donor arrangements.

Surrogacy UK
www.surrogacyuk.org
An organisation that was formed to support
and inform anyone with an interest in surrogacy
within the UK.

Surrogate Moms Online Surrogacy Support
Community
www.surrogatemoms.org
Online magazine covering topics relating to
conception and fertility from natural family
planning, to doctor assisted third party
reproduction techniques such as IVF, and
Surrogacy.

Surrogate Mothers Online (SMO)
www.surromomsonline.com
Provides information and support to individuals
who are interested in pursuing a surrogacy or
egg/sperm donor arrangement.

The American Surrogacy Center (TASC)
www.surrogacy.com
Website with tons of surrogacy information.

The Organization of Parents Through
Surrogacy (OPTS)
www.opts.com
A national surrogacy support organization
for both couples through surrogacy as well as
surrogate mothers.

UK Surrogacy Friends
www.excoboard.com/exco/index.
php?boardid=10316
Support group and message boards for people
in the UK.

Online Infertility Support Groups and List Servs

Donor Conception Support Group of
Austrailia
www.members.optushome.com.au/dcsg/
An organization of people considering or using
donor sperm, egg or embryo, those who already
have children conceived on donor programs,
adult donor offspring and donors.

E.I.N. Electronic Infertility Network
www.ein.org
A non-profit organization, providing
information about infertility and the work of
infertility support associations, within Europe
and the rest of the world.

Family First Fertility
www.familyfirstfertility.com
Informational website targeting many aspects
of fertility.

Fertile Hope
www.fertilehope.com
A national nonprofit organization dedicated to
providing reproductive information, support
and hope to cancer patients whose medical
treatments present the risk of infertility.

Fertility Neighborhood
www.fertilityneighborhood.com
Educational resource owned and operated by
Priority Healthcare Corporation, a specialty
pharmacy providing nationwide prescription
services and patient management support for
persons being treated for chronic conditions.

Fertility Plus
www.fertilityplus.org
A non-profit website for patient information
on trying to conceive. The information on this
website is provided by patients for patients.

FertilityNZ
www.fertilitynz.org.nz
New Zealand's national network for all
those who have an interest in or connection
with fertility problems; from people seeking
treatment for fertility problems, to gamete
donors, and people conceived as a result of
assisted human reproductive treatment.

FertiMagazine.com
www.fertimagazine.com
The mission of this monthly online journal is to
bring the latest news on cutting edge science in
human reproduction to fertility specialists and
healthcare professionals.

IHR - Infertility Resources for Consumers
www.ihr.com
Since 1995, IHR has specialized in developing,
hosting, and promoting infertility websites

InfertilityNetwork UK
www.infertilitynetworkuk.com
As well as providing authoritative information,
and practical and emotional support, it is
INUK's mission to raise the profile and
understanding of infertility issues in all quarters
and to strive for timely and consistent provision
of infertility care throughout the UK.

IVF-Infertility.com
www.ivf-infertility.co.uk
Designed by infertility specialists primarily
for couples who are experiencing difficulty in
having a child, and thinking that they might
need medical help.

Shared Journey
www.sharedjourney.com
Providing accurate, up-to-date information
on the subjects of infertility and pregnancy.
Community forum enables women to learn
about infertility, treatments, and alternatives and
to discuss and share their thoughts and hopes in
a caring environment.

The National Fertility Directory
www.fertilitydirectory.org
Founded and directed solely by physicians
specializing in the field of infertility and
reproductive medicine.

TheLaborofLove.com
www.thelaboroflove.com
For those trying to conceive, pregnant, or
already parents.

Stillbirth and Neonatal Death Support Groups

Hannah's Prayer
www.hannah.org
A Christian support network for couples facing
"fertility challenges" including infertility or the death
of a baby at any time from conception through early
infancy.

SANDS (Stillbirth and neonatal death support inc.)
www.sandsvic.org.au/
A self-help support group comprised of parents
who have experienced the death of a baby through
miscarriage, stillbirth, or shortly after birth.

SANDS (Stillbirth and neonatal death society)
www.uk-sands.org/
Working to support bereaved parents and families,
and to press for improvements in care during
pregnancy and when a baby has died.

About the Author

Like most young woman, Zara Griswold had dreams of becoming a mother someday. When she was faced with ovarian cancer and a complete hysterectomy at age twenty-three, however, her fantasies of motherhood were suddenly destroyed. For over eight years she worried if she would ever experience the joys of having children, yet deep down she knew it was a dream she would never dismiss.

In the spring of 2002, a friend of hers suggested something Zara had never considered before — surrogacy. Shortly thereafter, Zara found her surrogate mother Online, and about a year later, in June 2003, she and her husband, Mike, welcomed their son and daughter into their arms.

Zara is a former high school English teacher who is now a stay-at-home-mom. She has a Bachelor of Arts in English from Eastern Michigan University and a Master of Science in Education from Northern Illinois University. In addition to writing her first book, she is still involved in the surrogacy and infertility communities. She and her family live in the north suburbs of Chicago.

Printed in the United States
44837LVS00005B/79-84